GYPSIES OF BRITAIN

GYPSIES OF BRITAIN

An Introduction to their History

by

BRIAN VESEY-FITZGERALD

READERS UNION
Group of Book Clubs
Newton Abbot 1974

KI

AUGUSTUS JOHN, o.m., r.a.

O SHERAND 'PARL O ROMANĒ JUNIMÁSKO MALIBEN
THA KI SÂKON KOMONÉNDI TE KAMEN I ROMANICHEL TRUSHAL
O THEM SÂR

THA KI

AMOS CHUREN

ROMANÓ THA RAI, ODÂ-KAI MUKDÁS MAN TE KISTÉL
PESKO χUREDO GRAI KANA CHAVORÓ SHOMAS, THA ACHDÁS
MIRO PHAL POS-TE MUIÁS BISH-THA-SHOV BERSHA PALÁL

THA KI

JAMES ARIGHO

KAKKAVIÉNGERO AVRÍ χINDE-THEMÉSTI, THILIMÁNGERO, GILI-
ÉNGERO THA BOSHIMÁNGERO, LACHO PARAMISHÉNGERO, ZORALO
SOVEχERIMÁNGERO, ODÂ-KAI GOZHVERDÁS MAN DOSTA TRUSHAL
CHERIKLÉNGE THA STÂR-PIRENGRÉNGE DROMÁ AR'I VESHENDI
THA'I BÁRIÉNDI, THA SIKADÁS MAN SAR TE TARDÁ I MURENÉNGĒ
MACHÉ AVRÍ BITI PANIÉNDI THA TE LA CHOROχANÉS O BÂRO
SHOSHOI THA'I BÂRI KANI PENGĒ GARADĒ VODRÉNDĒ, THA TE
HAIAVÁ 'DOLA MURSHÉN THA JUVIÉN TE PHIRÉN OPRÉ O 'DROLANĒ
DROMÁ

CONTENTS

INTRODUCTION

I AM no Romani Scholar. I should like to make that clear straight away in view of the fact that this is a book about Gypsies, and it appears to be the fashion to describe anyone who writes a book about Gypsies, or even puts Gypsies into a book, as a modern George Borrow and a Romany Rye. I am not a *Romano Rai*—in the sense of a Romani scholar at any rate—but I hope I may properly be regarded as one of the " affectionatos."

People become interested in Gypsies for a variety of reasons. Many are first attracted by the halo of false romance that some writers have given them. This halo disappears pretty quickly and with it, as a rule, all interest in Gypsies. But there are yet some who remain interested after the halo has gone, and for them interest takes many forms. Some devote their attention to the past history of the race : some to the study of their language and its philological problems : some find their chief interest in tracing family pedigrees : some collect vocabularies, some folk tales, some music : some find their chief interest in Gypsies' customs : and some are content to leave all such matter to the specialists, and are satisfied with the simple contact, are happy in knowing a very lovable people.

If I belong to any one of these classes, it is to the last. But I have never sought out the Gypsy folk just because they are Gypsies or just because I happen to be interested in them. I have only sought their company when I have come across them accidentally. My interest in them and such knowledge of them as I possess has been incidental to my interest in natural history and the life of the country-side generally, and my contacts with them have been for the most part in the course of wanderings that were primarily concerned with birds and beasts and insects. My knowledge, such as it is, of their language has come just because I happen to pick up languages easily—I was born bi-lingual, and this no doubt is a help—and not because I have ever set out to collect a vocabulary from any Gypsy. There was, by the way, a time when I thought that because I had just sufficient *Romani* to *rakker* with the Gypsy in his *tan* that I knew something about him and his language. That was before I came across Dr. Sampson's great book and the *Journal* of the Gypsy Lore Society. I know better now. I am learning his language. No matter how fluently I can chatter when I am with Romanies—and I can rub along—each fresh number of the *Journal* shows me very clearly how much I have yet to learn ; which is very good for me. But I must confess that the language as it appears in Dr. Sampson's monograph and in the pages of the *Journal*—a beautifully balanced, constructed and accentuated language—sometimes seems to me very far removed from the speech I hear by the Gypsy fireside. In point of fact it is not—even though I not infrequently find it incomprehensible without the aid of a vocabulary and a good deal of intuition : what makes the two appear so different is that the one is a spoken and the other a written language. Romani is the language of an unlettered people : it was never a written language. It has only been recorded in fairly recent times, and only very recently has one mode of transcription come to be universally accepted—that used by the late John Sampson, the greatest of all *Romane Raia*. Sampson used the following alphabet :

a å b č d ð e ẹ f g γ h i j̈ k k̒ χ l ḷ m
n ŋ o p p̒ r ṛ s š t t̒ þ u v w̥ y z ž

Each of those symbols indicates a particular sound, and no other. There is no possibility of mistake. And quite obviously this is a much better method of taking down speech than the old phonetic method, since people are very apt to spell words differently to indicate the same sounds. All the same I have not used it in this book. Such Romani words as I have used (and I have deliberately reduced them to the minimum) I have spelt phonetically. Though this will not appeal to the gypsiologist (in any case this book is not written for him) it will, I fancy, be simpler for the general reader, who will, I believe, find *gorgio* easier to read than *gȃjo* and *hochay* than $\chi^{ȃčē}$, to take but two random examples.

Invariably when I talk about Gypsies—no matter to whom, individuals or clubs or societies or what not—I am asked how I first came to know Gypsies. I did not, rather unfashionably perhaps, make my first acquaintance with them in the pages of George Borrow. Indeed, I first read *Lavengro* when I was sixteen, and I first knew a Gypsy when I was seven or thereabout.

Then an itinerant harper came through the little country town where we lived. Father liked the harp and he liked characters too, and for several days the man came and played his harp outside our house. Father talked to him, and I would go out and listen, and the man would always talk to me also. I do not know what his name was, but I can remember him and his harp very clearly, more clearly than anyone or anything in my childhood. He was, I think, a very tall man. At least I remember him as being very tall, but he may not have been, for memory enlarges hugely. (At my public school, in my first year, I had an enormous admiration for the head of my house, a huge man, who was also head of the school and a forward in the School XV. I met him years afterwards and found to my astonishment that I was a good head the taller and much larger physically). But of some things I am as certain now as I was then. If I close my eyes now I can see him as clearly as if I was again standing before him and longing to pluck at the strings of his harp. He was very dark, dark skinned and with black hair. His hair was so long that it fell over his coat collar and he had a long black moustache. He had very black eyes with queer orangey pupils. They had a light in them that seemed somehow to be behind the eye itself. They never frightened me, but they did attract me strangely, even though they seemed to look deep inside me. He wore a black billycock hat and a sort of frock coat, and a handkerchief round his neck. It was a bright yellow handkerchief, and it had red spots on it. I was very impressed by that handkerchief. And the second year he came he gave it to me when he moved on. I have long since lost it, but it was a treasure for many years. It was from this old man (I knew he was an old man then, which now I come to think about it is rather surprising in view of the fact that his hair was black and my father's was white) that I learned my first words of Romani. I knew *diklo* meant handkerchief, and *mishto* meant good. Probably I knew many more words then too, but I cannot now remember them.

My father was a great walker. And from the time that I was eight he would take me with him on many of his walks. Sometimes we would take sandwiches and walk from the house and back again, covering a circle of country, and sometimes we would go by train to some wayside station and walk home by field paths and tracks. I did my first ten-mile walk when I was eight and when I was twelve I first did my twenty miles in the day. On these walks father would show me birds and animals, and interpret for me the sounds and sights of the countryside, but though he had a vast knowledge of birds and animals he was very much more interested in people, and he would stop and talk to anyone he could get to talk to him. I doubt if there was a farm labourer within a ten-mile radius of home whom father did not know. There could have been few cottages within that radius at which at some time or another we did not stop, few at which we did not at some time or another have a cup of tea or a glass of milk. Father collected people much as other men collect birds' eggs or stamps. And since he had knocked about the world a good bit he was not an unpopular visitor anywhere. Among the people we got to know on these walks were tramps and several families of Gypsies, who travelled the area. I had my first food in a Gypsy encampment with father when I was nine. I had my first meal alone in a Gypsy encampment when I was eleven. That was near Maidenhead, and I was playing truant from my preparatory school. There were a good many Gypsies around

Maidenhead in those days, and I spent many a stolen hour of a half-holiday in their company. Indeed when I was thirteen I was very deeply in love with a Gypsy girl. I cannot, now, remember who she was, but her name was Miranda. So, too, at my public school, where on Sundays we were allowed to go for walks by ourselves if we wished to do so. I got then to know several families who visited the area—Lees, Coopers, Stanleys, Scamps, Deightons, Drapers, Patemans, and can remember the names well. At sixteen I was more than a little attracted by Helen Scamp. So it was, very gradually and without motive, I got to know Gypsies. I learned my words of Romani by the simple method of listening. I learned one or two other things as well.

Another question I am invariably asked is : " Aren't you frightened ? I wouldn't like to get mixed up with Gypsies, a nasty cut-throat-looking lot." Well, people do frighten me as a rule : things frighten me much more. I think I can honestly say that I have never been frightened by a real Gypsy, for the simple reason that a real Gypsy has never tried to frighten me. I have been frightened once or twice by *diddikais* (half-castes) and more than once by tramps. In particular do I remember a *diddikai* named Best, whom I met near Nottingham. He was a hugely squat man with the largest and heaviest shoulders I have ever seen on a man, huge penthouse brows, a badly broken nose and a heavy jaw. His hands were hairy and square. I remember well noticing that his fingers were all the same length, the little fingers being abnormally long. He could not have stood above five feet four and he must have weighed a good fourteen stone, and none of it was fat. But the frightening thing about him was his eyes, which had the shifty brilliant glare of a wild animal. He himself was the colour of old mahogany, and his hair and heavy eyebrows were black, while his eyes were the palest yellow-green—the colour of downland grass in the heat of high summer. He had a nice van and a sullen-looking wife, who certainly had no Gypsy blood in her. Now, I had no contretemps with this man. He was, indeed, most polite and he had a pleasant low-pitched musical voice. But I was uneasy all the time I was with him—which was not long— and I have never been more thankful to leave anyone.

It must be remembered that if we look askance at the Gypsies and those that travel the roads, they regard us with equal distrust—and, taking it by and large, not without reason. It can take a long time to break down the wall of reserve and indifference built up against the gorgio, and things may sometimes become a little strained in the process. I have had my moments. One, only last year, was with a woman—not in the least frightening, but it might have been awkward. I do not look in the least like a Gypsy. I never could look like a Gypsy and I do not try to look like one. It has on occasions proved a handicap. Many of those who follow the Romani trail do look like Gypsies, and some can pass themselves off as Gypsies without very much trouble. Dr. Irving Brown, the greatest American *Rai*, can do so. George Borrow could do so, rather better perhaps than he made out. (But then I have always wondered how much Gypsy blood ran in Borrow's veins. He was so astonishingly unlike his father and his brother in every way, in looks, in build, in temperament.) But I cannot. I am an obvious gorgio. I am fair-skinned and blue-eyed, and large and rather solidly built. And so when I approached this van and asked, as I thought, a harmless question of the woman in charge (it *was* a harmless question !) I was greeted with a pail of cold and very dirty water over the hall door, and a torrent of abuse in the argot of the roads. My verbal reactions to this treatment quickly convinced her and her husband, who had come running up, that I could not possibly be what I appeared to be. And whenever I meet them now the occasion of my first visit is brought up amid shrieks of laughter. But I have never discovered the reason for that initial greeting.

No, there is nothing frightening about the Gypsies once you know them, or rather, since no gorgio ever really knows them, once you are accepted by them. They are no better and no worse than other men anywhere. But there is danger in knowing them. Do you remember Mathew Arnold's Scholar Gypsy ? He did not come back. And there are many more who have joined the travelling folk and have not come back. There is an overwhelming fascination about them and their mode of life. It is the fascination of freedom. We think that we are free : indeed we boast that we are. But of our civilisation we have made a tyrant. We are the slaves of money, of convention, of time-tables, of forms. We are the cogs in the gigantic machine of bureaucracy. The Gypsy, despite the unremitting attentions of the police, is still free. You know real freedom, real liberty, the moment you put foot on the road with the men and women who live on the road, the moment you sit, legs a-dangle, on the foot-board of a waggon, a good horse in front of you and fortune-knows-what around the corner. There is no romance, in the story-book sense, about the life of a Gypsy. It is a hard life and a rough life. It is not a life for those of weak stomach. But men have always to pay a high price for liberty. And it has rewards for the Gypsy beyond all price : true comradeship —a comradeship against all the world—and the clean air, sweet smells, and the earth and the sky, sun, wind, rain as God made them : there is truth.

For that truth the Gypsy has fought and lied and cheated throughout the centuries. In every country in which he has settled he has maintained in the face of all regulations and all oppression his own individuality, his own language, his own way of life. And he remains to-day what he has always been, a man apart, a member of the most mysterious race on earth.

INTRODUCTION

to the new edition

WHEN, almost thirty years after its original publication, a new edition of this book was mooted, the publishers naturally suggested that it should be revised and brought up to date. There is, however, nothing in the main body of the book that I would wish to revise: of Chapters I to IX, not one word that I would alter. The history, both of the people and their way of life, their customs, as set forth in those chapters is true. This is what happened: these are the customs that once were followed.

Of course, the final chapter of the original edition, "Gypsies To-day", is now completely out of date. Nevertheless, I have decided not to revise it. I leave it just as it was written, even the title unaltered. For that was the position at the outbreak of the Second World War. And that was what I thought, what I believed, in 1942. The years since the war have shown how wrong I was. But there is now no point in revising that chapter. Indeed, I believe that it would be a pity to do so. For already it has become history. Unaltered, it may serve as a measure of the change, of the revolution, that has taken place before our uncomprehending eyes.

So, all that I have done is to add a chapter bringing the story up to date.

Writing contemporary history—that is to say, recording events before they have become history in the generally accepted sense of the word—is a task fraught with danger. The most casual study of some passages in the introduction, some passages of the final chapter of the original edition, will show that I am a poor prophet. I would like to think that the title of my new chapter will prove to be as far from the truth as those passages in the original edition.

But England has shrunk since my youth and each year shrinks more rapidly. Space was essential to the Gypsy way of life. Speed has conquered space. But, of course, the Gypsy will survive: though not as the Gypsy I knew and so greatly admired.

B. V-F.

Throughout this book I have used the Borrovian form gorgio *(foreigner, non-Gypsy) in preference to the modern* gajo *or* gaujo. *I have done so because it has been my experience that few people, other than those acquainted with Romanes (which, it must be remembered is a spoken, not a written, language: only scholars actually write Romanes) know how to pronounce the modern form when they come across it in print. George Borrow had a good ear. His* gorgio—*the first* g *hard, the second soft—is as accurate a rendering of the correct pronounciation as one can get.*

I

EARLY HISTORY AND LEGEND

" Where we comes from the dear Lord only knows and He's too high and mighty to tell the likes of us."—CHARLEY SMITH, a Gypsy.

No race, except perhaps the Jews, is so widely distributed over the surface of the earth as the Gypsies. No matter where you travel in Europe, there you will find Gypsies. They are widely spread in America, both north and south. They are to be found throughout Asia Minor and Asia, except possibly in Southern India and the islands that stretch eastwards from the Malayan peninsular. They are settled in North Africa, along the Mediterranean coast and in Egypt, Darfur and Kardofan, and wandering bands visit South and East Africa from time to time. There are isolated bands in Australia and New Zealand. It would be idle to pretend that everywhere the race is the same— there is, for example, a clear distinction to be drawn between Oriental and Occidental Gypsies, though even the Gypsy long settled in the West is obviously an Oriental— but everywhere the race has resisted the onslaughts of the civilisations among which they dwell, and everywhere, even to-day, they exhibit the same, the old, characteristics. They are a migratory and nomadic people. Their wide distribution is due to migrations in the past. They are, and they always have been, wanderers. Even to-day, though in many parts of the world they are through force of circumstances sedentary, you have only to cast the most casual glance at the household arrangements of an apparently settled Gypsy to see that the nomad in him is very far from dead. No race, not even the Jews, has so successfully maintained its characteristics in the face of a hostile world. And no race has so strongly developed the power of handing on their characteristics. The half-bred

Gypsy is invariably more Gypsy than gorgio in temperament. Even a small drop of Romani blood in the veins is
sufficient to colour a whole life. A famous Lord Chan-
cellor—F. E. Smith, Earl of Birkenhead (though he had
more than a small drop)—is an excellent example. He rose
to great eminence in our legal and political life, but he
was always more Romani than gorgio in temperament.
And for one of his children at least a little Romani blood
has coloured all of life. Birkenhead was proud of his
Gypsy blood. He was no exception. I have met many
men and women only too eager to deny or conceal the
possession of Jewish blood ; I have yet to meet a man or
woman who is not proud of the possession of Gypsy blood.
Yet, despite the extraordinary success of the race in maintaining its characteristics in the face of an almost uniformly
hostile world, despite its astonishing vigour in handing
those characteristics on, despite many and varied talents,
despite pride of blood, and fierceness of independence,
despite an obviously great antiquity, the world at large
knows very little about the Gypsies, and they know practically nothing about themselves. We know the history of the
Jews from very early times. We have a fairly complete
history of the Gypsies (so far as the West is concerned : we
have none for the East) only from the fifteenth century.
Before that date history is swallowed up in conjecture.
Who are the Gypsies ? Whence did they come ? Of their
origin we know nothing. They remain what they have
always been, the most intriguing people on earth. They
remain so despite the fact that many great scholars have
interested themselves deeply in the problem.

There have, naturally, been any number of solutions.
They are, we have been told, Egyptians or at any rate
people who came into Europe by way of Egypt. They are
the Sudras, expelled by Tamerlane. They are Jats, Doms,
Dards, Changars. They are the heretic sect of the Athingani. They are the Sigynnæ of Herodotus. They are the
Sintians of Homer, a metal-working race speaking a wild
tongue. (It has even been suggested that Homer himself

was a Gypsy.) They are a prehistoric race that have lived in Europe for more than three thousand years. And so on. No doubt I have omitted several equally attractive solutions, but those will suffice to give some idea of the variety of theories that have been put forward from time to time in perfect good faith.

For many years now it has been recognised that the solution to the problem lies in their language. It was in 1763 that a Hungarian theological student named Stefan Vályi made the acquaintance in Leyden of three students from Malabar. It was in conversation with them that he discovered the fact that their language had much in common with that of the Gypsies from his part of Hungary. He drew up a vocabulary of one thousand words and put it before some Gypsies at Raab and found that they were able to translate the major part of it. It was an extremely important discovery. It showed that theirs was an Indian language of Aryan origin connected with the original Sanskrit. It shattered the theory, until then widely held (and not altogether dead to-day), that the Gypsies were, in fact, Egyptians. (But it did not, of course, remove the possibility that they may have come into Europe by way of Egypt.) Later Rüdiger and Grellmann and Bryant made the discovery more widely known, but it was not until Pott published in 1844–5 his magnificent two-volume work, *Die Zigeuner in Europa und Asien,* that the investigation of the Indian origin of the Gypsies began to be undertaken scientifically. (It is, by the way, worthy of note that Pott, whose work is still indispensable to serious students of the Romanies, never came into contact with the people themselves.) Pott was followed by Müller, Alexander Paspati, Miklosich, Weislocki, von Sowa, Kopernicki and many others. The earliest British worker in this field was John Beames, an Indian Civil Servant, who was an accomplished Sanskrit scholar and the author of *A Comparative Grammar of the Modern Aryan Languages of India,* the three volumes of which were published in 1872, 1875 and 1879. Beames regarded the Gypsy tongue as one of the Modern

Aryan languages of India, though he did not recognise it
as such until after the completion of his first volume. He
had no very profound knowledge of the language himself
and took many of his examples from Miklosich and Paspati
(he seems to have been unaware of the existence of Pott's
great work), but he was undoubtedly a great authority on
other points of importance. All these men were first and
foremost philologists. They all agree in assigning the
birthplace of the Gypsy language to India. But that is a
very different matter from establishing the exact locality.
Miklosich proved that some kinship with the Dardu and
Kafir dialects existed. M. de Goeje, a Dutch scholar,
believed that the Jats, Zott and Dom were related to
them. Beames considered the language more nearly
related to Sindhi. The localities suggested range from the
Hindu Kush mountain area to the deserts of the Indus.
More recent workers in this philological field include
Pischel, Woolner, Macfie, Finck, Kuhn, Littmann, Sampson (who, if primarily interested in philology, was a Rai of
outstanding attainment and no cloistered scholar), Macalister, Ackerley and Gilliat-Smith. They have done much
brilliant and suggestive work, but it is no good pretending
that the problem has been solved. Nor do I think it is in
the least likely to be. I am not a philologist and I lay no
claim to knowledge of philology, but it does seem to me
that any attempt to establish the original home of the
Gypsies by reference to their language is bound to fail, for
the very simple reason that we have no knowledge of the
dialects of India at the time the Gypsies left. And the
Gypsies have been away from India far too long in any
case. That much of their language is of Indian origin
cannot be disputed, but it cannot be referred to any one
dialect—indeed it cannot be identified with any existing
dialect—and it has all the appearance of having been collected from several, which seems to suggest that they were
already a nomad people at the time of their stay in India.

When did the Gypsies leave India? Beames and
Miklosich agree in dating the evolution of the Modern

Aryan languages of India from somewhere about 1,000 A.D. Most of the later philologists agree with them. This is taken to mean that the Gypsies could not have left India before that date and almost certainly left a good deal later, and that is, in fact, the opinion of the majority of those who have made a deep study of the language. But, as the late Dr. Sampson pointed out, while very great weight must be attached to such opinions, "it cannot be overlooked that the huge gap between the break-up of the Prakrits and our first knowledge of the modern vernaculars makes any positive statement rather in the nature of dogmatism." And, as a matter of fact, Miklosich himself does not altogether reject the possibility that at an earlier date when the Modern Indian dialects were taking definite shape, about the Middle-Indian period, the Gypsies may have left their home, taking with them in their language the germ of corruption, and far from their fellow-countrymen have developed an analytic form of language similar to that of the other Indian idioms.

Leaving out of account such theories as those that would identify the Gypsies with the Athingani (who, by the way, were a sect, not a race) and the Sintians of Homer, there is a good deal to suggest that the Gypsies were outside India long before 1,000 A.D. The Persian poet Firdusi tells us in his *Shâh Nâme* that the monarch Bahrâm imported into Persia, about the year 420, ten thousand musicians of both sexes from India. The same story is referred to by the Arabian historian Hamza of Ispahan, who wrote half a century earlier than Firdusi. Both writers agree in calling these musicians Gypsies. Firdusi uses the ordinary Persian Luri, and Hamza the word Zott, which is merely the regular Arabic pronounciation of Jat, and is one of the modern Syrian words for the Gypsies. Nor does the story end there. Chroniclers tell us that in the seventh century, during a war between the Arabs and the Persians, the Zott deserted from the Persian forces and settled in Arabia. Early in the ninth century these Zott had become so great a nuisance in the valley of the lower Tigris that twenty-

the bishopric of Würzburg, were Gypsies. I do not think that there is much doubt that the *Bemische* who were at Frankfurt-am-Main in 1495 were Gypsies, but Bataillard is not altogether successful in proving his theory for the earlier record. Bataillard was of the opinion that the Gypsies were in Europe in prehistoric times and that it was to them that prehistoric Europe owed all its knowledge of metal work, and he was a little inclined to stretch a point or two in favour of his theories. But there can be no doubt at all about Mr. Winstedt's records of the presence of Gypsies in central Europe in the fifteenth century prior to 1417. He has established the fact that there were Gypsy settlements at Hildesheim in 1407, at Basle in 1414, and at Meissen in 1416, which brings us to 1417, the popular date for the commencement of Gypsy history. In that year they were seen in Moldavia, Hungary, Germany and Switzerland, and from that year there are records galore.

It is rather astonishing that in view of all these early records it should still be the accepted view that the Gypsies, even though they were settling in south-eastern Europe in the fourteenth century or earlier, did not arrive in central and northern Europe until the fifteenth. The records I have mentioned are all well known to gypsiologists, and it is generally accepted that they refer to wandering tinkers, who indulged (as do Gypsies) in horse-dealing and fortune-telling. What is not generally accepted is that they were Gypsies. The main reason for this is the Romani language with its obvious affinity to Indian languages and the positive assertion of some philologists that it cannot have evolved much before 1000 A.D. Not being a philologist I do not know how much store should be set by the evidence of language. Paspati believed that the true history of the Gypsies was to be found in their language, and Paspati was a very great scholar. But even if you accept this, is it certain that the dates of the philologists are correct? The philologists are at work on something, an indefinite something at that, which happened at least eight hundred years before the earliest of them set to work.

Can they be definite to a century or two or three? The Arabian historian Hamza of Ispahan wrote about 950 A.D. and Firdusi about fifty years later. They record something that happened (and personally I have no doubt it did happen) four hundred years earlier. Is it certain that their dates are correct? Time is an elastic quantity—the early Hebrew historians provide sufficient proof of that—and it is at least possible that they predated the event by a century or two. The two schools of thought are not utterly incompatible.

The Gypsy word for men of their own race is *Rom*. That is the European Gypsy : the Armenian Gypsy is *Lom* and the Syrian and Persian Gypsy is *Dom*. All of these are, as Sampson has shown, in exact phonetic correspondence with the Sanskrit *doma* and the modern Indian *dom*, which means " a man of low caste who gains his living by singing and dancing." The Doms of modern India are vagrant tribes to be found mainly in Behar and the west and north-west Provinces, and they have many features in common with the Gypsies. They wander about with ragged little reed tents, which they pitch in the neighbourhood of villages, and they are adept at disappearing once they have got all they can out of the inhabitants. Some of them make baskets, mats and similar articles ; and in Dardistan, where they form a considerable part of the population but still, as elsewhere, constitute the lower caste, they are musicians, smiths and leather-workers. They eat the flesh of animals that have died a natural death, and are especially fond of carrion pork—the *mulo balo* of the English Gypsy. They do not appear to have any mother-tongue, but speak the language of the people among whom they live. Some writers object that the Indian Doms appear to be of Dravidian, not of Aryan stock. Dr. Sampson met this objection by pointing out that we know little or nothing of the early Doms or of those vagrant minstrels who left their fatherland more than a thousand years ago. There are to-day Doma and Doms, and the name may well have no more racial significance than our own " smith " or " tinker." H. L. Williams, a great authority on the wandering and criminal tribes of India, says : " I have also sought for pure unalloyed Doms, and I have never found them. I believe that Dom merely means a professional musician, and that the term is occupational, applied to any and every outcaste tribe." From this it would appear that *Dom* or *Rom* is the old name of the original caste and calling of the Gypsies, both Asiatic and European. But it does not, of course, connect the Romani with any particular dialect of India nor does it supply any clue to the migration route followed by the Gypsies.

John Sampson, at the end of his life, seems to have come to the conclusion that the Gypsies were in Persia before 900 A.D. He held to the belief that in Persia they divided into two bands, the one whom he called *Ben* Gypsies travelling southwards into Syria, and becoming the ancestors of the present Gypsies of Syria, Palestine, Egypt and Persia and Transcaucasia ; the other, the *Phen* Gypsies, settling in Armenia and then migrating westwards through Byzantine Greece. Personally I am sure that Sampson was right in assuming a division in Persia and two different routes of migration. I think he was right in believing that the Gypsies were in Persia before 900 A.D. (history, even if it is largely legendary, supports this), but I am not sure that he is right in assuming that the migration into Europe by way of Byzantine Greece was the first of such movements by the Gypsies.

It may be said that the people who came in 1417 would not have created the stir they did create had they not been new and different. But Mr. Winstedt has shown that they were, in fact, in Germany at least ten years before the stir, and that the bands who created the stir must have come from Hungary. The fact that the accounts of 1417 onwards are the first full accounts we have does not mean that they refer to the first appearance of the Gypsies in that neighbourhood. In 1866 a large band of English Gypsies visited Edinburgh : the Scottish newspapers of that date wrote as though it was the first visit of Gypsies to Scotland.

We know that it was not.   A similar error may well have been made by the European chroniclers of 1417–34—and it must be remembered that in those days few people could write.

History or legend, the evidence of language ; you may take your choice.   I do not believe that Bataillard was correct in asserting that the Gypsies were in Europe in pre-historic times.   I do not believe that the philologists are correct in their dates—I have noticed that philologists sometimes fail to see the wood for the trees—but I do not deny the Indian origin of the Gypsies.   I have no theory of my own.

II

RECENT HISTORY

WITH the fifteenth century we enter a new era in Gypsy history. From 1417 onwards we have many accounts of their visitations and can follow quite closely their journeyings across Europe. That there was a population of Gypsies in central and western Europe long before 1417 is, I think, beyond question. The year 1417 saw the beginnings of a fresh invasion of Gypsies, who had for long been settled in south-eastern Europe and who were moving because their provinces had either been invaded or were directly threatened by the Turks. But the invasion proper did not begin until about 1438. So much has been made of the invasion of 1417 that it is now difficult to realise that it was, in fact, undertaken by a single band of Gypsies, numbering no more than 300 in all, a reconnaissance party charged with the duty of spying out the land. They were a highly disciplined lot under able leaders. They split up as occasion demanded and met again at prearranged places. They travelled at astonishing speed and they went out of their way to force themselves upon the notice of the towns they visited. Now this is a most ungypsylike procedure, and it is to this extraordinary departure from the instincts of their race that we owe our comparatively full knowledge of their movements. Indeed it is very probable that had they behaved in the normal Gypsy fashion we should have heard nothing about them at all : it was because they were extraordinary that they were reported. Most of our information about them comes from chronicles and municipal accounts. Time and again we read in municipal accounts of a gift made to some duke or earl or count of Little Egypt and his followers and invariably we find that they presented themselves as penitents and pilgrims banished from their homes, and time and

again we read that they carried in support of their statement letters of recommendation from the Emperor
Sigismund and, later on, from the Pope as well. They
wanted to be seen—they were indeed exceptionally
ostentatious—and they wanted to be received in the
towns. They were spying out the land, and they wanted
to know how wealthy the land was and what chance of a
living their people would have if they came. The obvious
places in which to get that information were the towns,
and to the towns they went. It is evident that on their
return they reported very favourably, for from about 1438
onwards we find Gypsies spreading rapidly through every
country in Europe. Also, if they received a favourable
impression of the lands they had been sent to explore and
of the credulity of the people who inhabited them, there
can be no doubt that the inhabitants were equally, though
less favourably, impressed with them.

The first record of this exploring band is from Lüneburg.
Thence they proceeded to Hamburg, Lübeck, Weimar,
Rostock, Stralsund and Griefswald. We have accounts of
them from two chroniclers of Lübeck, who agree that they
numbered about 300, besides women and children, that
they came from " Eastern parts " or " from Tartary " (one
chronicler calls them Tartars) and that they called themselves " Secani " or " Tsigans." At their head rode a
duke and a count, richly dressed, wearing belts of silver
and leading hunting dogs in the manner of European nobles.
Behind these nobles came a motley ill-dressed crowd of
men on foot, and the women and children came in the
rear, riding in waggons. They bore letters of safe-conduct
from various princes and one from the Emperor Sigismund,
and they said that they were on a seven years' pilgrimage
imposed by their own bishops as a penance for infidelity
to the Christian faith. These letters caused them to be
well received in the towns they visited. But the Germans
of these merchant towns were not long deceived. We hear
that the Gypsies camped in the fields near the towns at
night, that they were great thieves, especially the women,

and that because of this " several were taken and slain."
These chroniclers agree in saying that they obeyed without
question the commands of their leaders, and that they
frequently broke up into smaller bands, but that they
followed each other very closely and marched more or less
as a whole.

Evidently they did not find the Baltic towns altogether
to their liking, for early in 1418 we find them at Leipzig
and at Frankfurt-am-Main, and later in the year at Zürich,
Basle, Berne and Soleure in Switzerland. The Swiss
chronicler, Justinger, writes of them as " more than two
hundred baptised pagans : they were from Egypt, pitiful,
black, miserable, with women and children ; and they
camped before the town in the fields, until there came a
prohibition because they had become unbearable to the
inhabitants on account of their thefts, for they stole all they
could. They had among them dukes and earls, who were
provided with good silver belts, and who rode on horseback ; the others were poor and pitiful. They wandered
from one country to another ; and they had a safe-conduct
from the King of the Romans." And so it goes on : at
Augsburg and at Mâçon, where they practised psalmistry
and necromancy, in 1419 : at Sisturon in Provence in the
same year they received large rations from the townspeople
who were frightened of them and called them " Saracens."
In 1420 we hear of them in the Low Countries at Deventre,
the town records saying : " Out of charity, to the Lord
Andrew, Duke of Little Egypt : on a Wednesday after
reminiscese (6th March) to the said lord, who had been
driven out of his country on account of the Christian faith,
and had come to our town with a hundred persons, men,
women and children, and about forty horses ; the same
having letters from the King of the Romans, containing an
invitation to give them alms, and to treat them with kindness in all the countries where they might go : given by
order of our aldermen, 25 florins, and for bread, beer,
straw, herrings and smoked herrings, for cost of the car-
riage of the beer, for straw, for cleaning out the barn in

which they slept . . . in all 19 florins, 10 plates." In the same year they were in Friesland and the north of Holland, and in 1421 at Tournai where " Sir Miquiel, Prince of Latingham in Egypt " received " out of pity and compassion " twelve gold pieces and bread and a barrel of beer.

In 1422 we hear of them in Bologna, and their leader, it seems probable, is the same man who did so nicely at Deventre. The Chronicle recounts how on " the 18th July 1422 a duke of Egypt, Duke Andrew, arrived at Bologna, with women, children and men from his own country. There might be a hundred. This duke having denied the Christian faith, the King of Hungary had taken possession of his lands and person. Then he told the King that he wished to return to Christianity, and he had been baptised with about four thousand men ; those who refused to be baptised were put to death. After the King of Hungary had thus taken them and re-baptised them, he commanded them to travel about the world for seven years, to go to Rome to see the Pope, and afterwards to return into their own country. When they arrived at Bologna they had been journeying for five years, and more than half of them were dead. They had a decree from the King of Hungary, the Emperor, in virtue of which they were allowed to thieve during these seven years, wherever they might go, without being amenable to justice.

" When they arrived at Bologna, they lodged themselves inside and outside the gate of Galiera, and settled themselves under the porticoes, except the duke, who lodged at the King's Inn. They remained a fortnight at Bologna. During this time many people went to see them, on account of the duke's wife, who, it was said, could foretell what would happen to a person during his life, as well as what was interesting in the present, how many children would be born, whether a woman was good or bad, and other things ; concerning all of which she told truly. And of those who wished to have their fortunes told, few went to consult without having their purse stolen, and the women had pieces of their dress cut off. The women of the band wandered about the town, seven or eight together ; they entered the houses of the inhabitants, and whilst they were telling idle tales, some of them laid hold of what was within their reach. In the same way they visited the shops under the pretext of buying something, but in reality to steal. Many thefts were committed in this way in Bologna. So it was cried throughout the town that no one should go to see them under a penalty of fifty pounds and excommunication, for they were the most cunning thieves in all the world. It was even allowed to those who had been robbed by them to rob them in return to the amount of their losses. In consequence of which several of the inhabitants of Bologna slipped during the night into a stable where some of their horses were shut up, and stole the best of them. The others, wishing to get back their horses, agreed to restore a great number of the stolen articles. But seeing that there was nothing more to gain there, they left Bologna and went off towards Rome.

" Observe that they were the ugliest brood ever seen in this country. They were thin and black, and they ate like swine : their women went in smocks and wore a pilgrim's cloak across the shoulder, rings in their ears, and a long veil on their head. One of them gave birth to a child in the market place, and at the end of three days, she went on to join her people."

On the 7th August of the same year they were at Forti, on the road to Rome. The chronicler says that some of them said they came from India, and he also says that for two days they went to and fro like wild beasts and thieves. They left Forti for Rome. The object of this journey is clear enough. Their original story told of a seven years' wandering, and the seven years were drawing to a close. They needed some further safe-conduct than that given by Sigismund. There seems to be no doubt that they did get an audience of Pope Martin V (though the Vatican archives have not got a record of it) for later in the year they were back again in Switzerland and they had with them papal as well as imperial safe-conducts. And there seems to be some evidence that they were here joined by a few Gypsies newly arrived from Hungary with a fresh safe-conduct from Sigismund.

For almost five years after this we lose sight of them. But in the August of 1427 they appeared outside Paris, then held by the English, and we have a very full chronicle of the event :

" On the Sunday after the middle of August, which was the 17th day of August of the said year 1427, came to Paris twelve penitents as they called themselves, that is to say, a duke, an earl, and ten men all on horseback, who said they were good Christians, and were from lower Egypt ; and said, moreover, that they had been Christians formerly, and that it was not long since the Christians had conquered them and all their country, and made them all become Christians, or put to death those who would not ; those who were baptised were lords of the country as before, and promised to be good and loyal, and to keep the faith of Jesus Christ unto death. And they had a king and queen in their country, who remained in their domains because they were Christianised.

" *Item*, True, as they said, a certain time after they had taken the Christian faith, the Saracens came and attacked them, and then, as they were but little firm in our faith with very little hope, without scarcely enduring the war, and without doing their duty towards their country, defending it very little, they surrendered to their enemies and became Saracens as before, and denied our Lord.

" *Item*, It happened afterwards that the Christians, such as the Emperor of Germany, the King of Poland, and other lords, when they knew that they had thus falsely and without great difficulty abandoned our faith, and that they had so soon become Saracens and idolaters, threw themselves upon them and soon vanquished them, as though they thought that they would be left in their country as before to become Christians. But the Emperor and the other lords, by a great deliberation in council, said that they should never hold land in their country unless the Pope consented, and that they should go to the Holy Father at Rome ; and there they went all, old and young, with great pain to the children. When they were there they made a general confession of their sins. When the Pope had heard their confession, he gave them as penance, after a great deliberation in council, to go for seven years following about the world, without sleeping in a bed ; and that they might have some comfort for their expense, ordered, as was said, that every bishop and mitred abbot should give them one payment of ten livres tournois ; and he gave them letters making mention of this to the prelates of the Church, and gave them his benediction ; so they departed. And they had been five years about the world before they came to Paris.

"And they came the 17th day of August in the year 1427, the above-named twelve ; and on the day of St. John the Beheaded the commoner people came, who were not allowed to enter Paris, but were lodged by authority at La Chappelle-Saint-Denis ; and they were not more in all, men, women and children, than about a hundred or a hundred and twenty, and when they left their country they were a thousand or twelve hundred, but the remainder had died on the way, and their king and queen ; and those who were alive had hope of still having worldly goods, for the Holy Father had promised them that he would give them a good and fertile land to inherit, but that they must finish their penance with a good heart.

"*Item*, Whilst they were at La Chappelle more people were never seen to go to the benediction of the Landit than came from Paris, from Saint Denis, and from the neighbourhood of Paris, to see them. And it is true that the children, boys and girls, were as clever as could be. And most and nearly all had both ears pierced, and in each ear a silver ring, or two in each, and they said it was a sign of nobility in their country.

"*Item*, The men were very black, their hair was fuzzled ; the women the ugliest that could be seen, and the blackest ;

all had their faces covered with wounds (tattoo marks ?), hair as black as a horse's tail, as only dress an old blanket, very coarse and fastened on the shoulder by a band of cloth or cord, and underneath a poor shift for all covering. In short, they were the poorest creatures ever seen in France in the memory of man. And, notwithstanding their poverty, there were witches in their company who looked into people's hands and told what had happened to them, or would happen, and sowed discord in several marriages, for they said to the husband 'your wife has played you false,' or to the wife, ' your husband has played you false.' And, what was worse, whilst they were speaking to folks by magic or otherwise, or by the enemy in hell, or by dexterity and skill, it was said they emptied people's purses and put into theirs. But in truth ; I went there three or four times to speak to them, but I never perceived that I lost a penny, nor did I ever see them look into a hand, but the people said so everywhere, so that the news came to the Bishop of Paris who went there, and took with him a Friar of the Minors named Little Jacobin, who by command of the Bishop made a fine preaching, excommunicating all those who had believed them and shown their hands. And they were obliged to depart ; and they departed on the day of Our Lady of September, and went away towards Pointoise."

Three weeks later, at Amiens, Thomas, Earl of Little Egypt, with forty followers, received pious alms from the mayor and aldermen after showing them the papal letters. Curiously, the mayor and aldermen of Amiens do not appear to have heard of these wandering penitents before they came and seem to have been taken completely by surprise and thrown into a considerable flurry. And so the story goes on. There is not need to follow it in detail, for each account has much the same story to tell. In the next seven years we have records of wandering bands of Egyptians at many places including Tournai, Utrecht, Arnheim, Bommel, Middleburg, Metz, Leyden, Frankfurt and so on. I think there can be little doubt that during

the five years' gap between the visit to Rome and the visit
to Paris some members of the band had returned to spread
the good news, for though the main invasion did not com-
mence until about 1438 there do seem to have been many
more wandering bands after 1427.   In 1438, however,
thousands began to pour into Europe, overrunning
Germany, Italy and France.   They were in Spain by
1447, in Poland and Russia by 1501, in Sweden by
1512.   And within a few years of their arrival steps were
being taken in every country for their suppression and
removal.

We do not know when the Gypsies first came to Britain.
The first mention of them by that name is in the accounts
of the Lord High Treasurer for Scotland under the date
22nd April, 1505.   But that reference obviously refers to
the Gypsies of this new invasion (the word Egyptian is
exclusively their own and was unknown before the entry
of the pioneering bands into Germany in 1417) and does
no more than indicate that they were in this country before
that date.   We do not know how long before nor do we
know for certain if we had Gypsies in these islands before
the great invasion swept across Europe.   Be that as it may
—and we shall not now I fancy get any nearer the true
date—there is some corroborative evidence for a date
before the middle of the fifteenth century.   And again it
comes from Scotland.   Simson says that " in the reign of
James II away putting of sorners, fancied fools, vagabonds,
out-liers, masterful beggars, cairds, and such like runners
about, is more than once enforced by Acts of Parliament " :
and we have for example an Act of the Scottish Parliament
of the year 1449 which is directed against " sorners, over-
liers, and masterful beggars, with horse, hounds, or other
goods."   Sorners were people who forcibly quartered
themselves upon others.   Now there is no mention of the
word Gypsy in this act, but it aims at a class corresponding
in every particular, even down to the " dogs of the chase,"
with the earlier pioneering Gypsies of the Continent.   And,
furthermore, when we do finally come to the word

" Egyptians " in Scottish Acts of Parliament we find it used to describe people with just those very habits so clearly outlined in the Act of 1449. I do not think, despite the lack of the word Egyptians, that there can be any reasonable doubt that the newcomers among Gypsies were in Scotland before 1449.

And it is to Scotland we must turn, for the first reference to the Gypsies, as such, in Great Britain which occurs in the accounts of the Lord High Treasurer for Scotland in 1505. It is very short : " 1505, Apr. 22. Item to the Egyptians be the Kinge's command vii lib." No more : we do not know what this payment of £7 was for, but it seems to be generally accepted that it was for some sort of entertainment. I think it is at least as likely that it was a charitable payment to pilgrims on the same lines as those made by so many people on the Continent nearly a hundred years later. The penance and pilgrimage tale was apparently never used in England (probably because the English had had plenty of experience of it in France) but it was certainly worked in Scotland, for in July, 1505, we find the King, James IV, writing to his uncle, the King of Denmark, commending to him, " Anthony Gagino, a lord of Little Egypt," who with his retinue had reached Scotland a few months earlier " during a pilgrimage through the Christian world, undertaken at the command of the Apostolic See." One of the most intriguing, and inexplicable, things about this period of Gypsy history is the marked change in the Royal attitude towards them. James II had shown no love for the sorners and masterly beggars of his time : James IV went out of his way to aid the Egyptians financially and to commend them to the ruler of the next country they were to visit. James V had them to dance before him at Holyrood House in 1530 and paid them for doing so. And this, moreover, at a time when they were rapidly losing their glamour and acquiring their merited reputation. In the Council Register for the City of Aberdeen under date May 8th, 1527, we read (I have modernised the English) :

" The said day, it was sufficiently proved before the baillies and a part of Council, present for the time, by famous divers witnesses, that the Egyptians took out of Thomas Watson's house two silver spoons, lying in the locker of a cabinet, which contained each one an ounce of silver, wherefore they charged Aiken Jacks, master of the said Egyptians, to deliver the said spoons again, or their equivalent, within twenty-four hours, because he answered and became good for his company in judgement : and as to the money the said Thomas alleged was taken away by them, the baillies adjourned the question because they got no witness to prove more clearly. And moreover, John Watson, and his mother and servant, were made quit of all annoyance from the said Egyptians, and that was given for doom."

Aiken Jacks is obviously an assumed name. It was a common name in Aberdeen at this time, and is good Scots. I think this is the first occasion on which we come across the Gypsy practice of adopting the names of the people among whom they stayed, or rather the first occasion of its use by the Egyptians. In this Aberdeen record we see the Gypsies in their traditional rôle of thieves. We find them in the same Council Register, and again for theft, on 22nd January, 1530. The names, this time, make very interesting reading, for the accused were Barbara Dya Baptista and Helen Andree, and they were described as the servants of George Faw, Earl of Egypt. Andree is probably the Scots Andrew, but Baptista is no Scots name at all and Dya is, of course, merely the Romani word *dya*, O mother. And this is also the earliest definite mention of the famous Scots Gypsy name Faw or Faa in connection with Gypsies, though a John Faw and a Patrick Faw are mentioned in the Register of the Great Seal of Scotland as holding land in Lothian in 1507. The chieftainship of this band seems to have been shared by two brothers George and John Faw, and they made themselves notorious in the Aberdeen neighbourhood, for we find them mentioned several times in the Council Register for various offences, including drawing the blood of one Sandie Barron. They were tried fairly on every occasion and indeed judged with leniency, but they were evidently too much for their hosts in the end, for on 21st February, 1540, this edict was recorded by the City Council :

"The baillies charged George Faw, Egyptian, and his brother, to remove themselves their company and goods out of this town, betwixt this date and Sunday next, under all penalty and charge that thereafter may follow : and in the meantime, that none of their company come into any house or close in this town, unless they be sent about, and if any does what may be away in the same house, that the said George and his brother shall refund the same."

The edict was never obeyed. Six days previously James V had signed a writ of the Privy Council of Scotland which granted to the Gypsies astonishing privileges, and I suppose knowledge of this document reached Aberdeen before the Council's edict was enforced. This writ was in effect a treaty between the King of Scotland and " John Faw, Lord and Earl of little Egypt " :

"James, by the Grace of God, King of Scots : To our Sherrife of Edinburgh, principal and within the constabulary of Haddington, Berwick, Roxburgh, Selkirk, Perth, Forfar, Fife, etc. etc., provosts, aldermen and baillies of our burghs and cities of Edinburgh, etc. etc., greeting : For as much as it is humbly meant and shown to us, by our loved John Faw, Lord and Earl of Little Egypt, that whereas he obtained our letter under our great Seal, direct you all and sundry our said sherrifs, stewards, baillies, provosts, aldermen, and baillies of burghs, and to all and sundry others having authority within our realm, to assist him in execution of justice upon his company and folk, conform to the laws of Egypt, and in punishing of all them that rebel against him : nevertheless, as we are informed, Sebastiane Lalow Egyptian, one of the said John's company, with his accomplices and partakers under written, that is to say, Anteane Donea, Satona Fingo, Nona Finco, Phillip Hatseyggow, Towla Bailzon, Grasta Neyn, Geleyr Bailzow, Bernard Beige, Demer Matskalla, Notfaw Lawlowr, Martyn Femine, rebels and conspirators against the said John Faw, and have removed them all utterly out of his company, and taken from him divers sums of money, jewels, clothes and other goods, to the quantity of a great sum of money ; and on nowise will pass home with him, howbeit he has bidden and remained of long time upon them, and is bound and obliged to bring home with him all them of his company that are alive, and a testimony of them that are dead : and as the said John has the said Sebastiane's obligation, made in Dunfermline before our master's household, that he and his company should remain with him, and on nowise depart from him, as the same bears : In contrary to the tenor of which, the said Sebastiane, by sinister and wrong information of false relation, circumvention of us, has purchased our writings, discharging him and the remnant of the persons above written, his accomplices and partakers of the said John's company, and with his goods taken by them from him ; causes certain our lieges assist them and their opinions, and to fortify and take their part against the said John, their lord and master ; so that he on nowise can apprehend nor get them, to have them home again within their own country, after the tenor of his said bond, to his heavy damage and hurt, and in great peril of losing his heritage, and expressly against justice : Our will is, therefore, and we charge you straightly and command that . . . ye and every one of you within the bounds of your offices, command and charge all our lieges, that none of them take upon hand to reset, assist, fortify, supply, maintain, defend or take part with the said Sebastiane and his accomplices above written, for no body's nor other way, against the

said John Faw, their lord and master ; but that they
and ye, in likewise, take and lay hands upon them
wherever they may be apprehended and bring them to
him, to be punished for their demerits, conform to his
laws ; and help and fortify him to punish and do justice
upon them for their trespasses ; and to that effect lend
him your prisons, stocks, fetters, and all other things
necessary thereto, as ye and each of you, and all our
lieges, will answer to us thereupon, and under all highest
pain and charge that may follow : So that the said John
have no cause of complaint thereupon in time coming,
nor to resort to us again to that effect, notwithstanding
any our writings, sinisterly purchased or to be purchased, by the said Sebastiane on the contrary ; And
also charge all our lieges that none of them molest, vex,
unquiet, or trouble the said John Faw and his company
in doing their lawful business, or otherwise, within our
realm, and in their passing, remaining, or away-going for
the same, under the pain above written : And such-like
that ye command and charge all skippers, masters and
mariners of all ships within our realm, at all ports and
havens where the said John Faw and his company shall
happen to resort and come, to receive him and them
therein, upon their expenses, for furthering of them forth
of our realm to the parts beyond the sea, as you and each
of them such-like will answer to us thereupon and under
the pain aforesaid. Subscribed with our hands, and
under our privy seal at Falkland, the fifteenth day of
February, and of our reign the 28th year."

Such a document can only be called a treaty. Endless
reasons for it have been given, the most convincing being,
I think, that advanced by Walter Simson, namely, that
James V had a fondness for Gypsies, was pretty gullible
and got well " led up the garden " by John Faw. What
had happened, Simson thought, was that the thieving and
general rascality of the Gypsies had reached such a pitch
that the Scottish court (at which Faw appears to have been

quite a personage) begged him to bring his pilgrimage to
an end, at least so far as Scotland was concerned. But
Scotland was a profitable place, and so Faw invented the
story of the rebellion and his tale that he could not return
to his own country without his full company. He said in
effect that, if he were helped to catch them, he would, as
soon as they were caught, depart, if ships were provided
for him. The rebellion at any rate was a put-up job.
Scotland was not a well-policed nor entirely law-abiding
country in the reign of James V, and any such rebellion
would have been quickly settled by Faw, or made complete
by Lawlor, by physical force. The Faas and the Baillies
did quarrel later on—the quarrel was said to be for the
Gypsy Crown—and this quarrel lasted for many, many
years, but it did not arise from this " rebellion " but more
likely from some unfortunate marriage between the
families. The names given in the treaty are of great
interest. Faw and Bailyow are the only ones that have
any Scottish connection, Bailyow being merely a variant
of Balliol or Baillie. Lawlowr is the old English name
Lawlor ; and the Christian name Notfaw is obviously due
to a painstaking but unintelligent clerk who copied down
the correction of a Gypsy who said : " *Not* Faw, Lawlowr."
MacRitchie suggested that Femine might be a spelling of
Fleming and that Matskalla might be Macskalla, in which
case it would be a Gaelic name. I have never heard
Macskalla as a Gaelic name nor can I find it in Gaelic
literature, and I think both suggestions a little far-fetched.
The other names are obviously foreign. The Gypsies had
not yet fully adopted the practice of taking the names of
good families for their own.

The treaty (which acknowledged to the Gypsies the right
to practise their own laws and customs within the Scottish
kingdom) was very short-lived. On June 6th, 1541, an
order in council was made respecting John Faw :

" The which day anent the complaint given by John
Faw and his brother, and Sebastiane Lalow, Egyptians,

to the King's grace, ilk ane plenizeand . . . upon other and divers faults and injuries ; and that is a greed among them to pass home, and have the same decided before the Duke of Egypt. The lords of the council, being advised with the points of the said complaints, and understanding perfectly the great thefts and hurts done by the said Egyptians upon our sovereign lord's lieges, wherever they come or resort, ordain letters to be directed to the provosts and baillies of Edinburgh, St. Johnstown, Dundee, Montrose, Aberdeen, St. Andrews, Elgin, Forres and Inverness ; and to the sherriffs of Edinburgh, Fife, Perth, Forfar, Kincardine, Aberdeen, Elgin and Forres, Banff, Cromarty, Inverness, and all other sherriffs, stewards, provosts and baillies, where it happens the said Egyptians to resort, to command and charge them, by open proclamation, at the market crosses of the head burghs of the sherriffdoms, to depart forth of this realm, with their wives, children and companies, within thirty days after they be charged thereto, under the pain of death : notwithstanding any other letters or privileges granted to them by the king's grace, because his grace, with the advice of the lords, has discharged the same for the causes aforesaid : with certification that if they be found in this realm, the said thirty days being past, they shall be taken and put to death."

This is reversal indeed, and all sorts of reasons have been given for it, including the tale that James V travelling with the Gypsies was hit on the head with a bottle by an irate husband for making advances to one of the women and that he was compelled to carry their goods on his back until he collapsed from fatigue (there is a similar story told of the English King John), the order being the result of his not unnatural indignation. I think Walter Simson is correct in maintaining that whatever may have been the true story the decree was the result of personal irritation, for it lapsed under his successor. It did not in any case succeed in banishing the Gypsies from Scotland, though it does seen to have driven the Faws south of the border for a while, for we find " Baptist Fawe, Amy Fawe and George Faw, Egiptians," in Durham in 1549. They were back again in 1553, however, and basking once more in the royal favour. Indeed, with the exception of the brief period of the decree of James V (and he died in 1542), the Gypsies lived in Scotland more or less as royal protégés from 1505 to 1579 when James VI took control and repressive legislature was really started.

The earliest mention of the Gypsies in England is a mention in *A Dyalog of Syr Thomas More, knyght*, which says that in 1514 the King sent the lords to enquire into the death of Richard Hunne, in the Lollard's Tower. One of the witnesses mentioned an Egyptian woman who had been lodging in Lambeth, but had gone overseas a month before, and who could tell marvellous things by looking into one's hand. Edward Hale in his *Chronicles* says that two ladies at a Court mummery in 1517 had their heads robed in a kind of gauze and tippers " Like the Egyptians " embroidered with gold : and again in 1520 he says that at a state banquet eight ladies came in attired " like to the Egyptians," very richly. The name appears again in Skelton's " Elynoure Rumminge " which was written about 1517, and again in his *Garland of Laurel* which was published in 1526 and in which the word " Gypsy " appears for the first time. The line runs :

" By Mary Gipsy, quod scripsi scripsi."

We know that some time about 1520 some " Gypsions " were entertained by the Earl of Surrey at Tendring Hall in Suffolk, and that in 1521 one William Cholmeley gave certain " Egyptions " at Thornbury forty shillings (equivalent to something like £40 in 1943 money), while in 1522 the churchwardens of Stratton, in Cornwall, received twenty pence from the " Egypcions " for the use of the churchyard. But in all these early English records there is not (in contrast to Scottish records) a single Gypsy name mentioned. Samuel Reid, in his *Art of Juggling* which was published in 1612, is the first man to name an English Gypsy. He gives 1528 as the year in which the Egyptians invaded England and says that they were then in the south and earned a good living by palmistry, fortune-telling and cheating. They rode on horseback and wore strange apparel and their king was Giles Hather and their queen Kit Calot. Thornbury, however, in his *Shakespeare's England*, published in 1856, says that their chief in Henry VIII's time was Cock Lorel and that he was followed by Ratsee. Harrison, in his *Description of England*, which is prefixed to Holinshed's *Chronicle*, describes various forms of roguery then practised in England and adds :

" They are now supposed, of one sex and another, to amount unto above ten thousand persons : as I have heard reported. Moreover, in counterfeiting the Egyptians rogus, they have devised a language among themselves, which they name Canting, but others pedlers' French, a speech compact thirty years since of English, and a great number of od words of their owne devising, without all order or reason ; and yet such is it as none but themselves are able to understand ; The first deviser thereof was hanged by the neck, a just reward no doubt for his desartes, and a common end to all of that profession."

By 1530—the year in which the Egyptians danced before James V in Holyrood House and received forty shillings for doing so—they had made themselves so great a nuisance in England that an Act—the first of many repressive measures passed in England—was passed dealing with them. It says that :

" Afore this tyme dyverse and many outlandyeshe People callynge themselfes Egyptians, usyng no Crafte nore faicte of Merchaundyce had comen into this Realme and gone from Shire to Shire and Place to Place in greate Company, and used greate subtyll and crafty means to deceyve the People, berying them in Hande

that they by Palmestre coulde telle Menne and Womens
Fortunes and so many tymes by crafte and subtyltie had
deceyved the People of theyr Money and also had
comytted many and haynous Felonyes and Robberies to
the great Hurte and Deceyte of the People that they had
comyn amonge.'.

And in order to stop further immigration it was enacted
that :

"From hensforth no suche Psone be suffred to come
within this the Kynge's Realme."

If any did, they were to forfeit all their goods, and to be
ordered to leave the country within fifteen days, and if
they did not do so they were to be imprisoned. Furthermore, if "any such stranger" thereafter committed any
murder, robbery, or other felony, and, upon being
arraigned, he pleaded not guilty, the jury was to be composed "alltogether of Englysshemen" instead of half
Englishmen and half foreigners, which they were otherwise entitled to claim under an Act of Henry VI. All the
Gypsies in England at the time the Act was proclaimed
were to leave within sixteen days, or to be imprisoned and
to forfeit their goods : but if any of these goods were
claimed as stolen, they were upon proper proof to be forth-
with restored to the owner. As an inducement—bribe
would be a better word—to enforce the Act zealously, all
Justices of the Peace, Sheriffs or Escheators, who seized the
goods of any Gypsies, were to retain half of them as their
own, and to account in the Court of Exchequer for the
other half, and they were excused paying any fees or
charges upon rendering the account.

The Act, of course, had no effect and does not seem to
have been enforced with any vigour. There was a prose-
cution or two, but nothing serious happened until 1544
when a large band of Gypsies was arrested in Huntingdon-
shire, convicted and sentenced to deportation. They were
taken to Calais, the nearest English port on the Continent.

Later in the same year some Gypsies arrested in Lincoln-shire were sent to Norway. But for the rest they wandered about the country much as before. The Act had, however, made one great change in the law and one greatly to the disadvantage of the Gypsies, who had hitherto had a great advantage. Up to its passing, a Gypsy who murdered or robbed an Englishman could demand a jury composed half of Gypsies. And anyone can see what that meant. It meant that an Englishman in the same position was at a great disadvantage, and this meant inevitably that a number of the more rascally English took, if they possibly could, to the Gypsy way of life and consorted if possible with Gypsies, and the prospect was the more alluring to those with a distaste for work by reason of the Gypsy aversion to hard work. That it was not uncommon for English-men to consort with Gypsies is shown by the legislation against it. Indeed men and women were hanged for doing so. A severe penalty, but in Tudor times methods of dealing with vagabondage were as crude as they were unsuccessful.

The Act of 1530 was but the first of many. Though they were cruel and comprehensive—just to be a Gypsy was sufficient to bring a sentence of death (the last occasion on which this death penalty was enforced seems to have been at the end of Cromwell's dictatorship when thirteen were hung at one Suffolk assize)—they were not effective. It was estimated that in Queen Elizabeth's reign there were 10,000 Gypsies in England, and from this time onwards we find records of their baptism in parish churches. Gradually they came to be accepted as a part, if a regrettable part, of English life, though repressive legislation was enacted as late as 1908.

Deportation, however, was common. In 1665 at Edin-burgh an order was passed banishing certain Gypsies to Jamaica and Barbados. In 1715 nine Scottish Gypsies—named Faa, Finnick, Lindsay, Roberston, Ross, Stirling and Yorstoun—were transported to Virginia. These seem to have been the first British Gypsies to be sent to America

(France probably deported some of hers), the forerunners
of the many thousands now in the States. Portugal and
Spain deported Gypsies to Africa and South America, and
we did the same to Australia, where some of them rose to
affluence. Almost every country in which Gypsies have
settled has at one time or another banished them. Germany did so in 1497, Spain in 1499, France in 1504, England in 1531, Denmark in 1536, Moravia in 1538, Scotland
in 1541, Poland in 1557, Venice in 1549, 1558 and 1588,
and so on. But the Gypsies remained. No race, not even
the Jews, have so firmly held to their way of life in the face
of such vigorous attempts at suppression.

It would not be right to close this brief account of the
beginnings of Gypsydom in Britain without some mention
of tinkers and their speech. In England we do not use the
word tinker much nowadays. It used to indicate a wandering smith, and then came to mean any wandering person
who lived a certain sort of life and followed certain recognised and generally unconventional occupations. It soon
became synonymous with Gypsy, since the Gypsies led the
same sort of life and followed the same occupations, and it
rapidly gave way to the new word. Nowadays we divide
our wandering population quite arbitrarily, and very
inaccurately, into tramps and Gypsies. The Gypsies are
those that have caravans or wear rather odd clothes, the
tramps are all the rest. We pay no attention to race.

In Scotland the word is still used : and in Scotland, too,
it is synonymous with Gypsy. But the Scots speak of
tinkler-Gypsies where we speak of Gypsies, and the combination suggests that there was at one time a recognisable,
though small, distinction between the two. The tinkler
was known in Scotland long before the arrival of the
" Egyptians." He followed the same way of life, practised
the same deceits, had the same occupations, but was yet
different from the Egyptians. He was different in appearance, in the clothes he wore, in the language he spoke. (He
was different, perhaps, because he had been there so very
much longer. The English Gypsy after four hundred years

of England has forgotten a great deal of his language—
Anglo-Romani is now a very corrupt tongue—and has
married so frequently with the gorgio that often he does not
resemble a Gypsy physically.)   Anyway he was different,
and the Scot recognised the difference.   But the similarity
in the way of life and customs was so close that before long
he classed the two together as tinkler-Gypsies.   In Scotland
the original tinkler population more than held its own with
the newcomers : in England it failed to do so.

Until comparatively recently Scotland was much more
closely associated with Ireland than with England, and
there was a constant traffic between the two countries.
The tinkler-Gypsies, isolated from England and English
Gypsies and helped by the wildness of the country they
inhabited, have evolved a language of their own, which is
a compound of Gaelic, Romani, cant and Shelta.   Shelta
is the language of the Irish tinkers.   The word tinker is
very far from dead in Ireland : the word Gypsy has never
had any currency, for the Gypsies have never invaded
Ireland in any numbers and if there is a Gypsy population
in the island it must be a very small one.   The wandering
folk of Ireland are tinkers and they are quite distinct from
Gypsies.   Quite distinct : and yet obviously closely allied,
so closely allied, in fact, that it has been suggested that they
are a branch of the Romanies.   They follow the same way
of life ; are smiths, horse-dealers, fortune-tellers ; have
many of the same customs.   They are not just Irishmen
who have taken to the road.   They are a race.   (One of
them told Dr. Sampson that he could always recognise a
tinker woman by her appearance, and James Arigho, a
tinker friend of mine, supports this, maintaining that he
can always tell a tinker of pure blood by his appearance.)
They are a race distinct from, yet similar to the Gypsies.
And they have a language of their own.   It has long been
known, of course, that itinerant tinkers have a jargon of
their own.   Shakespeare, who knew something about
everything, refers to it in the first part of *King Henry IV*
(Act 2, Sc. 4), when he makes Prince Henry boast that he

" can drink with any tinker in his own language." That cannot, however, be taken to mean that Shakespeare knew of the existence of Shelta, only that he knew of the existence of cant. Shelta is not a jargon, it is a language. Furthermore, it was, until recently, a secret language—how secret will be realised when it is said that George Borrow was completely unaware of its existence.

Ireland was rich in secret languages—they are not as melodramatic as they sound—having no less than six, of which we have some knowledge to-day, and it is quite possible that there were others which have vanished altogether. The six are Ogham, Hisperic Latin, the corrupted Irish of the Dúil Laithne (which Professor Macalister has called Bog Latin), Bérlae na Filed, Béarlagair na Saer, and Shelta. All these languages are artificial. That is to say, they were made by learned men who introduced all sorts of archaic words and forms, borrowed from the Greek and the Latin, indulged in such devices as the use of words in a figurative sense, the reversal of words, the omission of a letter or a syllable, or the addition or insertion of letters or syllables. They were originally languages manufactured by scholars for the use of scholars, a means of concealing knowledge, of preserving certain knowledge within a comparatively narrow circle. Ogham is the most ancient of the six. There are those who maintain that it was the Druidical language, and was in existence at the time of Cæsar's invasion of Gaul. (Druidism was the religion of Gaul at the time and Cæsar hints strongly that the headquarters were in Britain.) That the Druids had a secret language of their own is beyond doubt, but I confess—I am no authority and put this forward humbly—to doubting whether Ogham as we know it was that language. And there are those who maintain that it was still in existence in 1328. It is true that we are told that in that year there died one " Morish O'Gibellan . . . an exact speaker of the speech that is called ogham." But I do not think that it was the Ogham of the monuments, of the Druids if you will. I think that Ogham at the time of O'Gibellan's death meant no more than " good literary Irish " as opposed to ordinary everyday Irish talk. Next in age comes Hisperic Latin (it should be Hisperic Latin and Irish) which was a language manufactured by the students in the monasteries, and dates back to somewhere around 600 A.D. The corrupted Irish of the book Dúil Laithne dates from the late fourteenth or early fifteenth century. I do not know what dates are given by the authorities for Bérlae na Filed (the language of the poets) and Béarlagair na Saer (the vernacular of the masons), but they, too, belong to the Middle Ages and were connected originally with the monasteries. The impact of Irish monasterial life and thought upon the Irish nation was very wide, and many people must have had the opportunity of picking up a word or two here and there of these secret languages. No doubt, too, there were from time to time adventurous or rebellious souls who cut adrift from the monasteries and took to the roads (as renegades they would find hospitality nowhere else) bearing with them the language of their craft. And finally, with the religious upheavals the masons and the smiths would be forced, many of them at any rate, to take their skill elsewhere. It is indeed not surprising that these secret languages should have spread by degrees beyond the bounds of their craft ; what is surprising is that having done so they should still have remained secret.

Four of these six secret languages are altogether dead. Two, Shelta and Béarlagair na Saer, survive. Attention was first drawn to the existence of the latter as long ago as 1808 when a list of twenty words was given by P. McElligott in *The Transactions of the Gaelic Society of Dublin*. In 1859 Edward FitzGerald, a Youghal architect, published a vocabulary of 250 words and six phrases. To-day we know some 400 words.

Shelta was discovered in 1876 by Charles Godfrey Leland, who stumbled across it near Bath. His own description of the discovery is given in his book *The Gypsies*. He came across an itinerant knife-grinder and talked to him in Romani. He found that he knew a little of it (there are very few men on the roads who do not know a word or two) but the knife-grinder was not impressed. " We're a-givin' Romanes up very fast—all of us is," he remarked. " It's a-gettin' to be too blown. Everybody knows some Romanes now. But there *is* a jib that ain't blown," he added reflectively. " Back slang and cantin' and rhymin' is grown vulgar, and Italian always was the lowest of the lot. Now Romanes is genteel. I've heard there's actilly a book about it. But as for this other jib, it's very hard to talk. It's most all Old Irish, and they calls it *Shelter.*"

From that humble beginning sprang great things. The Bath knife-grinder apparently knew no Shelta, and Leland admits that he was not impressed, assuming " that the man merely meant Old Irish." Leland meant by Old Irish, Gaelic (the expression is used by tramps on the roads to this day to indicate a man who speaks Gaelic) and was no more impressed by that than he would have been if a tramp had told him that Shelta was mainly Welsh. But a year later he was in Wales at Aberystwyth with E. H. Palmer, a brilliant linguist and an astonishing eccentric. Here they met a tramp, who was a man of some education, and who, hearing them talking Romani, spoke to them. Asked what he did for a living, he replied *Skelkin gallopas*, and shook both Leland and Palmer, both of whom had very extensive knowledge of Romani and the various jargons of the road, to the core. Asked what on earth he meant, he said " selling ferns," and that it was " Minklas Thari " (that is how Leland wrote it : more correctly, *Minker Tāral*) tinkers' talk, or Shelta. From this man Leland obtained the first vocabulary of the language. Some time later he had the luck to come across an Irish tramp in Philadelphia, named Owen MacDonald. He talked to this man in Romani, found that he knew a fair amount of it, and also " Old Irish," Welsh, Gaelic—I think that by this he must have meant Scots tinkler talk—and Shelta, though he only owned to the last after a good deal of pressure. From this man Leland took another and much longer vocabulary. Ten years after his discovery of the language he published a long article in *The Academy* in which he suggests that knowledge of the language was very widespread, in fact he says, " I doubt if I ever took a walk in London, especially in the slums, without meeting men and women who spoke Shelta "—an obvious exaggeration. This article in *The Academy* aroused interest and brought forth short lists of Shelta words from T. H. Crofton and T. W. Norwood. These in turn brought forth another short list from G. A. Wilson, who was given it by a lady who had taken the words down from a tinker child on the island of Tiree, and who told Wilson that the child's mother, when she discovered what had happened, tried to persuade her that they were only the fruits of an active imagination ; and also one from the Rev. J. F. M. ffrench taken down in Co. Wexford. Crofton had already pointed out that a good deal of Shelta was merely Gaelic reversed, in other words, Gaelic back-slang, and Wilson went one better by showing that the numerals given by Leland were merely Gaelic numerals mis-spelt. This threw a pretty douche of cold water on the idea of a new and secret language, and might well have drowned it altogether but for David MacRitchie. MacRitchie had himself taken down a long list of words from tinkers in Arran, and believed that Leland was right. He wrote to John Sampson and persuaded him to take the matter up. He could not, and of course he knew it, have made a better choice. Sampson was a genius at this sort of thing. He had an enormous knowledge of Romani, a very wide knowledge of most of the jargons of the road and of the men and women who spoke them, great experience in taking down Romani from the lips of deep speakers, an expert knowledge of phonetics, and in addition to all this he was a man of great courage, indomitable will and incurable curiosity.

Sampson began work in 1890. He started in the slums of Liverpool (then, as now, very largely an Irish city) and the slums of Liverpool in those days were almost as dangerous as they were dirty. Indeed he describes them as " safe

only for the dispensary doctor and the Catholic priest."
His first lists were taken from an itinerant knife-grinder
named Brennan. This man, however, did not know, or
pretended that he did not know, much Shelta (though he
admitted to having an uncle who never spoke anything
else unless he was obliged to do so), and Sampson soon
moved on. He met, a little later, three men who worked
together—two knife-grinders and an umbrella-mender—
and he spent some time with them collecting words. One
was called " Manni " Connor, another was called " The
Shah " and the third was known as *Re-Meather*, which
means Double Devil. They were an unpleasant trio.
Indeed Sampson, who was not unaccustomed to unpleasant characters, said that he had never seen three
more uncleanly and evil-looking men. But they spoke
with astonishing fluency a language of their own which
was made up of Romani, Shelta, flying cant and rhyming
slang, and this was just what Sampson wanted. He collected from them in tinkers' taverns. His association with
these three obviously could not last long under any circumstances, and the places in which he had to collect his words
made it certain that it would come to an end under
unpleasant conditions. Sampson described it thus : " On
the last occasion I was in their company we were seated
in an inner room with wooden table and sanded floor.
For obvious reasons I had placed them on the bench
against the wall, occupying, myself, the other side of the
table. Something, I forget what, aroused suspicion in their
minds, and there was an air of immense trouble which I
hoped at any rate would not be mine. I saw Manni rise
to get between me and the door, while Re-Meather was
surreptitiously unbuckling his belt. Grasping the table
with both hands, I turned it on its side, jamming them to
the seat, the three blue and white pots of beer sliding down
on them. Glancing back as I left the room, I saw those
three worthies framed in a kind of triptych against the
wall, and as I passed through this door I wished that I had
more time to admire their astonished faces." If you have

ever seen the havoc that can be worked by an angry man armed with a heavy belt—and I have—you will realise how wise he was to leave quickly.

Quite undeterred by this experience he set about finding another Shelta speaker, and this time he was very lucky. He fell in with John Barlow, a tinker aged seventy-nine, and he managed to make friends with him. Barlow really spoke the language. He learned it from his mother and father in childhood, and he spoke it unmixed with cant or Romani. Furthermore, he was honest, refusing to make up a word if he did not know it, and he could recognise, and invariably did, a Gaelic as opposed to a Shelta word, for he was also a natural and fluent Gaelic speaker. From him Sampson obtained a most extensive vocabulary, some stories in Shelta and other useful bits of information. He also introduced Professor Kuno Meyer, a great Celtic scholar, to him. Sampson had little or no knowledge of Gaelic : Meyer had a great knowledge of it and was thus able to probe deeper into Barlow's words and to put the whole enquiry on a rather more advanced footing. Barlow was himself convinced that Shelta was not only a secret language (he frequently stressed the fact that his father had warned him never to divulge it to strangers) but a very ancient one. He maintained, in fact, that the speakers of Shelta originally were not Irish at all, but the old travellers who first came to Ireland. Sampson believed that it was a secret language of great antiquity, which had acquired a basis of Irish at an early stage of its development. Professor Meyer after his investigations came to the same conclusion, and went further, in that he allied it to the other secret languages of Ireland.

There can be no doubt at all that Shelta is the language of the Irish tinkers, handed down from father to son, and spoken habitually, and in preference to Gaelic and English, by certain families. But I do not think that any great antiquity can be claimed for it. Some of it certainly goes back about as far as it can possibly go back, some of it certainly has connections with the ancient secret languages of Ireland, but much of it is merely Gaelic reversed, a good deal of it is merely old Gaelic left unaltered, and some of it, it seems to me (but Professor Macalister, who is the authority on the subject, makes no mention of it in his book, so I am probably wrong), is Welsh in origin. Professor Macalister has given in his book a complete—as complete as is known, that is—vocabulary of the language and shows the etymology of many, indeed most words. Some, like *kam* = son, *i.e.*, *mac* reversed, are easy : others are not at all easy, and for some he gives no etymology at all. *Dāl'on*, meaning God, is one of these : though I cannot imagine why he has rejected the possibility (probability to my mind) of its being a corrupt form of *Dúilem*, which means Creator. After that temerity, let me hasten to say how right he is in stressing the Englishness of Shelta. In its idiom and construction it is, as he very properly stresses, much more English than Irish. Obviously an Irish language originally it must have been fashioned into its present form by speakers whose main language was English. The words, many of them, are Irish words in common use, but they are used in a manner which no native speaker of Irish would dream of using. I know that he is absolutely right here. And I have had the truth of it driven home to me many times, albeit unconsciously, by a man who spoke Irish fluently as his native tongue and knew Shelta very well indeed. He used the same words in the two tongues— you could make him do so with a little care—but he used them quite differently. This Englishness of Shelta is, I think, most intriguing. It makes the whole thing so much more mysterious. And no one, so far as I know, has attempted the task of showing how it came about, nor even suggested a theory.

There seems to be an idea that Shelta is no longer used very much by the tinkers and that Béarlagair na Saer is no longer used at all. It is a completely erroneous idea. Shelta is still used considerably, even in England, no longer perhaps as a connected whole, a vital and separate speech (though I do know a Shelta speaker), but many words and phrases are very much alive. And the same is true of Béarlagair na Saer. This has long since ceased to be a language, but many of the words are used habitually by Shelta speakers, or at any rate the Shelta speaker I know best. Many of the words in this language are ordinary modern Irish corrupted—*i.e.*, *cabhaill* = horse, modern Irish *capall*—others are older forms, and there is some back slang and rhyming slang. I do not know where or how James Arigho picked up Béarlagair na Saer (I think that probably many of its words have been incorporated in Shelta), but he uses a number of words from it in his speech, and uses them absolutely naturally as he does Shelta and Romani words. He is a native speaker of Gaelic, knows Shelta very well indeed and quite a bit of Romani. He does not know Béarlagair na Saer as such, but he does know when he uses words from it that they are not Shelta words. He never muddles them up. If asked what they are he says (without hesitation as a rule) " Old Irish." It is interesting, too, to note the connections in which he uses some of them and their Shelta and Romani equivalents. For example, he is interested (what Irishman is not ?) in horses. His usual word for horse is *capall*, which is modern Irish, but if he desires to be explicit and to indicate a gelding, as opposed to an entire, he invariably uses the word *kuri*, which is Shelta. He uses the Béarlagair word *cabhaill* on occasions, but only when he is talking about horses that are dead, *i.e.*, " I once had a horse." I have twice heard him use *lapac* for horse (the word is not given by Macalister, but Arigho maintains that it is good Shelta, and it is obviously back slang for *capall*) and on both occasions he was referring to a Derby favourite that did not win. He uses the Romani word *grai* only when talking to Gypsies. So, too, with the word " woman." Normally he uses the Béarlagair word *be* (but this is a good Irish word that has fallen into disuse, except occasionally in poetry, rather than a true Béarlagair word) to indicate any young woman of pleasing appearance. He invariably uses the Shelta word *bewer* to indicate any woman of doubt-

ful morals or unpleasing appearance. This word, by the
way, has become current among English vagrants. I have
frequently heard it used by men and women who have no
connection whatsoever with either tinkers or Gypsies.
Another Béarlagair word that is quite commonly used by
English tramps is *long-shuain*, meaning a bed, which they
pronounce *longan*, not a bad approximation to the Irish
pronunciation.

None of the Romani words for tinker are complimentary
and most are the reverse. Gypsies do not like tinkers,
though they do on occasions marry with them—Dr.
Sampson knew a Liverpool tinker named Murray who had
married a Romani woman ; Helen Shevlin's husband was
an Irish tinker ; two of James Arigho's sons and one of his
daughters, though themselves pure-blooded Irish tinkers,
married Gypsies. I think the Gypsy dislike of the tinker
springs very largely from the similarity between the two in
the way they live and the way they earn a living, and
because wherever the two meet the Gypsy is blamed for sins
that more often than not are the tinker's. This is certainly
the case in Wales and down the Welsh border, a region
that experienced a big invasion of travelling Irish, but
elsewhere in England the Irish tinker is a rarity and the
Gypsy dislike has been transferred to the tramps and
vagrants for whose sins they too often get blamed. Equally
the tramps and vagrants of England blame the Gypsies,
generally I think unjustly, for the petty crimes of the road-
sides. The Irish tinker, however, and this applies equally
to the travelling Irish of Wales and the border counties,
has no particular dislike for the Gypsies. He either admires
them openly or is utterly indifferent to them.

III

TABOOS

ONE does not connect the word " taboo " with the quiet lanes and wind-swept heaths of Britain. It is too closely bound up with the names of Fraser and Crawley and Malinowski for that, with ancient religions or with the most primitive and pagan of savages. Or, if we do not happen to be familiar with *The Golden Bough* or *The Mystic Rose* or *Savages and Sex*, we may perhaps connect it with retired Anglo-Indians in a " school-tie " sense. In fact, we are likely to connect it with almost anything but the English countryside. Yet not so many years ago, certainly within the memory of many men and women now living, there was an elaborate system of taboos in force among English Gypsies, and, though that system in all its elaboration has died out, it would be a mistake to suppose that all the taboos have been discarded. So far from that being the case, there has, I think, been a perceptible increase in the observance of some in recent years.

Somebody once said—I have searched an extensive library but cannot at the moment give the reference—that a race without taboos is a race without virility, and it is a fact that the dropping of taboo observance is frequently the prelude to decline. The majority of taboos are connected with women, death and food, and the vast majority with women. It is when these begin to loosen that a decline not infrequently follows ; of that it would be possible to give innumerable examples. And it is a fact that until about the close of the third quarter of the last century an extensive system of taboos connected with women was observed by English Gypsies, and that at that time the English Gypsies were more coherent, purer in blood, and generally more prosperous than they have been since.

Of this branch of Romani lore, the great authority is

Mr. T. W. Thompson, and I am indebted to him for much of the information contained in this chapter. His enquiries were made among midland and northern Gypsies, who seem to have retained more of the ancient customs of their race than those in the south, but it should be remembered that they were made when the taboos he mentions had ceased to be widely observed, and that the men and women from whom he obtained the information themselves for the most part only knew of these taboos, elaborate as they were, in decline. We have no information about the full elaboration of taboo among English Gypsies, for it was in decline before a *rai* arose to record.

But I wonder sometimes if any taboo ever dies absolutely. I have heard a young English Gypsy declare something to be *mochardi* (unclean) when he could have had no experience of the ancient taboo, and when no other member of his family had any ideas on the subject. And I also knew an old south-country Gypsy, a man who had never travelled widely, who regarded many matters in much the same light as some of Thompson's midland Gypsies, and this old man observed certain food taboos punctiliously until the day of his death.

The word *mochardi* means unclean. Dogs and cats are *mochardi* in the sense that they are regarded by many Gypsies as dirty animals. Thompson was told that this was because they lick themselves all over, and that the horse was not regarded as *mochardi* because it does not. So Thompson's Gypsies would drink after a horse, but not after a dog. Amos Churen (who loathed cats) was an exceptionally clever trainer of dogs and treated his dogs with unfailing kindness, but nevertheless he regarded them as dirty animals. He would not allow them in his tent nor would he allow them to lick his face, though he did not mind them licking his hands. I do not know if he would have drunk after them, for I did not unfortunately come across Thompson's work until after his death, and so did not ask him, but I imagine not, although he had no misgivings about eating rabbits that they caught. This does not look as though he regarded dogs as particularly unclean, and some German Gypsies (according to Wittich, quoted by Thompson) train their dogs to steal meat from the butchers' shops, which indicates that they, too, do not regard the dog in quite the same light as the midland Gypsies of the middle of the last century. But I think the fact of the meat they catch being cooked makes all the difference. Incidentally, some Hungarian Gypsies I knew, who would cheerfully eat carrion, regarded cats as unmentionably dirty. A cup washed in water in which hands or face had been washed would be regarded as *morchardi*, dirty, by the vast majority of Gypsies to-day.

A definite distinction must be drawn between the word *mochardi* as applied to women in general and as applied to certain acts and things that may legitimately be described as dirty. It is a definite distinction, but it is at the same time indefinable. Thompson's informants would not define it nor explain it more clearly than by describing it as part of their religion. In this sense *mochardi* has nothing to do with dirtiness. It means unclean in the ceremonial sense only. At one time there can be no doubt that English Gypsy women, even when in normal health and circumstances, were regarded as unclean by their men ; not unclean in the dirty sense, but as a source of pollution, as dangerous to the health and strength of man. While this is no longer so, traces of it still linger here and there, and a woman not in full health is still in many families the subject of taboo.

I first came across taboo in connection with Gypsy women when I came to know Amos Churen fairly well, and almost all my personal experience of taboo among English Gypsies has come from the same source. Amos would not eat or drink anything that a woman had stepped over, nor would he touch a plate or a cup or any food utensil that a woman had stepped over. Indeed in such an event the food would be given to the dogs and the utensils destroyed. It would all be *mochardi*. This taboo is mentioned at some length by Thompson who gives many examples. Among the strictest midland Gypsies it was taken to great lengths—one man refusing to drink any water from a tap in his house because the pipes ran underground and the women must therefore step over them. Another made his women take a detour of three miles to reach a village only a mile away rather than allow them to cross the stream from which he drew his drinking water and which lay across the direct route. This prohibition against stepping over water is, of course, very old and is not confined to Gypsies. Fraser in *The Golden Bough* mentions the prohibition in Greece against a woman at the time of menstruation crossing a running stream, and a similar ban exists in many parts of the world. The Gypsy prohibition, however, is not confined to the time of menstruation nor, of course, only to English Gypsies. Coppersmith Gypsies have just the same taboos, and so have some of the most primitive of the Hungarian Gypsies. Thompson mentions an extension of this taboo among some south-country Gypsies so far as food and food-vessels are concerned in that the prohibition is made to apply to men as well. This, as he points out, is obviously a modern addition. I have not myself come across it nor have I heard of it, but another taboo mentioned for the same south-country Gypsies, and divulged to Thompson by the same man, was known to and observed by Amos Churen. Any food in which a hair was found was instantly thrown away. I did not see this happen to Amos, but he told me about it, and I have no doubt he meant what he said.

He did not, however, have any misgivings about women's hair. Among the midland Gypsies a woman was not allowed to let her hair down and comb it out in the presence of men; in fact, she could not do so anywhere except in her tent unless she was quite certain that only women and girls were present. This applied even to the woman's husband, for Thompson's informant told him that his mother never let her hair down outside her tent even when alone with her family. But this taboo was evidently not common to all midland Gypsies, for this man knew of families in which it was not observed and told Thompson how his father and his uncle reacted to the breaking of the ban by the ignorant—his father by getting up and walking away and his uncle by outspoken remonstrance. Amos had no knowledge of any such taboo, or if he had ignored it, for I often saw women combing their hair in his presence, and I have, in fact, not noticed any inhibitions about hair in the south country Gypsies I know, beyond the hair in food taboo mentioned to me by Amos. Nor do I think it has ever been a widespread taboo in Britain, for in one English and one Welsh family it was the custom for a girl already betrothed to warn off any other man who attempted to court her by letting her hair down, a custom I have also heard described by Gypsies in Denmark.

The deportment of women in camp was also a matter of regulation. Here, as in the stepping over food or water, there could be defilement without any actual contact. Even the way in which the women sat was a matter for regulation. According to Thompson's information, there were two recognised postures. Unmarried girls were allowed to sit only with their legs crossed and their feet tucked underneath them : married women might sit with their legs straight out if they so desired provided that they did not separate them, and this proviso was most important. On this point Thompson's two informants were quite definite : if in the presence of men the women must sit with their legs pressed tightly together. One of his informants was not definite about the distinction between married and unmarried women, but both made it quite clear that the legs-together position was not due to any question of modesty, for the rule applied with equal force if the only man present was husband or father or brother. I cannot say that I have ever noticed anything of this sort in force among the Gypsies with whom I am personally acquainted. The most usual sitting position for Gypsy women is cross-legged with the feet tucked under them, but in the families I know the women sit as they please and there is certainly no prescribed difference as between married and unmarried women. This was not the only rule of deportment in force among the older midland Gypsies by any means. Indeed, there were a great many and some of them were taken to great lengths in a few families. Only one other concerning the actual deportment of women in the camp need be mentioned here. A woman must never pass in front of a man when he is sitting down, even if he is her husband she must pass behind him. This taboo is widespread among Gypsies. It occurs all over Europe, though it is not observed with equal force everywhere, and I have met it in France, Italy, Austria, Germany, Hungary and Denmark. In England, Thompson mentions several families in which it was scrupulously observed, and I know a number in which it is still observed. Indeed it is probably true to say that the rule that a woman must pass behind a man who is sitting down is known to almost every English Gypsy of middle-age and over, and is still observed by a great many of them. I am not, however, certain that the reason for the rule (which is, of course, the fear of defilement) is known. Amos Churen, in whose family it was scrupulously observed, knew that it was *mochardi* for a woman to pass in front of a sitting man, but in the other families in which I have seen it observed I have never heard anything to suggest that the *mochardi* idea in this connection was known to them. It has, in fact, become a mere custom unrelated now to the ceremonial uncleanness taboo.

" At and following childbirth a Gypsy woman is considered a greater potential source of danger than at other times, and special precautions are necessary to protect men from possible contamination," says Thompson. It is a commonplace of Gypsy folk-lore that a woman has her own set of crockery for some time after she has given birth to a child. There is also a period of quarantine during which she is regarded as particularly *mochardi*. This period varies. A month is usual among English Gypsies. One family observed a month and a day, another three months, but regarded only the first really strictly, another three weeks, while I met a woman not long ago who told me that she was subject to restrictions from the time she first knew she was going to have a child until three months after the child was born. She lived in central Cornwall all her life and for England she must be regarded as very exceptional. But so long a period is not, I think, exceptional for the Gypsies of German Silesia, though over most of Germany a month seems to be the accepted period. In Hungary it seems to be two months and in Italy only a fortnight, but my experience of Central European Gypsies is not really sufficiently wide to justify generalisations.

Amos Churen told me that his grandmother had a separate tent put up for her whenever she was going to have a baby and that this tent was destroyed a month after the birth. Thompson states that Lias Boswell's grandmother always had a separate tent for the birth of her children. The two women must have lived at about the same time, the one in the midlands and the other on the Welsh-English border, and this suggests that at one time the practice was widespread in England. And there is a good deal of evidence to suggest that it is the ancient Gypsy practice. Wittich says that among German Gypsies births are not allowed to take place inside a living waggon as it and all its contents would have to be destroyed or sold to the gorgios ; and that the woman is usually delivered on a makeshift straw bed underneath the waggon. In an unpublished manuscript, quoted by Thompson, he varies this by saying that a woman is usually got out of her waggon into a tent for childbirth. Should she be taken ill too suddenly to permit of this, as many things as possible are thrown out of the waggon, anything that remains becoming defiled by the birth. On such occasions, he states, men may not offer the least assistance. When the late Dr. Sampson visited the Greek Gypsies at Liverpool in 1896 he noticed that a woman who had recently given birth to a child had a special tent reserved for her. In 1930 in Italy, near Susa, two women of a Gypsy tribe had babies on successive days—they were married to the same man—and each had a special tent. The father, who was quite unperturbed by this family crisis, lived in the big family tent. A fortnight after the births the tents were burned by the roadside and the wives returned to a normal existence. I do not know if the special tent is used and destroyed nowadays by any English Gypsies, but I do know that births do take place in the living-waggons in some families at any rate. In one recent case of which I have personal knowledge everything that could be moved out was moved out beforehand, and such movable objects as were in the van at the time of delivery were afterwards burnt. And this was in a family with a large admixture of gorgio blood ! Amos, so he told me, always put up a tent for himself and saw to it that everything that was in his wife's tent at the time was destroyed at the end of her quarantine.

As might be expected, a woman at menstruation is especially *mochardi*, and there is a wealth of material on these taboos. Very young babies are *mochardi*. Amos Churen, as was the case with many old Gypsies, would not touch, let alone kiss, a very young baby, even, as he told me himself, his own. This taboo appears to have died out entirely among Engish Gypsies, though babies' napkins are still regarded as *mochardi*. During childhood no taboos apply. A female child from babyhood to young womanhood is not accounted unclean, nor is it considered possible that she can be defiled. Her underclothes, for example, can be washed with the men's clothes. She can be with her mother after childbirth and yet live with the men and boys of the family, though she must be careful not to touch the food or crockery until she has washed her hands.

At one time, in some of the midland families at any rate, it used to be the custom for the husband to give his wife a new pair of gloves on the last day of her quarantine and she would wear them for some weeks afterwards when cooking or handling food or crockery. This seems to have been a local taboo entirely. Thompson mentions it for only four of the midland families—Boswells, Herons, Grays and Smiths—and I have never heard of it among south country Gypsies.

But the taboos connected with women's clothing were known at least in part to both Amos Churen and David Burton. These taboos are also known to German and Hungarian Gypsies, and so are probably of great age. It was a strict rule that women's clothing must not be washed with the men's. Women's clothing was strictly *mochardi*. Thompson gives an excellent account of this taboo as described to him by Caroline Boswell. Wittich, himself a Gypsy, described it for Germany. Not only must women's clothes not be washed with men's, they must not be brought into contact with food, they must not even be hung out to dry with the clothes of the men, and under no circumstances must a man touch them. In varying degrees the midland Gypsies and the German Gypsies observed these taboos. Neither Amos Churen's family nor David Burton's observed them in their entirety, but both Amos and David knew all about most of them, and neither would allow male and female clothing to be washed together. David would not allow female clothing to be dried where he could see it.

No distinction is drawn between the sexes during childhood. They are, in fact, regarded as neuters. At what age a male child becomes defilable is uncertain. Probably the majority of Gypsies in England no longer give the matter serious thought, but in any case it varies from family to family—as early as ten in some families, according to Thompson, and as late as thirteen in others. A female child becomes subject to uncleanness taboos at her first menstruation. Thompson is not definite on this point, because the Boswells from whom he obtained most of his information never mentioned women's periodic disability. David Burton was very reticent on this point also, but Amos Churen had no inhibitions about mentioning it and was quite definite about it, as also is another friend of mine, James Arigho, who is not unacquainted with Romani ways, having rubbed shoulders with them most of his long life. And as the change takes place at this time among most other people who have similar taboos, I think it may safely be presumed for all Gypsies, though one or two families may make the change a little earlier.

Among German Gypsies the taboos connected with menstruation are many, and so far as I know or have been able to find out (it is, in my experience, harder to get information on this subject than on any other) are observed as scrupulously now as they were when Wittich wrote. I think it probable that among the purer-blooded English Gypsies there are to-day more taboos observed in this connection than in any other, but I have very little information on this point, and for once Thompson is not completely satisfying. On this point, however, there can be no doubt. Women at this time are regarded as especially dangerous. Wittich, quoted by Thompson from an unpublished manuscript, is very definite on this point and gives many examples of what may not be done by a menstruous woman. I do not know how many of these prohibitions are current among English Gypsies ; probably they all were at one time, probably only a few are now. But two that are mentioned by Wittich have come within my personal experience. A woman may not mention her infirmity, even to her husband. A menstruous woman may not cook food or touch food intended for a man. Both these taboos are observed to-day among English Gypsies, though I do not know how widely.

Amos Churen told me that the only way he knew when his wife was temporarily unwell was because someone else did his cooking for him. David Burton would never mention this sort of thing at all, partly I think because he was an exceptionally nice-minded man, but mainly, I am sure, because he did regard all this as his religion, a thing to be observed and not discussed. So I do not know what happened in his family, but I think that any taboos were probably more faithfully observed there than in that of Amos Churen. James Arigho, whose travels are constant and far-flung, told me that all true Gypsies observe this taboo, that a woman shall not mention her infirmity to a man, no matter how intimately she may know him. That a menstruous woman shall not cook food or touch food intended for a man seems to follow as a matter of course, though it need not do so. Amos did not tell me that his wife would not tell him when she was temporarily unwell, he told me that he knew it because she would not cook for him. I have no doubt that this happened, too, in David Burton's tent, for David was as particular on food matters as Amos. James Arigho also observed this taboo. He had no objection to his wife discussing her infirmity at the time, but every objection to her cooking for him at that time. And I have found this to be the case also, even in such half-bred families as the Mathews, Lanes, Pages, Toogoods, Smallbones and Whites of the south country. That being so, I am prepared to believe that it also exists in the purer blooded Stanleys, Coopers, Burtons, Smiths, Lees, Ayres, Lovells, Boswells, Grays and so on. It is, in any case, not an entirely Gypsy taboo. Fraser in *The Golden Bough* gives a number of examples, from English folk-lore, of the same thing. Thompson has come across one gorgio family (who claimed Gypsy descent) in which it is firmly believed that if a menstruous woman touches raw meat that is going to be kept for any length of time, in pickle for example, it will rot. This family once had two hams from one of their own pigs go bad, and attributed this to the woman who was employed to salt them being menstruous at the time. They maintain, too, that meat that is going to be cooked straight away will not be so nice if touched by a woman during her menses, and one of the family at any rate believes that this also applies to cakes, pastry and other things made of flour. The head of this family did not approve of women handling meat at any time. I could give several similar examples from Hampshire, Wiltshire and Dorset peasantry, and I am quite sure that the fear of menstruous blood is even in these days much more general than might be believed. One Hampshire shepherd, whom I knew well and who died only last year, always made his wife wear gloves when she handled raw meat. I do not know that he prevented her cooking when she was menstruous (I think not, but he was an excellent cook himself), for she was dead before I really got to know him, but I do know that he would not allow her to touch flour while she was menstruous. He maintained that bread so touched went sour. I have found this belief in connection with flour more common than in connection with meat myself, but the belief that meat that is going to be pickled will quickly go bad if handled by a woman in her menses is still common in the isolated districts of Hampshire and Wiltshire, and, so I understand, in Yorkshire.

When the full elaboration of taboo was in force among English Gypsies there must have been punishments enforced upon those who wilfully or thoughtlessly broke them. There are such punishments enforced to-day among German Gypsies. We have no record of them unfortunately. Gradually as the taboo weakened families began to contain both clean and defiled members, and the realisation that nothing very terrible happened to the latter yet further weakened the taboo. With the weakening came a gradual but increasing influx of gorgio and mumper blood and a consequent further weakening. Time was when a Boswell would not shake hands with a gorgio. That time is long past, and many a Boswell has taken a gorgie to wife. Yet even so, even though the full elaboration of taboo is altogether dead and forgotten, even though many of the taboos are now not observed though not perhaps wholly forgotten, there lingers something at the back of the Gypsy mind and, like the language, it is apt to well up again in unexpected places. And the man who observes taboos to-day is not laughed at. He is regarded with respect, even with some little awe. The religion is not wholly dead. I do not myself believe that it will ever die.

IV

MARRIAGE

" Lees recordin' to rights should marry wi' Lees," said Ira Lee to me once. " We didn't oughter marry outa de name." And he went on to tell me that in the past it had been a rule in his family that they should marry Lees. He himself married his first cousin Sophia Lee, but the rule has long since lapsed, for I have met many Lees who have not observed it. In any case I very much doubt if it was ever a rule so much as a custom, and as a custom it can be found in several other Gypsy families such as the Smiths, Grays and Herons. Beyond any measure of doubt, as anyone who cares to study the genealogical tables that have been prepared of some of the best families can see for himself, in-marriage was the common practice. For that matter, though many if not most of the old rules and customs have largely collapsed under the pressure of time and the growth of towns, in-marriage is still very common among Gypsies, and particularly so in the best Gypsy families. Thompson finds from a long and close study of the genealogy of English Gypsies that ascendant and descendant relatives, and brothers and sisters, have been regarded by all but one or two people as prohibited mates : that a small but appreciable minority of men have married their nieces or aunts, the former more frequently than the latter, and their brother's daughters most frequently of all : that alliances between first cousins have been very popular and in some of the best families exceedingly common : that, generally speaking, first cousins have been preferred to second as marriage partners : that in two out of the three families for which very full particulars can be given ortho-cousins have married much more often than cross-cousins, and it is noteworthy that these two families are composed of Gypsies who have preserved the old customs, or, alternatively, the Romani language, rather better than most. In the matrilineal families these ortho-cousins have generally been the children of two sisters, the children of two brothers in the remainder. Thompson, of course, goes much deeper into the matter than that, but enough has been said to show that in-marriage is a common practice. Indeed the only marital bar would appear to be common parentage. There is one certain record of a man marrying his grand-daughter and another of a man marrying his half-sister, while there is another case of marriage with a half-sister that was strongly suspected but not proved. These are isolated incidents though, and do not in any way invalidate the common parentage bar. So far as marriages between uncles and nieces, and aunts and nephews are concerned they have never been common, though a list compiled over all the years in which Gypsies in this country have been studied would probably reach formidable, but misleading dimensions. Almost all these marriages have proved to be permanent partnerships, and not a few of them have been productive.

Gypsies, it will be realised, hold rather different views on marriage to those current elsewhere in the country. Polygamy among English Gypsies has not been uncommon, though I think that here again the formidable list that no doubt could be compiled would be rather misleading. There are, of course, some well-known cases in literature : George Borrow's reference to Riley Boswell and his two wives in *Ramano Lavo-Lil*, for example, and Francis Hindes Groome's reference to Charlie Pinfold and his three wives in *Gypsy Folk-tales ;* and I think that a certain measure of polygamous households has always existed among English Gypsies. It is a rule, or at any rate a custom, that is enforced, among certain primitive peoples who allow polygamy, that a man's co-wives must be sisters, or at any rate near kinswomen : and judging from the composition of the more permanent polygamous households that we know to have existed among English Gypsies in modern times, it would seem that this was so with their ancestors. Anyhow, sixteen of the twenty-four men recorded as having had more than one wife at the same, and for a considerable, time were living during the period in question with either two or three sisters : whilst it is likely that two more were similarly circumstanced, and probable that another two had been earlier in their lives, though for only a short time. Moreover, one of the latter had a mother and her daughter as co-wives during the last ten years he spent in England. One of the four who remain for consideration had a mother and her two daughters as co-wives for the greater part of a long married life. The three remaining men did not, it would seem, at any time share their homes among near kinswomen. In general, in polygamous households, two or three wives seems to have been usual, and these have almost always been Gypsies. There is, I believe, a record of a Gypsy with two gorgie wives. And there are, of course, records of more than three wives. Thompson has a record for 1922 of a man with seven wives. I have known one man with two wives and one with three, the former marrying two unrelated gorgie women. These wives are not married all at once (though one midland Gypsy is reputed to have married two sisters at the same time), but acquired as time goes on. And it may be that a younger sister just follows in her elder's footsteps. These co-wives in English Gypsydom do not live together, but have separate tents and run separate families, and there does not seem to be, or to have been, any difference in status between them, no " senior " wife or anything like that.

It is all very shocking, of course, if you care to look at it like that. But it should be remembered that Gypsies, no matter how anglicised they may have become, are not " English." They are orientals. Other races, other manners. I well remember some years before the war staying at the same hotel in France as a fabulously rich oriental. He had four " wives " (three of them English and the fourth German) and they all lived together. It was a good hotel, too. Other races, other manners. And, if you find the eastern view of marriage among English Gypsies shocking, there are yet some shocks to come.

At one time it does appear to have been the custom among certain English Gypsies that a man had " rights " over his wife's younger, or supposedly younger, sisters before they acquired official husbands.   There are, in fact, substantiated records of this for one family, and it may well have been a general custom in the distant past.   And in this connection it is worthy of note that, among the Santals, a man's unmarried younger brothers are permitted to share his wife with him until they acquire permanent wives of their own, while it is considered perfectly correct for a man to cohabit with his wife's younger sisters provided they are agreeable.   So far as I know the custom has now completely died out among English Gypsies—it was still practised by some German Gypsy families a few years ago—and for that matter polygamy is dying very rapidly.   These customs had their roots in the dim past of the race, they were never merely licentious practices.

The fact that a woman might be an unmarried wife to her sister's husband, even the fact that she might have a child by him, did not prevent her from acquiring a husband of her own.   Indeed, such cases as there have been among English Gypsies in comparatively recent times have been rather on the lines of trial marriages—a few might even perhaps rank as examples of unstable polygamy—than on the lines of " automatic " rights.   Trial marriages have not been uncommon among English Gypsies, for I think that many of the brief first marriages of women who have after-wards settled down to a long and happy married life with a second husband can truly be described as " trial " mar-riages, and I have come across examples myself quite recently.   Here, of course, the practice is no whit different from that of some gorgie who make a commonplace of divorce, except that very few Romani women appear to marry more than twice.   And, even so, the deliberate prac-tice of trial marriage appears to have been confined in the main to one family.

It is difficult to reconcile much of this with the very high standard set by Gypsies for their women so far as modesty and chastity is concerned. It is quite beyond dispute that among pure-blooded English Gypsy families there is still a very strong insistence on pre-nuptial chastity. At one time Scottish Gypsies demanded definite proof of a bride's virginity at the time of her marriage. And at one time— even perhaps within the last hundred years—English Gypsy girls used to wear a virginal girdle, made of wool mounted on catskin, from about the age of twelve until the wedding day. It was fastened on by the mother every morning and removed by the mother every night, and it was carried before the girl as a token of her maidenhood when she was married. Moreover, according to Philip Murray, who told the late Dr. Sampson about it, it was then kept by the husband until it was required by his eldest daughter and so on. Thompson has never been able to confirm this statement by Murray—Murray was an Irish tinker who married into one of the many Gypsy Smith families—but as proofs of a bride's virginity were customarily demanded by Spanish and French Gypsies, and are still demanded by many of the Gypsies of eastern Europe both in Europe and in the United States, to which country many families have migrated, and as it is known that virginal girdles were worn by the Spanish Gypsies, it is not improbable that some steps of a similar nature were taken in this country. In this connection it is, perhaps, worth noting that Amos Churen once said to me : " Our gels was proper looked arter times. Morn' an' night I heard tell." I could not get anything more out of him, and it may have no relevance, but we were talking of marriage. So far as I know, no proof of maidenhood is now required by any English Gypsies—indeed, in view of the prevalent way of getting married, it would scarcely be possible—but a very high standard has always been set in these matters in Gypsy families. There seems to be some evidence, or rather some suggestion of a tradition, that in the dimmer past a Gypsy girl found guilty of prostitution was buried alive. Certainly up to quite recently a girl found guilty of prostitution was invariably disowned by her family. Furthermore, in Scotland, at any rate and within perhaps the last hundred years, the man who wronged an unmarried Gypsy girl did so at the risk of his life. But prostitution among Gypsy girls is very uncommon. Crabb, writing more than a hundred years ago, found it to be so among the New Forest Stanleys and Lees. George Borrow found it to be so, and Ursula showed him clearly enough what she thought about loose-living, even the merest suggestion of it. And modern investigators have found no reason to think that things have changed, at least so far as the purer-blooded families are concerned. Among them the standard is as high as ever it was. In some other families there has, I think, been a slight falling off recently, due, I am convinced, not to any fault in the Romani blood, but rather to an infusion of gorgio blood. Marriages between *Romanichals* and gorgios are much more common than they used to be, and, even more important in many ways, there is now much more intercourse between the Gypsy and the gorgio, and, unfortunately, it is rarely that a Romani marries the better type of gorgio, rarely that they associate at all freely with the better types. This has undoubtedly had some effect, but the cases in which it has had any marked effect, in which the standard has been markedly lowered, are few and far between. But they do exist. It would be a mistake, however, to judge by the few *diddikai* families, in which a moral standard is noticeable mainly by its absence ; a still greater mistake to judge by the young women, who garbed as Gypsies used to infest the downs at Epsom of a night in Derby week, who none of them could boast a drop of Romani blood, who came from the back streets of Soho on return tickets, and who mixed pilfering and prostitution as occasion demanded.

I have myself always found Gypsy girls to be most modest and chaste in their bearing (this does not apply to their speech : verbal chastity is not noticeable among Gypsies) and in this my observations agree with those of other modern investigators. How to reconcile this with the undoubted, if infrequent, occurrence of cohabitation between a man and his wife's unmarried younger sisters is a problem. Custom notoriously dies hard, and it may well once have been customary. It does not in any case invalidate the general rule. But if there can be little or no doubt about the exceptionally high standard of pre-nuptial chastity, there does seem to be some doubt about the general standard of morals after marriage. I am not, here, referring to the frequency with which young Gypsv couples have married only to part again after a short time. Some of these marriages last only a few days, some a month or two, some perhaps a year. In some cases they may properly be termed " trial " marriages—though, as I have said, the deliberate practice of trial marriage appears to have been confined to one family—in some it means no more than that the couple quickly discover they have made a mistake and as quickly take steps to remedy it. Almost invariably the persons concerned marry again soon and remain steadfast to their second partners. The number of marriages that collapse after a year or two are few, and the number of men and women who change their partners more than once are also comparatively few, though in a minority it does occur more often, and in some of them (as in some gorgios) it develops into what might almost be called a disease. But none of this is anyway different from events in other and more " advanced " races. Certainly it cannot be taken as a sign of immorality. But there are hints to be found in this writer and that that the morals of Gypsy women apparently permanently married are not all they might be. Miss Eileen Lyster, in her book *The Gypsy Life of Betsy Wood*, states that while a casual love affair with a gorgio was uncommon and did not meet with the approval of the other women, there was no disapproval of a woman " who lured another woman's husband to be her lover for a season, and the forsaken spouse, after a transport of rage and grief, would usually set herself to win another mate. But although these prac tices were rather admired as feats of skill than condemned, most of the family elected to live faithfully with the lover of their choice." That does not sound to me as if the practice was very widespread. And I must say that I have found nothing myself to suggest that the standard of morality among married Gypsy women in this country is low. Against this must be set the punishments for infidelity on the part of women—men do not appear to have been punished—that were once imposed by English Gypsies. To cut off an ear or the nose, even to slit the nose and take a piece out of each ear, to scar the cheeks—these are not light punishments. They would not have been applied in any but a race of the highest moral standard, but that they were applied is sufficient evidence that once at least delinquency was sufficiently frequent to require drastic measures for its suppression. How long since these drastic punishments have been inflicted in England I do not know, but they are known to many elderly Gypsies to-day as the traditional punishments of their people. And one old man, whom I met some twenty years ago, remembered a woman in his family who had actually had her nose slit. But old Gypsies are sometimes apt to confuse experience and tradition, and I was not sure that he had himself seen her. The tying of erring wives to a cart-wheel or a stake and thrashing them with a horse-whip (the woman being naked), the tying-up naked in an exposed place, the shearing of hair, these punishments for infidelity have been inflicted quite recently. Amos Churen had seen the thrashing of an erring wife when he was a young man, and told me that one of the Patemans had shaved his wife's head and forced her to wear no covering either to her head or body for two days when, on his return from Germany where he had been a prisoner for three years, he found that she had been unfaithful. But the sum total of all this only proves that in a race with exceptionally high moral standards severe penalties were exacted for infidelity in wives : it does not prove that there was a generally low moral standard in married women. I think it probable that the standard is lower to-day than it was in the days of punishment because of the infusion of a fair amount of gorgio blood, but I must stress again that I have no evidence to support this and no modern *rai* who has actually travelled with Gypsies of recent years even suggests that it is so.

Undoubtedly the early age at which English Gypsy girls, in common with other oriental races, have married in the past helped in maintaining the high level of pre-nuptial chastity. Marriages at twelve, thirteen, fourteen and fifteen were once common. The average age at which the girls now marry is, of course, appreciably higher. Marriages at sixteen still occur, but nowadays that is regarded as rather young, and, generally speaking, girls marry at nineteen or twenty and men at a year or two older. It is very uncommon to find a man or a woman unmarried at thirty, though in one or two families there seems of recent years to have developed a strong disinclination to marry at all. Marriage at a very early age does still occur, though I do not know how frequently. A few years ago I came across a young woman of twenty-one with five children. She had been married when she was thirteen and was very happy with her husband, who was ten years older and obviously adored her. Indeed I have not seen a more contented, and yet vital, looking woman.

Another factor in the maintenance of pre-nuptial chastity is undoubtedly the extreme brevity and astonishing restraint of the Gypsy courtship. Thompson records an instance in which the couple had not been out together and had not kissed each other before marriage, and says that this was told him not as an extraordinary occurrence but as an illustration of the customary courtship in that family. I have never myself come across anything quite so restrained, but I do know more than one couple who had not been out by themselves before they married. And there are any number of recorded instances of restraint in courtship, so much so indeed that the ordinary uninitiated gorgio might be forgiven for wondering how on earth man and maid even manage to communicate their desire to each other. Signs played a big part in Gypsy courtship until comparatively recent times, and though many of them seemed to have died out completely some remain even in these outspoken days. The coloured handkerchief, for example, is still used. It is given, to-day as formerly, by the man to the girl of his choice, who will not wear it unless she is willing to marry him. But for the most part nowadays these matters are arranged by word of mouth. There is no recognised engagement or betrothal period among English Gypsies. Most of the old authorities suggest that there was (though it is noticeable that Crabb does not) and some even go so far as to suggest that it was two years. If that was ever so, and I doubt it, it most certainly is not so now and has not been so for many years. In a few families it was the custom to pledge the lovers as a preliminary to marriage, but I do not think this ever carried any importance. In some families, however, it was the custom to test the suitor, and this presumably was a matter of importance, but it does not seem to have been a widespread custom at any time. The testing differed—in some families it consisted of making the suitor fight one or more of the girl's menfolk, in others it consisted of stealing a horse or a sheep. The latter method was also applied by some families to eloping bridegrooms. Usually it was a horse that had to be stolen and there does not appear to have been any time limit, but an Ingram in Co. Antrim told me that a sheep was chosen in his case.

Most Gypsies' marriages are elopements. It is customary for the suitor to ask the girl's father for the hand of his daughter in marriage, and it is customary for the father to refuse. The young couple then elope, but in due course they come back again and are accepted, sometimes after a pretended fuss, sometimes at once. And this brings me to the vexed question of the Gypsy marriage ceremony, about which reams have been written.

The popular idea is that Gypsies marry by jumping over a broomstick in the presence of their families. That, so many people and particularly novelists have maintained, is the traditional ceremony. Undoubtedly it is a marriage ceremony, but it is only one of many, and in origin it is, I believe, tinker and not Romani at all. It came to England, in my opinion, from Ireland *via* Scotland. In Ireland it was, and is, called " jumping the budget," and tinkers are married " over the budget," which is the name of the box in which tinkers keep their tools. One modern Irish novelist, Maurice Walsh, has, in his *The Road to Nowhere*, given a few refinements to the performance by placing lighted candles on the box, but I have never heard of this being done in real life. One of my best friends was married " over the budget " in Co. Clare, and he said the ceremony was simplicity itself. He and his wife-to-be held hands, jumped the box, and that was that—though it must be done before witnesses from both families.

Jumping the broomstick is the Gypsy version of this ceremony. So much is obvious. But whereas "jumping the budget " does appear to be the traditional tinker ceremony, a good deal of doubt attaches to the Gypsy practice. Crabb does not mention it, and Crabb knew the Gypsies of the New Forest pretty well. On the other hand, *diddikais* in the New Forest some fifty years or so ago (that is considerably later than Crabb's day) undoubtedly did jump the broomstick as a wedding ceremony, but Harry Lee stoutly denied that true New Forest Gypsies ever did so. In Wales, however, pure-blooded Gypsies certainly jumped a besom made from flowering bloom until quite recently, and perhaps, here and there, individuals still do so. In view of their long seclusion, it is to be expected that Welsh Gypsies would have rather different rites, and in view of the fact that they have preserved their language so very much better than Gypsies elsewhere in Britain, it might be expected that they would also preserve some at least of the ancient customs and traditions. There is no evidence to suggest that jumping the besom was one of them. It was not, so far as I can discover, ever the whole of the ceremony, nor was it essential to jump over a besom made from

flowering broom ; a plain pole was used on occasions. It
seems to me probable that they copied the practice from
the travelling Irish already in Wales, and that there were
evolved and practised by individuals elaborations (the
flowering broom evidently has roots in a fertility cult) that
were not accepted by the Welsh Gypsies as a whole. So
far as English Gypsies are concerned, Morwood appears
to be the only authority to describe a broomstick wedding.
He witnessed one in Yorkshire, and his account rings true
in every respect. We have no other eye-witness account.
Plenty of Gypsies speak of marriage over the broomstick,
and it is very difficult to say just when they are speaking
metaphorically or not. It is a phrase used by some to
indicate that they were not married in a church or a
registry office, but it is possible that some of them do mean
that they were actually married in that way. If the New
Forest *diddikais* were (and I have no doubt about that), it
is at least possible that some pure-blooded Gypsies were
also. But I am sceptical, for there is no doubt at all that
many Gypsies have staged " faked " weddings over the
broomstick as an additional way of getting money out of
the gorgios, and I cannot imagine the Romani, however
tough, deliberately prostituting his proper wedding ceremony for the amusement of the gorgios. I can imagine
him benefiting by the adoption of another's ceremony
and deriving much amusement as well as profit from so
doing.

The marriage rite that has been most widely practised
among English Gypsies is the simplest imaginable—the
mere joining of hands in the presence of witnesses. Its
validity has been upheld in the English courts. As this is
the custom in Germany (where a legend of broomstick
marriages in the past also exists), in Hungary and elsewhere, it seems possible that it is the ancient rite or the
remains of it. Simple enough in itself, there has been
attached to it at one time or another, and varying from
family to family, many interesting and sometimes complex
customs.

Amos Churen was married " by de liddle stream " near Rhayader. "We joined hands and promised ourselves afore our own people." That done, Sarah (the bride) took a bucket and went down to the stream and filled it and brought it to her husband. And he took a cup and filled it and then they both drank from the cup. That was an additional pledge. " Yer didn't never drink from de same cup else." And then the cup was broken. " It were allus done so among our people." With that the ceremony ended. But Amos and Sarah, though man and wife, did not immediately live as man and wife. Sarah returned to the tents of her people for that night, and the next morning she and Amos went away by themselves for three days. That marriage took place in or about 1876. Amos always maintained that the carrying of water, the drinking from the cup, and the breaking of the cup were the proper practices at a true Gypsy wedding, but he did not seem to have any definite ideas about Sarah's return for one night to her people. He did not seem to think it was a Gypsy custom, and I gathered that he had never heard of anyone else doing so, but he was always a bit vague about this episode : not vague as to its happening, nor ashamed of its happening, but vague and, I think, a little uneasy when asked questions about it. It may have been that the young couple could not for some reason move from the camp that day (though I can see no good reason why two young Gypsies should be unable to move), for Amos was always very definite that newly married couples must leave the camp for a few days.

David Burton's marriage was rather different. It took place in or about 1878 and consisted also of joining hands and pledging each other in the presence of witnesses. But after that things were different. There was a loaf of bread, and this was broken in two. A drop of his blood and a drop of hers (obtained by the prick of a thorn in the thumb) was dropped on each half, and then each ate the little piece covered by the blood of the other. This was the additional pledge similar to the drinking from the same cup that distinguished Amos Churen's marriage. And there was another similarity in that, as in that ceremony the cup was then broken, so in this the remaining bread was broken over the heads of the couple. After that David and his wife left, but returned the next day to take part in the rest of the festivities. I do not know how long these lasted, for David had forgotten. " Dey was *motto* (drunk) *pal*. Alayin' on de ground helpless dey was, ah, bloody helpless dey was."

Amos Churen was married in Wales in 1876. David Burton was married near Bentley, on the borders of Surrey and Hampshire, two years later. Amos had never heard of the breaking of bread as part of a Gypsy marriage ceremony—he regarded it as one of " dem *ratvali gorgio* ways " —though the drawing and mixing of blood evidently did not seem foreign to him. David Burton had never heard of the drawing of water by the bride, and he regarded the drinking from the same cup as no more than a pledge between sweethearts. Yet there is no doubt that the drawing of water was once practised fairly well by English Gypsies (though it was never a common practice), while the drawing of blood in connection with bread and flour has been practised by a number of Romani families. It seemed to me that both are offshoots or remnants of what was once a much more complex ceremony, and I think this is supported by the number of different customs connected with the marriage ceremony that have been recorded for families in different parts of Britain, customs which are one and all based on the same idea and differ only in detail. Furthermore, many of them are to be found in only slightly different form among Continental Gypsies.

There are one or two records of English Gypsy couples drawing their blood and mixing it with flour which is afterwards baked into a cake, and Thompson records one case in which bride and bridegroom drank each other's blood from a cup. There are not many records of this " blood " ceremony, and it might therefore be supposed that it was uncommon and practised by only a few families.

But I am not so sure about that, for no Gypsy that I have talked to about it has ever seemed surprised at the idea, although Burton was the only one who had practised it or had definite knowledge of it. And it is worth pointing out that among certain Indian tribes it is the custom for the bride and bridegroom to eat food in which their blood has been mixed.

There are rather more records for the mixing of flour—the use of a loaf is no more than a refinement of this—among British Gypsies at the marriage ceremony ranging from the elaborate procedure described by Simson as being in use formerly by the Scottish Gypsies to the simple stirring of flour in a bowl or the simple breaking of bread or cake over the heads of the bridal pair. This latter practice has many forms in English folk-lore—the cutting of the cake by the bride at a modern wedding is a degenerate remnant of it—and it might be thought that it had been borrowed by the English Gypsy from the English peasant, if it were not for the fact that it is in use to this day among various Continental Gypsies. More probably it is the remnant of some ancient earth and fecundity rite that has crept into the peasant-lore of many countries—and so been acquired by the Gypsies. Of the vast elaboration of the Scottish Gypsies—the use of wine in the flour and of a ram's horn to stir it—nothing now remains, but the horns of a ram still seem to be regarded with some reverence by the Gypsies of the Basque country, though I have no evidence that they are ever used.

In Germany I have seen bread broken at a marriage ceremony in just the way that was described to me by David Burton as having occurred at his wedding. But blood was not used at any time during this wedding as far as I could tell. Salt was sprinkled liberally on the two halves of the loaf and then these were broken over the heads of the bridal couple. In Austria I have seen blood used. The couple in this case were married in church, and feasting took place afterwards at the village inn. The bride smeared blood from her finger on the cheeks of her groom, and he in turn smeared blood from his finger on her feet. In Denmark, nearly twenty years ago, I saw bride and bridegroom mix the flour in a bowl. The mixture was baked, and when this had been done the couple came before the headman of the tribe (he had travelled almost all over the world and spoke excellent English) and the cake was handed to him. He said a few words to them, which I could not hear, and then they joined hands and turned to face each other, standing very closely together. The old man lifted up the cake and broke it over their heads. The bridegroom kissed his bride, and the wedding was over. Something very similar I have no doubt happened at the wedding of David Burton and Emmy White all those years ago in a glade in an English wood.

Nowadays the majority of English Gypsies get married in church or in a registry office. Gypsies always adopt many of the customs of the land in which they sojourn, and among these customs is that of the dominant religion. It is, too, nowadays convenient to have things properly done from the point of view of registration and so forth. I am not suggesting that the adoption by English Gypsies of that form of Christianity prescribed by the Church of England is absolutely insincere. Religion, as a matter of fact, scarcely enters into the matter—I have seen very few signs of its forms being practised (except in the case of one Roman Catholic family) and I can just imagine the stir that the arrival of a Gypsy family in most churches would occasion. And I am quite certain that the increase of marriages " recordin' to law " has not in any way altered the normal Gypsy view of marriage.

Church marriages have occurred among Gypsies for many years. It is by no means a new departure. But it has increased greatly of recent years—there has been an even greater increase of marriages before a registrar—and presumably therefore a decrease in the old practices. But I am not sure about that; I think most Gypsies, except those that have become excessively genteel, still cling in one way or another to some old Romani way.

Just before the outbreak of war a young Gypsy travelling the New Forest district with a wife of only a few days' standing told me that they had been married by a registrar " recordin' to law." " But it's what we say to each other that matters, sir, now ain't it ? "

V

DEATH AND BURIAL

On April 17th, 1926, there was buried at Crediton, Devonshire, Mrs. Caroline Penfold (the name should be Pinfold, but has been corrupted), a Gypsy. After the burial the living-waggon in which she died, together with all her personal belongings that could be burned, were reduced to ashes, all her crockery was smashed and buried, and all her jewellery, with the exception of one heavy gold ring, was also buried.

Though the burning of the belongings of the deceased is the best known and most characteristic of all English Gypsy funeral rites (and I shall return to the funeral of Caroline Penfold, which was remarkable in many ways) it is by no means the only one. There are, as is to be expected, a considerable number of customs connected with the death and burial of English Gypsies. Moreover, though not all of them are observed now, and though there is a considerable variation as between family and family, many more of them are still observed than is the case with other customs and taboos, and as they are from their very nature more noticeable and so more easily recorded than the customs and taboos connected with birth, marriage, uncleanness and so forth, we have a considerable amount of material concerning them. There are very few published accounts of Gypsy weddings, for example, but there are quite a number of accounts, in books and newspapers, of Gypsy funerals. For, curiously enough, though few Gypsies in the past took the trouble to get married in church, or indeed thought it necessary, the vast majority insisted on Christian burial.

There are, of course, many stories of Gypsy burials in unsanctified ground. For example, there is supposed to be a Gypsy burial ground at Strethall in Essex, which in times past was used by the Shaws, East Anglian Grays and

Dymocks, which last is not a Gypsy name. This story has been investigated by Thompson and others, and they have found nothing to support it. The Shaws profess no knowledge of it (and Gypsies do not mind admitting past burials in unsanctified ground) and nobody in the parish at the time enquiries were made could recall it. All the same there were mounds in that field, and skeletons were dug up. Some people at some time were buried there, but that is no proof that they were Gypsies. Again, there are places in Buckinghamshire where Gypsies are supposed to be buried. At Quainton, near Fenny Stratford, at Mursley and in Towersey Field. There is a possibility that those at Quainton and Mursley are genuine ; there seems to be no evidence to support the others. These are only a few examples. It would be possible, I imagine, to duplicate them for almost every county in England. But, as Lias Boswell said to Thompson, " there's no compass to the lies gorgios 'll make up about *Romanichals*."

Naturally there is very little evidence of unofficial burial, and such as there is is indirect. It seems to have been confined within recorded time at least, mainly to the Herons, the East Anglian Smiths, the northern Youngs and to some of the families connected with them by marriage. It is best substantiated for the Herons. Remarkably few records of the interments of Herons occur in the old parish registers, only one between the years 1650 and 1830—that being of " Mrs. Hearn a Gypsey Queene " at Stanbridge, Bedfordshire, in 1691. And, as Thompson points out, she may not have belonged to the family by birth nor have adhered to it after her marriage : " Whilst ' his majesty's ' failure to provide a shroud or winding sheet of woollen cloth, in consequence of which he was distrained upon, ' but no distress to be found,' may imply that he possessed so little experience of ordinary burials as to be ignorant of a law relating to them already twelve years old." The very fact that interments of Herons do not appear in parish registers, coupled with the tradition of unsanctified burial current in the family, is proof enough of such

burial ; and additional weight is lent to this when we find
in the same period of 180 years no fewer than eight records
of Herons marrying in church.   While in conversation with
Thompson modern Gypsies of Heron blood have been very
definite about it.   Kadīlia Brown, a Heron in the male
line, would not hear of Christian sepulture among her
ancestors.   " ' Bury in churchyards ! ' she exclaimed.
' Not they ! They was too a-*trash* (frightened) to go nigh
them. No : they'd just dig a grave thersel's, and bury the
poor things there where they died, on some bit o' common,
or down an owld lane.' "   Her cousins, Katie Smith and
Adelaide Lee, were equally sure about it.   " It was kept
secret, they declared, sometimes from relatives, even, until
after the body had been disposed of, as quickly as might
be, in a ditch, or on some little frequented heath ; and
again fear, this time of strangers handling the corpse, was
given as the motive."   Then Genti Gray, a granddaughter
in the female line of " No Name " Heron, assured him that
several of her mother's kin were buried " up there on the
Mussel," meaning Mousehold Heath near Norwich.   In
fact, it may be taken as certain that Herons, Grays, Youngs
and Smiths did bury their dead in unsanctified ground.
Why they did is another matter.   I cannot accept the
reason that they were frightened to go near churchyards,
since they were not frightened of going to church to get
married.   Nor can I accept the idea that they were afraid
of the gorgios handling the body, since it is the common
Gypsy practice to get them to lay out the body, and, in
fact, Gypsies show a strong disinclination to handle the
dead at all.   It seems to me much more probable that it
was the ancient custom to bury the dead where they died,
by the roadside or on some unfrequented heath, and that
the custom took longer to die in the notoriously diehard
Heron family.   Personally, I think that the occasional
preference expressed even to-day by Gypsies (and expressed
much more frequently a few years ago) that they should
be buried as close to the hedgerow of a churchyard as
possible, and the desiré still quite frequently expressed that

a thorn bush should be planted on the grave, is also a relic of wayside burial.

Naturally we have no record of any ceremony or other custom connected with these burials by the wayside. The impression given by the descendants of the Heron family who discussed the matter with Thompson is that they were hurried and secretive affairs. But I find this hard to believe in view of the fact that there are to-day so many customs observed, most of which have nothing to do with Christian burial and which must have their roots deep in the past, and also because, in one case at least (I have an idea that Blackwater in Hampshire might be another), the burial place is so well known. If these wayside burials were hurried hole-in-corner affairs scattered up and down the country one would hardly expect them to be remembered. But Mousehold Heath is remembered. More than one Heron lies buried there " in a hollow screened by gorse, on that part of the heath farthest from the barracks," as Fred Gray told Thompson. The very fact that more than one lies buried in the same spot (and Genti Gray said " several ") indicates a return to the place for the particular business of burial, and that in itself indicates some sort of ceremony, some customs attached to the actual act of interment. But if we have no knowledge of what occurred at these wayside burials, nor yet of what occurred before them, we have a considerable amount of material connected with Christian burial.

It appears to be the custom in many families for the body to lie awhile " in state " so that it may be viewed by relatives and friends. There are several records of this for the Boswell family, who did not apparently mind the gorgios viewing their dead. In each instance the coffin was left open until it was nearly time for the procession to start for the graveyard, as is often done at gorgio funerals, so that mourners from a distance might see the body. When Urania Buckland died at Reading in 1912 a similar proceeding was adopted, and when Thomas Pinfold died in Cornwall in the same year the coffin was taken out of the van an hour before the time fixed for the interment and laid on the grass with the lid off for friends to view the body. Many other examples could be given of this practice, and Thompson also mentions that the body of a Gypsy woman who died at Littlebury in Essex about 1830 is said to have been laid on trestles by the encampment whilst awaiting burial, a procedure that appears to be unique. Against these examples Thompson lists some in which a sight of the body has been refused even to relations. " When Lawrence Boswell's eldest son, Moses, died at Etwall, near Derby, in 1855, his widow, Trēnit Heron, excluded visitors from the ' death tent,' and even refused to allow relations to view the body. The East Anglian Smiths and Browns, the latter being Herons under an assumed name, secreted their dead in the same manner, according to Katie Smith, a granddaughter of ' Jasper Petulengro ' and her cousin, Kadīlia Brown ; and similar behaviour has been noticed recently by O'Connor Boswell's family (who are descended from Major in the male line, and a succession of gorgios in the female) among relics of the Ambrose Smith–John Chilcott ' clan ' settled at Green Lane, Birkenhead. The colony there consists of Lurēni and Lenda Young, daughters of Trēnit Heron's brother, Taiso, and of Shūri Chilcott, together with their children and grandchildren, who bear the names Boswell, Smith and Robinson ; and one of the Robinsons is married to a son of O'Connor's. Yet, despite this connecting link, the latter's wife, Angelina Finney, declares that she and her family have twice been denied a sight of their dead. ' And we're not the only ones,' she said, ' for ther's some as is more nearer to 'em nor what we are bin served the same, though they've gone a-purpose to take a last look.' " The fact that Angelina Finney complains, and evidently feels bitter about it, is sufficient to show that it is not the usual custom. I have not personally come across a single instance of refusal. At Caroline Penfold's funeral, where things were carried through with a most punctilious regard for custom, and at Helen Shevlin's funeral (and Helen had

the true black blood of the Ingrams in her veins) the body
was exposed to view.

Most bereaved Gypsies fast while their dead lie un-
buried. In one family of Boswells there is a definite taboo
against the eating of " red " meat at such a time and this
taboo remained in force until the camping place had been
deserted. This family also abstained from preparing meals
of any sort, and normally declined any cooked food offered
them. The East Anglian Smiths and Browns, according to
Thompson, neither cooked nor ate cooked food, contenting
themselves as a rule with bread and water, and Būi Boswell
and his many daughters neither ate nor smoked, and drank
only water, whilst his wife, Savaina Lovell, was awaiting
burial. The same practice has been recorded for Herons
and Grays and Smiths, Lees and Lovells and Loveridges,
Bucklands and Burtons, Stanleys and Coopers. I have
known it in Ayres, Lees, Deightons, Pinfolds—indeed I
have not yet come across any family in which this custom
of fasting until the time of burial is not observed. Normally
fasting ends with the return of the mourners from the graveside, and then sometimes a special meal is served. Thompson records that this happened after the burial of Thomas
Pinfold in 1912, when " tables placed on the moor were
laden with provisions and wine." This must be a very
rare occurrence indeed—and is obviously an imitation of
a common gorgio custom—for Thompson gives only the
one occasion. I have not myself ever come across it.
Children are not expected to share the fast, so far as I
know, in any family, and Thompson bears this out. All
the same, while an Ayres was awaiting burial a year or so
ago his grandchildren, aged fourteen, twelve and eleven,
fasted as rigorously as their parents.

Frequently while the body is awaiting burial it is
watched over by relatives. This " vigil " is a very old
established custom among Gypsies. Thompson was told
by aged members of the Derby gypsery that Vashti Carlin's
body (Vashti was a Boswell who married a gorgio, per-
suading him to travel) was watched continually by two

kinswomen from the time of death until burial and that her
body was illuminated the while by candles at her head and
feet. Vashti was buried on April 10th, 1839. Thompson
then records similar vigils for Mary Buckland in 1909, when
her two surviving sisters sat by the corpse without sleep
until it was removed for burial, and for the wife of Ōni
Lee some ten years earlier, when her sister and a daughter
performed the same feat. Giving examples of vigils during
which the watchers were changed, he instances the death
of Abraham Buckland at Cowley near Oxford in 1923, and
quotes from Frank Cuttriss's account in *Romany Life* of a
New Forest vigil. Cuttriss says : " The coffin was placed
in a tent a short distance from the rest of the camp, by its
side stood a tiny clock . . . the little chamber being lit
by a lantern suspended from one of the tent rods. Two
were keeping watch until midnight when they would
arouse two others to take their places until dawn." Cuttriss
does not give the name of the dead person, but I am pretty
sure he was writing of the death of Sarah Churen in 1912.
His reference to a lantern is interesting, because the usual
illumination is by candles, or more commonly I think by one
candle at the head, and I know that a lantern was used at
the death of Sarah Churen. As a rule these illuminations
continue day and night, but in some cases, as at the death
of Abraham Buckland, they are lit only at night, which is
a departure from normal Christian practice. Another
interesting point in Cuttriss's account is the mention of the
tent at a little distance from the rest of the camp. The
erection of a death-tent is not usual among English
Gypsies. As a general rule the body is left where death
occurred, in the van or tent, and removed only when the
procession to the grave is due to start. The laying of
Thomas Pinfold's coffin on the grass, so that people might
view the body, is an exception to this, and Thompson
records an instance in 1811 when a tent was erected over
the coffin of a Boswell who died in Birmingham, an
instance which he regards as altogether exceptional.
Cuttriss's example was not, however, exceptional for New

Forest Gypsies, nor did he regard it as such. I have not heard of a case recently, but it was certainly the common practice among the *poorer* New Forest Gypsies until quite recently and, a little further back, among those of purer blood. As soon as death had taken place the body was removed from the tent, or van, carried to a little distance from the camp, laid upon a board or folded blankets, and an old tent or a rough, but rainproof, makeshift put up over it. After the burial (and a light was kept burning until the burial was over) this tent and its contents were burnt. There were, I think, two reasons for this departure from the normal practice : a desire to remove the dead body from the camp as some precaution against the return of the spirit (all Gypsies are mortally afraid of ghosts : but more of that later) and common or garden thrift, the desire not to destroy more than absolutely necessary.

The keeping of formal vigils is not confined to Gypsies, of course. I have known it to occur among Hampshire peasantry ; in fact, it occurred as recently as 1940 near Winchester, when, by the way, a single candle was kept alight at the head of the corpse. It occurs among Irish tinkers, according to James Arigho, who maintains that the " wake " has never been a tinker custom. It occurs among the northern potters who have a faint Gypsy strain in them. These northern potters do not feast and drink in the presence of the dead as was once the custom among north-country or Scottish Gypsies, according to Simson, and Thompson records that there was no feasting at the death of George Miller, a potter, in 1909, although there was no fasting. Scottish Gypsies had very different customs from those in use among English Gypsies, and while they may well have infected the Gypsies of the north country I find it hard to believe in view of the contacts the latter undoubtedly had with strict English families. The feasting among north-country Gypsies must, I think, have been among tinkers strayed over the border. Vigils also are kept among the Welsh Gypsies, and Thompson quotes from a letter written to him by a Mr. Alfred Jones from Llanelly in 1912 : " Gypsies about here do not go to bed until after the funeral. They sit in company round the fire, and now and then fall back dozing, but at least three must keep awake. If there were only two, one of them might drop off to sleep, and that would leave one by himself. Afraid of the ghost, they said ; that is why they sit in company and lie around the fire." The keeping of vigils is, nowadays, less common and seems to be commonest among south-country Gypsies and particularly amongst those in the New Forest.

I have said that Gypsies have a strong aversion to handling a corpse and that the laying out is almost invariably done by gorgios. One might as well say " invariably," for Thompson, in all the long and careful research he has done into Gypsy death and burial customs, has come across only one instance of a Gypsy assisting at the laying out of a corpse. This aversion to handling the body is sometimes accompanied by a strong objection to anyone else doing so. Sometimes on these occasions the normal preparations are very much curtailed. Thompson cites as examples two comparatively recent deaths at Birkenhead. Both were youngish men and both died fully, even carefully, dressed, though both had been ill for a considerable period. The only attention either received subsequently was to have his eyes and mouth closed, and his face sponged over very lightly and rapidly by his mother. " On each occasion the body was then laid on a strip of carpet at the back of the tent, and covered with a white sheet. The undertakers were not allowed to make any measurements, and when they brought the coffin their instructions were to lift the corpse into it by taking hold of the carpet only." A similar procedure is said to have been followed in the case of earlier deaths at Birkenhead, notably in the case of Ambrose Smith's sister, Elizabeth, in 1883.

This custom of the Ambrose Smith family may be regarded as rather extreme, but the practice of dressing up for death was formerly quite common and I have known it to occur as recently as 1930 or thereabouts.

When Louis Boswell was buried on January 26th, 1839, he was fully dressed and shod in buckle shoes. In his pockets were his watch, his pocket-knife and some money, beside him lay his walking-stick, his silver tankard and, perhaps, his fiddle. When his daughter Vashti was buried later in the same year she, too, was fully dressed and had on her buckle shoes. Round her waist was a broad belt ornamented with silver, and having concealed pockets in which money had been placed. There are other records of Gypsies being buried in shoes, notably Absolom Smith, who was buried at Twyford in Leicestershire in 1826 wearing shoes adorned with silver buckles each of which weighed half-a-pound. But the custom of being buried in shoes seems to have been confined in the main to the midlands. Thompson only gives two examples outside the midlands, and says some Gypsies, including a Gray, a Heron and a Lee, have informed him that it is contrary to Gypsy custom. Dressing up, however, is certainly not. It has been a common practice not only in England, but in Germany and throughout Eastern Europe. In England and Germany best clothes are worn, but they are always clothes that have been worn before. In Eastern Europe there seems to be a preference for new clothes. Covering the head does not seem ever to have been a common practice among English Gypsies. Eliza Heron was buried in Norfolk about 1887 in a scarlet bonnet, and this seems to be a unique record. There are two records of midland Gypsy women being buried with kerchiefs arranged in the usual manner on their heads. There is one similar record for a Norfolk Gypsy, Tom Brown, and Eliza Boss was buried with the hood of her cloak turned up. The practice seems to have been more prevalent among Scottish Gypsies, who were otherwise buried naked more often than not. Simson says that a paper cap was used and that paper was also put round the feet of the body. Otherwise the body was naked except that on the breast, opposite the heart, a small circle of red and blue ribbons was placed.

G.B.

Burying a corpse naked is unknown among English Gypsies, and so is the use of paper or of ribbons of any colour to adorn the body. But the circle on the breast idea is not unknown, for instead of ribbons some English Gypsies have used, and perhaps still do, a round sod of turf. The exact purpose of this custom is not known. I find it impossible to take seriously the Smiths' explanation (the custom was commonest among Smiths), as quoted by Thompson, that it was to prevent swelling. It is, in any case, not entirely a Gypsy custom. It was formerly common among the peasantry of the lakeland counties, in Staffordshire, in Cornwall, and even occurred occasionally in Hampshire. It was known and practised by the northern potters. And related customs—the use of a few tufts of grass (which would certainly do nothing to prevent swelling) by midland Gypsies, of grasses or flowers by southern Gypsies, and of a pebble by Irish tinkers—are many. It is curious to find no explanation in all the pages of *Folk-Lore* (if there is one I have missed it) and even Fraser is unhelpful. The same reason—prevention of swelling—has often been given for the placing of a saucer of salt on the breast. This is a generally accepted survival of saining ; so it looks, as Thompson points out, as if the motives that once prompted the adoption of these rites had been forgotten or had become confused.

If dressing-up for death was at one time a fairly common practice among English Gypsies, the burying of possessions including clothes with the dead was very much more common and is not yet extinct, nor, in fact, does it show any signs of becoming extinct. And this is the reason why many Gypsies' coffins are so exceptionally large. There is nothing else out of the way about Gypsy coffins. In my experience they are always very good and solidly made and the inscriptions short, plain and neat. Clothes are the most usual possessions buried with the dead. Thompson gives a fairly full list of well-known burials of this type. Her entire wardrobe was buried with Ethelenda Heron, the greater part of Santīnia Smith's with her : Isaac

Heron was buried with a suit and an overcoat, Savaina Lovell with one or two dresses, a silk shawl, and other "bits o' finery." All these Gypsies were buried only in under-garments and a shroud. It was probably less usual to bury additional clothes with a fully-dressed corpse, but it undoubtedly did occur, and Thompson, who gives two examples, thinks that it would be easy to obtain many more and that it may once have been customary to do so. On the other hand, the East Anglian Smiths, who normally buried their dead fully dressed, regarded any loose enclo-sures in the coffin with disfavour, though one of this family, Elizabeth, was buried with two Brussels carpets, one a "large one" as well as the strip upon which she was laid out. The clothes very rarely include boots or shoes. Boots were placed in the coffins of Thomas Penfold and Supplista Smith, but this is most unusual, and I think the inclusion of a pair of new boots in Job Cooper's coffin, as mentioned by Leland, must be a mistake on the part of that great *rai*. There is no other record of a similar occur-rence among English Gypsies, and it is absolutely contrary to accepted English Gypsy practice, though it has occurred among foreign Gypsies in England as recently as 1936. Indeed there is a strong aversion to unworn clothes belong-ing to the dead, and Thompson mentions that when Theo-philus Boswell was buried his large coffin was almost filled up with clothes, but a new suit which had just come for him from the tailor was left out, and subsequently cut up and sent to a rag-shop.

The clothes buried with a corpse are sometimes turned inside out. There are not many recorded instances of this among English Gypsies, but for all that I think this custom was once fairly widespread, and it is not dead even to-day. The three best known examples are all for members of the Heron family who died within a year or so of each other— Isaac Heron, his niece Amelia Heron, the wife of Elias Gray, and her niece Ethelenda Heron. Isaac and Amelia died in the midlands, Ethelenda in South Wales, and in each case the clothes were folded inside out and laid beneath the body. According to Thompson, these are the only three records of this practice in England, but he mentioned related practices in the coat of a fully dressed corpse being turned inside out and of bodies being buried clad in underclothes turned inside out, both being practices regarded as normal by his informants. I can add one further example of clothes being folded inside out and the corpse laid upon them—Caroline Penfold was buried thus. I know of no case of a fully dressed corpse having any of its clothes turned inside out, but I do know of two, and perhaps more, cases in which underclothes have been turned inside out. This at least seems to have been a widespread custom, for James Arigho maintains that the true tinkers were always buried so. The reversal of garments, so Thompson was informed, is a practice in Bulgarian mourning. I do not know about that, and cannot find confirmation anywhere, but the reversal of clothes is a well-known safeguard against ill-luck among many peoples. Thompson gives one or two examples, including one from a Gypsy tale. Among peasant peoples in England it is uncommon now, perhaps it was never common, but it does still occur and the remnants of it still linger among the educated classes. I have been told by highly educated people that it is good luck to put a sock on inside out, I have even been told that it is good luck to put on a jumper or pullover inside out. I have known a Hampshire farm labourer turn his jacket inside out before taking part in a ploughing match, and I have known Irish peasantry reverse their hats before any big event in which they particularly desire to be lucky. I think it not improbable that this reversal of clothing as a burial custom is no more than a desire to ensure that the corpse has a lucky journey to the next world, though it would be easy to produce much more complex reasons for it.

I think consideration of the journey that must be taken after death plays a large part in deciding the other articles that are frequently buried with a corpse. All sorts of things are buried, but jewellery and trinkets seem to be the most usual. Occasionally a vast amount of material is buried with the deceased. Rodney Smith, the Evangelist, in his autobiography, *Gipsy Smith, his Life and Work*, says : " When an uncle of mine died my aunt bought a coffin large enough for all his possessions—including his fiddle, cup and saucer, plate, knife, etc.—except, of course, his waggon. My wife and my sister pleaded hard for the cup and saucer as a keepsake, but she was resolute. Nobody should ever use them again." Such wholesale methods are unusual, and, as a general rule, Gypsies destroy a dead person's crockery and table cutlery. There have been few exceptions to this rule, though a Constance Smith had a knife, fork and plate buried with her, and Mordecai Boswell a cup, plate, knife, fork and spoon, all carefully wrapped up in a " crumb cloth." His daughter Ambrozina, as Thompson records, remarking that " he'd likely have need of 'em."

These are, however, exceptions : jewellery and personal trinkets are not. Most Gypsy women wear rings, necklaces and ear-rings or ear-pendants, and these are often— probably even to-day more often than not—buried with them. Leland heard of Stanleys buried with rings on their fingers, and Thompson says that the Derby Boswells regard stripping a dead woman of her jewellery as both wicked and dangerous. In this family it was usual to place in the coffin with the body any trinkets that the deceased was not wearing at the time of her death, but in most families Thompson thinks it is probably more usual to break them up and either drop them into water or bury them in a hole. It is recorded that at Alice Barney's funeral, at Otterbourne in Hampshire in 1911, her jewellery was interred underneath the coffin, a practice intermediate between those commonly favoured. Actually the heavy gold ring that she was wearing at the time of her death was removed and is still being worn by a descendant. Alice Barney was buried, except for this, in the jewellery she was wearing, and all the rest, a considerable collection, was dropped into the grave just before the coffin was lowered. A point

I have not seen mentioned is that a golden sovereign was thrown on to the coffin before the grave was filled in. Watches are sometimes buried with the men, and so are all sorts of oddments that might conceivably be thought useful in after-life or on the journey, for example pocket-knives, walking-sticks, tankards (many old Gypsies carried drinking mugs in their tail pockets), tobacco boxes, and so forth. There is one record, at least, of a fiddle being buried and one of a whip. They were the things that the deceased used most frequently or was fondest of, but, curiously, I can find no record of a snuff-box being buried, and as I have seen some very old and exquisite snuff-boxes in the possession of Gypsies it would seem that these were always kept as mementoes.

Food, curiously enough, seems to have been buried with the dead only by Hampshire Gypsies. Thompson quotes a very curious record which he says was originally published by the Hampshire Field Club in 1922 of a Gypsy burial at Blackwater in 1912. (I cannot find any record of this in the Club's publications.) At this funeral there was placed in the coffin the deceased's best set of harness, some grain and some bread. The reason for this is evident enough. Harness and corn would be needed for his horse in the next world or *en route* to it, and bread would be needed for his own sustenance. Thompson very rightly casts doubt on this record. For one thing it is supposed to have taken place in Blackwater churchyard, but there is no church at either of the Blackwaters in Hampshire nor is there one at the Blackwater in the Isle of Wight. Again, the man is described as " a Gypsy king," and Thompson has no knowledge of anyone who could possibly be described as such dying at any of the three Blackwaters in or about 1912. The last objection is easily disposed of—all Gypsy men who die and achieve print in so doing are " kings," all Gypsy women who achieve print at their death are " queens " (even poor Caroline Penfold was " a Gypsy queen "). It means no more than that. The objection about the churchyard is more serious, at first sight indeed insur-

mountable. Since there are no churchyards at any of the
Blackwaters the man could not possibly have been buried
in one. But he might, I think, have been buried at Blackwater. As I have already said, I have wondered once or
twice about one of the Blackwaters as a possible burial
ground analogous to Mousehold Heath. The late date,
1912, makes an unsanctified burial very unlikely I admit,
but——. I do not know anything more definite about this
mysterious burial than this—that early in 1912 one Job
Churen, almost the last of that mysterious and respected
family, died, and that at his funeral his favourite horse
(Thompson wondered about the horse and if one was
slaughtered at the Blackwater funeral) was slaughtered.
So much I have heard, but I do not know where Job
Churen was buried. One more point : bread and grain
are believed by many Gypsies to afford protection against
ghosts, witches, evil luck generally, and even against the
devil. Gypsies have been known to sew bread inside their
horses' collars to safeguard the animals against " witching."
Thompson states that Sandi Lovell used to clutch a loaf
of bread to his naked breast whenever he was assailed by
wandering spirits, and that Tom Lee crumbled a whole
loaf around his tent when his son, Bendigo, was born.
Furthermore, tales are not infrequently told by Gypsies of
men and women who habitually carried wheat or other
grain in their pockets as a measure of safety, or ran into
cornfields when followed by the *beng* or a *mulo*. " The dear
God's bread " and " the dear God's grain " are common
expressions among old-fashioned Romanies. Amos Churen
always carried some bread in his pocket. He set very great
store by it. It was something much more than a talisman
to him.

Money is frequently buried with the body. Leland, on
the authority of one of the Deightons, says that £3,000 was
buried with one of the Chilcotts, which is, I think, improbable. The sums are usually small. Twopence was buried
with Zachariah Smith, " a copper or two " with Kenza
Smith, a penny each with Supplista Smith, Noah Holland

and Thomas Penfold. Some of the Boswells were apparently buried with a pound or two, for the Derby branch
of this family used to put in the coffin any money the
deceased had about him when he died or had handled just
before he died. The largest sum that I have knowledge of
is the sovereign thrown on to the coffin of Alice Barney.
The custom of burying money with the dead is not confined
to Gypsies, of course. The Prussians used to put money in
the coffin so that the deceased could buy refreshment on
the way, and the custom is not yet dead in Germany and
Austria, and I believe is still followed in parts of the
Balkans. Thompson records that at the funeral of James
Hedges, one of a half-blood family that travels chiefly in
Essex, a friend dropped half-a-crown into the open grave,
saying as he did so : " Here, Jimmy : here's something
for a drink on the way." The old Irish tinkers used to drop
a coin into the grave and, when the grave was filled in,
spill some liquor on the soil.

The inclusion of a coin in the coffin was not unknown in
gorgio funerals, particularly, it is said, among Roman
Catholics, though it is generally strenuously denied by
them. Some details of this may be found in *Notes and
Queries* * : " Cuthbert Bede," writing about the burial of
a Roman Catholic lady of title not then very long dead,
states that tenantry and others saw her in her coffin and,
according to " two or three cottagers," a hammer rested
in her right hand and a gold coin in her left : " with the
hammer she was to knock at the gate of heaven, and with
the coin to pay St. Peter for admittance." He discredits
these statements and suggests that a crucifix and a reliquary
were mistaken for the secular objects named. Then follows
some correspondence during which one " C. B." thought
that the " hammer " must have been a crucifix and suggested that the " coin " was a medal, perhaps granted by
some religious order. He denied that it was a Roman
Catholic practice to furnish the dead with a hammer and

* 5th Series, Vol. XII (1879), pp. 148, 236, 478, and 6th Series, Vol. I (1880),
p. 132.

a coin, but added : " I have heard of such equipments for a corpse spoken of among Montgomeryshire peasantry." Next comes R. H. Hampton Roberts, who said that once he had been told by some aged Welsh people of the burial with Roman Catholics of a candle to light the way, a loaf of bread for refreshment on the journey, a hammer to knock at the door of heaven and a coin to pay St. Peter for opening it. Lastly, J. W. Smith wrote to say that a similar story, with the addition sometimes of a billhook or hatchet to clear obstructions from the road, and a tinder-box, flint and steel to strike a light, was current in Essex. He declared this to be an absurd Protestant idea arising from ignorance of Roman Catholic usages. If so, as Thompson points out, it is odd that an Irish Roman Catholic of the late Mr. Hall's acquaintance should have told him that he had witnessed the putting of a hammer, a candle and one or two pennies into the coffin at gorgio funerals and for the purposes mentioned, even supposing he did not imply priestly sanctions or tolerance of the practice.

Both candles and hammers have been placed in Gypsy coffins. I know of no recent inclusions of candles, but a hammer was placed in the coffin of Caroline Penfold in 1926, and there are records of this as far back as 1864. Whether it is Gypsy custom that was copied by some gorgios or *vice versa* is a nice point. Myself, I incline to the latter view.

There does not seem to be any special order about Gypsy funeral processions nor any unusual feature common to all, nor is there any evidence that there was in the past. The majority of Gypsy funeral processions are, as processions, perfectly ordinary, but a few have odd and outstanding features and some of these are worth recording. For example, when Dinah Boswell was taken to her grave at Newington Butts in 1773 chimney sweepers' boys were substituted for plumes on the hearse. When Charles Organ was taken to the cemetery at Newport, Monmouthshire, in 1912 the mourners wore horseshoes for luck and, refusing to ride in the vehicles provided, walked behind the body. Thompson records that at the funeral of an unknown Gypsy at Winterton, Lincolnshire—perhaps as recently as the middle of the nineteenth century—the hearse is said to have been drawn by a pair of donkeys with their inside ears cut off. This information was given him by the late Mr. Hall, whose son heard of it from a native of Winterton. (I think this must be a legendary tale of some long distant Gypsy funeral, based as most legends are on a thin foundation of fact, for when I was a boy and beginning to show an interest in Gypsie. I was told by an old fisherman that their coffins were drawn to the graveyard by donkeys with their ears cut off.) When William West died at Oswald-twistle in 1913 his body was taken by road to Astley Bridge near Bolton where he was buried in the family vault. For this purpose a team of six Belgian horses was employed, and on one of the first pair a postilion dressed entirely in black was mounted. This procedure was followed fairly closely in two more modern funerals, and is perhaps the nearest we can get to the true Gypsy funeral procession.

The wearing of black by the mourners is now quite common among Gypsies, though it is by no means universal. White has been worn by maidens in funeral processions, but this is an adaptation of an English folk usage and is not a common Gypsy custom. Thompson gives several examples, including the funeral of Sinaminti Buckland. When she was buried a white sheet held by eight girls dressed in white was used instead of a pall, since she was considered " young and single " although she was the mother of at least three children. At one time red was favoured as a mourning colour by women, and the women of the Lawrence Boswell family, until quite recently, invariably wore red cloaks, though black or dark clothes, supplemented by mourning scarves and crepe hat bands with long streamers were customary for the men. At Aaron Boswell's funeral, in the middle of the last century, all the little girls as well as the grown women wore red cloaks, and some were provided with new ones for the

occasion. At Sinaminti Buckland's funeral red cloaks
were also worn, and many Gypsies have told Thompson
that red was formerly the mourning colour for women,
some maintaining that it used to be so for men as well.
Louis Lovell was buried in a suit of red flannel and Eliza
Heron in a red cloak and bonnet. Among south country
Gypsies generally the wearing of some sort of red ornament
—a rosette or ribbons—rather than the wearing of red
clothes seems to have been more usual, and is not yet
extinct—I have seen it within the last eighteen months.
This has also been noticed in the north, for Thompson says
that at the funeral of Muldobriar Heron, at Birch-in-
Hopwood in the 'eighties, some of the male mourners had
red ribbons in their button-holes or pinned to their coat
lapels. It has been carried across the Atlantic, too, for
when Matilda, the wife of Levi Stanley (who migrated to
America about 1860) was buried at Dayton, Ohio, in 1878,
" red was the predominant hue of her funeral trappings,
each mourner wore a scrap of crimson and the hearse was
decked with red plumes." The circle of red and blue
ribbons placed on the deceased's breast by Scottish
Gypsies is, I think, connected with this rite and also, in all
probability, the painting of some Gypsy tombstones at
Yatton red, white and blue. So, too, is the tying of red
ribbons to the rose tree that was planted on the grave of
Louis Boswell. Andree says that Gypsy visitors to the
tomb of two of their race at Volkmarode in Brunswick tied
red ribbons and pieces of rag to it, and Wittich, writing of
south German Gypsies—an unpublished article quoted by
Thompson—says that graves are adorned each year with
red wool, plaited into ropes, and " hung crosswise from the
grave cross," but Thompson says that the Louis Boswell
incident is the only one known to have occurred among
English Gypsies. This is not so, however, for although I
have not personally come across any similar incident I
have talked to an old woman (not a Gypsy) who remembered it being done at the grave of Gerania Lee at Otterbourne in Hampshire, and I have talked many times to the

Gypsy who did it year by year until the thorn tree that was planted in the grave grew too large and had to be cut down. Gerania was credited with more than one hundred years when she died (in point of fact she was forty-two) and she came from the midlands. A thorn tree was planted on the grave and a quickset hedge all round it, and to this tree on the anniversary of her death red ribbons were tied by relatives who came from the Nottingham district for some years after her death, and for many years after that by Amos Churen, who lived in the neighbourhood.

Death means a great deal to Gypsies and their expressions of grief are sometimes more unrestrained than our own. Gorgio accounts of Gypsy funerals rarely seem to agree, and very little reliance can be placed upon newspaper reports. Sometimes, as at the funeral of Urania Boswell at Farnborough, Kent, on April 28th, 1933, which was very widely reported, every account differs, so much so that it is difficult to believe that they refer to the same event. One newspaper described the mourners at this funeral as " a gay and happy throng," and went on to say that this was the Gypsy custom (another described them as " silent and respectful," another as " weeping aloud "), but I find it hard to believe that the mourners at any Gypsy funeral have been " a gay and happy throng," and it most certainly is not the Gypsy custom that they should be so. It is entirely contrary to everything I know about Gypsies and their ideas about death. It is also contrary to all the authoritative accounts of Gypsy interments. True, it was formerly the custom among Border and Scottish Gypsies to feast and drink in the presence of the dead, but this custom was certainly not prompted by joy, and in any case the fast, to which I have already referred, has always been the common practice.

Keening is not usual among English Gypsies as apparently it is among those of southern Germany, for Wittich says that among his people when a man dies it is the custom for all the bereaved except the widow to howl loudly. Crabb says that when James Smith was buried at Launton, in Oxfordshire, in 1830, his widow " tore her hair, uttered the most frantic exclamations, and begged to be allowed to throw herself on the coffin that she might be buried with her husband." Charlotte Yonge, in *An Old Woman's Outlook*, says that the relatives of Gerania Lee, at her funeral at Otterbourne, " lamented her with loud cries like the Easterns." And after the burial of " Queen Grannie Jeffers " in the Stanley vault at Dayton, Ohio, in 1884, her sons and daughters climbed " down to the coffin to take their last farewell. Their sobs and cries filled the air, and were echoed by the mourners that stood on the brink of the grave . . . threw themselves prostrate on the coffin, kissing the hard wood, and it was only with great difficulty that they could be prevailed on to come out of the grave." Thompson gives other records of this sort of behaviour also, but says that he regards the behaviour of those who followed Isaac Heron to his final resting-place in Manston churchyard, near Leeds, as more typical of Gypsy funeral custom. The Rev. D. M. M. Bartlett has published a very full account of this funeral in the *Journal* of the Gypsy Lore Society : " After the body had been lowered into the earth the mourners came to the foot, and there crouched down, bending themselves nearly double and leaning forward right over the grave, staring down at the coffin as if they would pierce the wood with their gaze. Thus they remained for some little time, rocking themselves backwards and forwards in grief, and then quietly rose and walked away." At two recent Gypsy funerals that I have witnessed the behaviour has been somewhat similar, silent, undemonstrative, but most impressive in its sincerity. Among Welsh Gypsies there is a traditional belief that tears disturb the repose of the dead, and so lamentation at funerals is tabooed.

The return of relatives to the grave on the anniversary of the death, or, as formerly, at some special time of the year such as Christmas (according to Crabb), but never so far as I know on the anniversary of the burial, is an established Gypsy custom. Nowadays there are no rites attached to the customs—the visitor may kneel in prayer for a moment or so, but that is all. It is a decorous and respectful pilgrimage. It was not always so. On January 30th, 1708, Charles Boswell ("a mad spark, that, having an estate of about two hundred per annum, yet runs about. He is mighty fine and brisk and keeps company with a great many gentlemen, knights and esquires") was buried at Rossington in Yorkshire. Nearly one hundred years later Edward Miller recorded in his *History and Antiquities of Doncaster* that "for a number of years it was the custom of Gypsies, from the south, to meet at his tomb annually, and there perform some of their accustomed rites, one of which was to pour a flagon of ale on the grave" : hot ale, according to a letter written by the rector of the parish in 1820 and quoted by Thompson. Another Boswell, buried at Selston in 1821, was also visited annually and ale was also spilled upon his grave, and it is said that the visits, but not necessarily the spillings, continued until 1870 and perhaps even later. Ten years later, on the eve of Horncastle August Fair, No Name Heron and Taiso Boswell were "slayen by thunder and lightning and a fire Ball" at Tetford on the Lincolnshire Wolds, and every Horncastle Fair time for some years afterwards members of the clan visited their tomb. We have, in fact, an eye-witness account of this, for Harriet Williams, who in 1831 was already married to Jack Gray, a son-in-law of both No Name and Taiso and who survived until 1906, clearly recollected these visits and told the Rev. George Hall about them. According to her the men of the party on each occasion walked bare-headed to the grave, with mugs of beer in their hands, and after spilling some, drank the rest in silence, each "making a bit o' prayer to hisself." And when that was done the women visited the churchyard in twos and threes. Crabb says that "most families visit the graves of their near relations once in the year ; generally about the time of Christmas. Then the depository of the dead becomes a rallying spot for the living ; there they renew their attachments and sympathies and give and receive assurances of continued good will. At such periods, however, they are often addicted to intemperance." There is no doubt that at one time funeral feasts were held at the grave on the anniversary of the death or at some particular season of the year (both Wittich and Liebich record the custom for German Gypsies), and this drinking at the grave and spilling of liquor on the grave is a survival of the ancient custom, though survival is too strong a word, for I think the custom so far as British Gypsies are concerned is wholly dead. Crabb's reference to intemperance is supported by an incident at Odstock in Wiltshire, recorded by Thompson. One Josiah Scamp was buried there in 1801, and annual visits were paid to his grave by relatives until they were prohibited by the church authorities because of the nuisance caused by drunken brawlers. This prohibition called forth a curse from one of the deceased's daughters : " May the parson never be understood when he preaches—may the churchwarden be a bankrupt—may the clerk die before the year is out "—a curse that is said to have been fulfilled in every particular. Generally, however, the anniversary gatherings, of which there are many records, were decorous affairs, for they have not elsewhere provoked any complaints and, indeed, have more than once been remarked upon for their extreme reverence. Thompson says that one of the Grays, when visiting his wife's burial-place during the first Christmas season following his bereavement, lay on her grave silently grieving for three hours or more, oblivious of the cold rain pouring down, and barely aware of the presence at his side of an aged sister, who had made the long journey with him " to keep him from harm." Neither of the mourners ate anything at all that day : nor did they on the first anniversary of the death, when a similar pilgrimage was undertaken. Such behaviour, though in this instance rather extreme perhaps, is not untypical of modern Gypsies. I know a Gypsy woman who has spent each of the six anniversaries of her husband's death sitting all day at his graveside, fasting.

After the burial comes the sacrifice. And this is the best known of all Gypsy funeral customs, and the one most widely practised in the past, though to-day it has almost died out. There are innumerable accounts of these Gypsy holocausts, varying only in the extent of the sacrifice made, and it will not be out of place to mention a few here.

In 1769, following the burial of a Gypsy woman at Tring in Buckinghamshire, " the survivors took all her wearing apparel and burnt them, including silk gowns, silver buckles, gold ear-rings, trinkets, etc., for such is their custom." In 1773 " the cloaths of the late Diana Boswell, Queen of the Gypsies, value £50, were burnt in the middle of the Mint, Southwark, by her principal courtiers, according to ancient custom." After Absolom Smith's funeral at Twyford in Leicestershire, in 1826, his tent, bedding, panniers, and fiddle were burnt ; and after Constance Smith's burial at Highwater in 1830, " the whole of her wardrobe was burnt, and her donkey and dog were slaughtered by her nearest relatives, in conformity to a custom remaining among her tribe."

George Borrow, in *Romano Lavo-Lil*, says that after Riley Boss had been buried in Brompton churchyard, Shurensi Smith (his last remaining wife) and a large number of his relatives returned to Notting Hill, " not to divide his property among them . . . but to destroy it. They killed his swift pony—still swift, though twenty-seven years of age— and buried it deep in the ground, without depriving it of its skin. Then they broke the caravan and cart to pieces, making of the fragments a fire, on which they threw his bedding, carpets, curtains, blankets and everything which would burn. Finally they dashed his mirrors, china and crockery to pieces, hacked his metal pots, dishes and what-not to bits, and flung the whole on the blazing pile." And when the fire had died down the remains were collected and buried furtively at nightfall, but as the gorgios heard there was silver among them, and began rooting about in search of it, they were dug up again and thrown into a deep pit of water at some distance from the " Arches."

But everything, says Thompson, was not destroyed at this funeral, for Shuri insisted on keeping two small copper cauldrons in memory of her *rom*, and these cauldrons were in the possession of her grandchildren at Hull, who told the late Rev. G. Hall about them.

Though there are very few records of mementoes being kept I think it was probably a fairly general custom. Crabb, writing of Hampshire Gypsies, says that they " have a singular custom of burning all the clothes belonging to anyone among them deceased, with the straw, litter, etc., of his tent," but a little later on he says that " their attachment to the horse, donkey, rings, snuff-box, silver spoons, and all things, except the clothes of the deceased relatives, is very strong. With such articles they will never part except in the greatest distress ; and then they only pledge some of them *which are redeemed as soon as they possess the means*." This surprising statement had been taken to mean that *none* of these things were destroyed, but I do not think that Crabb, who was a most careful and accurate reporter, intended anything of the sort. He meant, I am sure, that one, or perhaps some, of these things were kept from the sacrifice as mementoes of the dead. Certainly there is no evidence to support his statement if he did mean it to be taken in the wholesale sense. But a ring or a snuff-box, a silver spoon or a watch, these things have been kept out of the holocaust by Hampshire Gypsies in the past, and also, I feel sure, by Gypsies elsewhere. I, at least, have seen a good many heirlooms of great age among modern Gypsies.

Riley Boss died somewhere about the middle of the nineteenth century and at about the same time the funeral pyre of a Gypsy, supposed to have been Henry Lock, was raised by the Severn, probably in Worcestershire. " Cuthbert Bede," writing in *Notes and Queries*, says that he was informed by an eye-witness that " first they burnt his fiddle and then they burnt a lot of beautiful Witney blankets, as were as good as new ; and then they burnt a sight of books —for he was quite a scholar . . . and then there was his grindstun . . . they couldn't burn *him* ! so they carried him two miles, and hove him right into Siv'un ; that's true, you may take my word for it, sir ; for I was one as helped them to carry it."

The Locks, like the Bosses, were, of course, Boswells before they changed their name. The Boswells were a large clan, and the Aaron Boswell, who was buried at Long Whatton in Leicestershire in 1866, belonged to another branch. Thompson records that after his funeral " his clothes, bedding, tent, cart, grinding barrow and harness were burned ; and his crockery and iron pans pounded to fragments, and then buried in the earth together with two copper kettles previously battered out of shape, some pewter jugs and plates which were first hacked to pieces, and a quantity of cutlery, forks, spoons and tools ; whilst his horses and donkeys were dispatched to Nottingham for sale, in charge of a man who did not belong to the family, but had been appointed by them to dispose of animals, and of things like the iron tyres of the cart wheels that could not be made away with at all easily. He was employed because the mourners themselves might sell nothing, according to Caroline Boswell, Aaron's granddaughter, who also insisted that any article touched by a dying man shortly before he expired must be destroyed whether it was his own property or not."

There were plenty of funeral sacrifices in the 'seventies and 'eighties, but as these were very similar in detail they need not be dealt with here. In 1894 occurred a funeral pyre rather different in detail, when Oli Heron was buried at Withernsea. On the evening of the day of the funeral his widow, Wasti Young, " having removed her personal belongings from their living-waggon, had it taken down to the seashore, where, early next morning, and as the tide was rising, some of her kinsfolk set it alight. Towards evening, by which time the ashes of the fire had been carried away on the ebb, they returned to the incombustible wreckage, to break up the iron stove and pans, and any crockery or glass unshivered by the heat, and to cast the refuse into the sea when the water was at its lowest."

A year or two later, after the death of Ambrose Smith's daughter, Lavinia, in a house at Yarmouth, " her clothes and bedding and what little furniture she possessed were burned on the foreshore just beyond the north end of the town ; and her jewellery, the fragments of a tea service valued at £10, some broken or battered domestic utensils, the remains of an iron bedstead, and the carcase of a pet dog poisoned by the survivors, were rowed out to sea more than a mile ; and then thrown overboard." In January, 1899, Savaina Lovell was buried in Liverpool. Immediately the mourners returned from the service they broke up " her crockery, and beat her silver teapot, tray, sugar-basin and spoons into shapeless masses, as a preliminary to filling them, and her jewellery, into two or three small sacks, which were unobtrusively dropped into the Mersey from one of the ferry boats later in the evening ; but her clothes were not destroyed until some days afterwards, when her husband, Būi Boswell . . . and those of the funeral party who had accompanied him to Jackson's Bridge, near Ormskirk, made a fire of them, close to a canal, on the surface of which they strewed the ashes."

In the early years of this century two funeral sacrifices stand out (there were many more, and probably as many again which were not recorded), that of Isaac Heron and that of Crimea Price. Isaac Heron was buried at Manston, and a very full account of the whole procedure has been published in the *Journal* of the Gypsy Lore Society. At 5.30 a.m. on February 25th, 1911 (the day after the funeral), his son, Iza, by arrangement with the blacksmith at Sutton-on-Trent, brought the old man's waggon on to a bare patch of garden behind the smithy. " He next re-moved the shafts, and wheels, and placed them, together with the harness, inside the van, which already contained a quantity of bedding, some old clothes, a hat, a pair of boots, and several small articles in a sack ; and then, having thrust straw inside as well, and saturated it with paraffin, he applied a light." A considerable crowd of villagers, not unnaturally, quickly gathered round, and one woman persistently begged for a charred spindle as a memento and was as persistently refused. After the fire had burned itself out, the ashes were strewn about the garden and the scrap iron was given to the blacksmith. The stove, iron pans and the crockery were broken up and the fragments buried in the ground. The horse was taken to Doncaster where it was sold, probably to a slaughterer. But the hub caps and some hooks were kept by Iza himself, for some reason which no one has ever found out.

Crimea Price was four years old when, in September, 1911, he accidentally set himself on fire while his parents were away hop-picking near Dormington, in Herefordshire, and was so badly burned that he died in hospital next day. When news of his death was brought to the camp " members of the family took their living-van, which cost £80 to build, into the centre of the field, and then, amid much grief, broke it to pieces with axes, and making a funeral pyre of parts of the vehicle, set it alight and burnt it to ashes." Apparently a year or two previously a party of Smiths, stopping on Norton Common, near Weobley, which is another of the Herefordshire hopping centres, broke up their van and burned it on the death of a child. But this wholesale holocaust is most uncommon in connetion with the death of children. It is then not customary to do more than destroy their clothes and perhaps a few of the things most intimately associated with them. This is the practice described by Miss Lyster in her book, *The Gypsy Life of Bestsy Wood*, and it has occurred this year in a *poshrat* Hampshire family with which I am acquainted. Wittich says that the same custom is current among German Gypsies. It is noteworthy that the Prices, though on one side they spring from the true black blood of the Ingrams, are a family with very little good Gypsy blood in them, and it is supposed that the Smiths referred to above are also largely gorgio in origin. Such families often cling most tenaciously to the old Gypsy customs and are often more wholesale in their observances of them than are the true Romanies. Thompson gives a number of instances in support of this view : " On the death, near Madeley, in Cheshire, in 1898, of Vernon, son of Edward (alias Richard) Taylor, an itinerant barber who married Margery Lock's sister Lucy, his widow, Kodi Jones, not a thoroughbred Gypsy by any means, burned his waggon, and ridded herself of his other property ; and when Kodi herself died, on Sound Heath near Wrenbury, in the same county, her sons set fire to her caravan and broke up and buried her crockery and pans." Among Lincolnshire mixed stocks, too, vans have been destroyed on their owner's demise—Frank Elliot's, for example, in 1913. But Scottish tinklers, and the north country potters or muggers of similar origin, apparently do not make extensive sacrifices, if any at all, in these latter days, though the families settled at Kirk Yetholm used to burn the clothes of their dead, according to a writer in Blackwood quoted by Sir Walter Scott ; and so did the Cumberland Stewarts, even within the memory of William Stewart, who was barely sixty when I saw him in 1913 ; whilst in 1871 or 1872 a relative of mine residing near Windermere witnessed the burning of some clothes and bedding belonging to a member of the Miller family who died close to his house.

With the outbreak of the Great War the number of funeral sacrifices seems to have decreased. No doubt there were sacrifices during the war years that were not recorded —people were too busy making and recording other and greater sacrifices—and no doubt there were sacrifices in the years of the Long Armistice that passed unnoticed, but if so they were few, and few also have been recorded. Thompson records three, all in 1924. One of these was after the funeral of Levi Boswell on May 8th at Bromley, Kent. Levi, who had two crippled sons, had lived in the neighbourhood for close upon thirty years and was well known and well liked by many people. By profession he was a horse-dealer—he had a truly remarkable knowledge of horses even for a Gypsy and a great reputation for honesty—and he was also a showman, and these two callings naturally brought him much into touch with the gorgios. His funeral procession was interesting : "He went to his rest wearing—as marks of his chieftainship of the clan Boswell—bright yellow socks and a muffler of brilliant red. Buried with him, according to custom, were also many little gifts most treasured by him. These were placed in the coffin secretly, and the members of his family are pledged never to disclose what they are. The coffin, half-hidden among flowers, was in a hearse drawn by six black horses richly caparisoned in purple and gold. On one of the front horses rode a postilion wearing a tight-fitting black tunic and purple knee-breeches and a black jockey cap. The widow rode in a motor car with her two sons, who, like herself, are crippled and use crutches. She wore a black dress with a bodice of Victorian fashion and a heavily-plumed hat. On foot followed a long procession of relatives." * We have already seen the use of postilion and six horses in the Lancashire funeral of William West and we shall meet it again. The colours red and yellow are the Gypsy colours, but the use of yellow at British Gypsy funerals is unusual. After Levi's funeral there does not seem to have been a holocaust—no burning of living-waggon or slaughtering of horses—but many of his personal possessions and all his clothes were destroyed by fire.

But later in the same year, when Mrs. Sarah Bunce died at Reading, there was, following the funeral, a regular old-fashioned holocaust on the fair ground. Sarah was the daughter of Gypsies whose belongings at their death had been burned, and in her case everything was destroyed with the van and only money was saved. Still later in the year a Smith died at Chasetown, in Staffordshire, and was buried by the side of his wife at Wilnecote, near Tam-worth. The body was dressed only in a shroud and no clothes were placed in the coffin, which did, however, contain his pipe and tobacco and a potato he had picked up on the road just prior to his last illness. After the funeral one of his daughters smashed up his crockery, and then his son placed the harness together with all his other

belongings in the van, into which he also poured a gallon
or two of paraffin and then threw in a bundle of lighted
straw. The van caught fire, but it did not burn well, and
so one of the onlookers, a Gypsy, threw a stone through the
back window, and thus caused a draught that soon encouraged the flames. When everything had been burned the
son collected the metal trappings of the harness and threw
them into a pond some little distance away.

There were two funeral pyres in 1926. On October 2nd,
Plato Buckland, who was reported to be 102 years of age,
was buried in Reading cemetery. He died at Marlow, and
after the funeral his van and harness and all his belongings
were burned at Marlow. There seems to be some doubt
about his horse. Those papers that reported the occurrence, and they included the thoroughly reliable *Observer*,
all maintain that it was shot. Thompson does not believe
that it was, and there does seem to be some ground for
believing that it was sold to a knacker in Maidenhead.
But the more remarkable sacrifice occurred earlier in the
year after the funeral of Caroline Penfold at Crediton,
Devon, on April 17th. In some ways, indeed, this was the
most remarkable holocaust of recent years.

Caroline Penfold was only twenty-six when she died
from tuberculosis on April 15th. (Her husband, Christopher Penfold, had died only some three weeks earlier.)
Penfold is not a Gypsy name, but a Devon name, though
Penfolds appear to have married Gypsies on a number of
occasions. Caroline was of good Gypsy blood, for her
father was Thomas Roberts and her mother Defiance Pinfold, a daughter of the Thomas Pinfold whose funeral has
already been described. In this case the ancient rites were
observed to the letter—I think Caroline probably left
instructions, for she was fiercely proud of her Romani
blood, proud to an extent that I, personally, have met in
no other Gypsy save Amos Churen—and the funeral was
attended by Gypsies from a wide area, and also by many
poshrats. Among the names of those that attended were
Roberts, Pinfold, Gray, Birch, Holland, Stanley, Lee,

Smith, Penfold, Manley, Pateman and Darling. For twenty-four hours before her burial she lay in state in the waggon in which she died. A lighted candle was placed by her head and this was the only illumination in the waggon. Female relatives watched over the body, but anybody who so desired was at liberty to enter the waggon. So far as I know the whole camp fasted during these twenty-four hours and until after the holocaust. Caroline was buried in a shroud only. Her best dress and her finest underlinen were carefully folded inside out and placed in the coffin and her body was laid upon them with the arms straight down at her sides. In the coffin was placed all her jewellery except for one heavy gold ring. This jewellery was said to be very valuable, but I do not think she had very much and I do not believe that what she had was of any particular value. The ring, however, was undeniably good, a broad and heavy gold band of considerable antiquity. Also in the coffin were placed a silver comb, some small trinkets of which she was very fond, her snuff-box and a hammer. After the funeral a female relative smashed all the crockery, and her father packed everything else into the van, poured in paraffin and set it alight. When the fire had burned itself out the remaining metal was taken away and buried. The horse that normally drew the van, a young and strong piebald, was taken away by her brother and sold, but two other horses and one or two ponies were retained. Caroline was reputed to be wealthy and to keep a considerable amount of loose cash about her as well as having a very substantial balance in the Post Office Savings Bank. I do not know how true this is : certainly no money was destroyed. She was also reputed to have second sight, and for this there certainly seems to be some foundation. Nothing was planted on or around her grave, and there is nothing to indicate where she is buried. Curiously enough, when her father died the traditional Gypsy ceremonies were not observed. Nothing was buried with him, nothing was planted on the grave, nothing was burnt. Again a large number of Gypsies from a wide area attended the funeral (most of the same names but also some Coopers) and at the conclusion of the service they surrounded the grave, peering down intently, repeating some Romani words and each throwing in a handful of earth. One man, whose name I do not know, also threw in a florin.

On April 28th, 1933, at Farnborough, Kent, Urania Boswell was buried. This is the funeral to which I have already referred. It created a great deal of interest and was widely reported in the national Press by an army of reporters, all of whom saw something different and none of whom seemed able to agree on any major point. Urania Boswell was the widow of Levi Boswell whose funeral I have already mentioned. Urania was the daughter of Gypsy Sarah, the Brighton " Queen," and Abraham Lee, who was, according to some of the papers, the original Gypsy Lee. I have yet to meet a Lee of any age who is not the original Gypsy Lee, and I have met a large number of Gypsies and an equally large number of *poshrats* who have laid claim to the same title. Indeed on Epsom Downs one Derby Day some years ago there were no less than three original Gypsy Lees doing a thriving trade, and none of them was truly Gypsy. Be that as it may, Urania Boswell —she was generally known as Reni—undoubtedly came of the aristocracy of English Gypsydom and married into an equally renowned family. And her funeral did attract much attention. The crowds that gathered were variously estimated at 15,000, 20,000 and 50,000, but it is beyond question that some hundreds of Gypsies attended and that the mourners did number fifty-two. As with her husband's funeral, so with hers, the coffin was drawn by six horses draped in black and with a postilion, dressed in black and wearing a black jockey cap, mounted on one of the front pair. The crippled sons, Herbert and Kenza, her daughter Nora (who got up from a hospital bed to come) and her brother Job Lee followed in one car, and another son and daughter, Levi and Georgina, with some other relatives in a second car. But the outstanding feature of this funeral is that after it was over the living-waggon and the possessions of the deceased were not destroyed. Having regard to the lineage of Reni and the family into which she had married, this departure from tradition is truly astonishing, and shows all too clearly the waning strength of Romani customs in this country. Instead of burning it was decided that the waggon should be left exactly as it was when she died until it rotted away. I suppose this decision may be taken to show some faint remnant of the traditional Romani attitude towards the dead, but as it was an exceptionally well-furnished waggon I cannot think that it was left untouched for long.

Later in the same year, on November 22nd, another Gypsy queen was buried at Newport in Shropshire, and on this occasion the ancient tradition was observed to the letter. As the lady's name was Helen Shevlin, which is not a Gypsy name at all (though it is not unknown among Irish tinkers), this is at first almost as astonishing as the Boswell departure from tradition. Helen Shevlin, however, came of the very old, very deep Romani stock. She was Helen Price and she married Cornelius Shevlin, an Irishman of tinker stock. She was said to be the daughter of Bob Price and Jane Stevens. I knew her fairly well and she was actually the daughter of Amos Price (Bob's brother) and an Irishwoman of tinker stock named Mary Ann Duffy. She was thus the granddaughter of that Henry Price who married Helen Ingram. Now the Ingrams—the name has disappeared from the English roads (a very ancient man who died near Petersfield in 1907 or 1908 may have been the last of the male line)—were the true black blood of the Romani. They and the Chilcotts were regarded with something akin to awe, even by such old Gypsy families as the Herons and Boswells and Grays, nor is the name forgotten to-day. Helen Shevlin was very proud of her Ingram blood (very proud also of her Irish blood) so it is not surprising that ancient tradition was followed at her funeral.

It, too, was a funeral that attracted much attention. At

the time of her death Helen was near Crewe, and she was brought to Newport at considerable expense. The whole funeral is said to have cost some £300. A great concourse of Gypsies, some of whom came from long distances, attended and the *Crewe Chronicle* published a list of ninety names—a truly remarkable achievement on the part of the reporter, considering that this was a Gypsy funeral. These names make interesting reading. They include several Finneys, Duffeys, Toogoods, Braddocks, Egertons, Rollinsons and a Gorman, in addition to the Shevlins present. That surely is an amazing list of Irish names to be found at an English Gypsy funeral. Finney, Duffey, Braddock, Egerton and Gorman, as well as Shevlin, are names to be found among the travelling tinkers on the Irish roads to-day. I have not met either Toogood or Rollinson as Irish tinker names, but in view of the obvious connection between this English-Irish Gypsy woman and Irish tinkers I suspect that both are good tinker names. Of the other names there are many Locks and many Smiths, three Burtons, and one Price—all good English Gypsy names. The Locks and the Prices are very much intermingled, but, even so, it is rather strange that there should have been only one Price present.

After the funeral the whole crowd returned to Crewe and the four men who had acted as bearers at the funeral pulled the living-waggon away from the others into a corner of the field and, after they had taken out all the crockery and breakable possessions, packed the undercarriage with straw and poured paraffin over it. Before they could set it alight, however, some of the younger members present protested against what they considered waste. Their leader was one Jack Taylor and he had considerable support, particularly from other Taylors and a very tough individual named Carloman. For some time it looked as if a real old-fashioned *chingaripen* was going to develop, and blows were, in fact, exchanged between one of the Taylors and one of the Finneys (I think it was Arthur). But finally, after an impassioned address by Cornelius

Shevlin, the eldest son, the straw was set alight and all was well. A great change came over the assembly as soon as the fire started, and what had a few moments before appeared an angry crowd stood in complete and reverent silence until the *vardo* was consumed. The crockery was smashed and buried, and the horse (who was a great age) was sold in Crewe about a week later. There have been holocausts since Helen Shevlin's, of course—Jemina Brazil's led to a lawsuit—but the custom does not, I think, require further description.

It is, perhaps, worthy of mention that both Urania Boswell and Helen Shevlin were wealthy women. Urania was reputed to have left £15,000 or so—though there has been some argument about the actual amount—Helen Shevlin left £30,000 and there has been no argument about this. She carried in her *vardo* a great deal of money, which was taken before the burning and divided by Cornelius between the sons and daughters, and Urania Boswell is reported to have had a hundred £5 notes kept in her waggon. Both women owned considerable house property.

Probably we have seen the last of Gypsy holocausts, at least on the grand scale. Economic conditions and the great infusion of gorgio blood have done their work, and the present generation of travellers think more of utility than of tradition. It is very often said that the Gypsy has no superstition and knows no God. I do not think either statement is in the least degree true. He has a very great respect for the dead, a much greater respect than is normally to be found among gorgios, and he is undoubtedly frightened of the spirits of the dead. It is this *trashiben* of the *mulo* that has been at the bottom of all Gypsy funeral rites. Hard as the sacrifice has been on the remaining members of the family on many occasions, sinful as the waste may have appeared to our materialistic and utilitarian minds, it has for the race as a whole been a beneficial custom, for it has kept very much alive the spirit of independence and endeavour. More has been sacrificed with the passing of sacrifice than ever was lost in the flames.

VI

SOCIAL ORGANISATION

IT is difficult to believe that there is any social organisation among the Gypsies. A Gypsy family on the road, a casual visit to a Gypsy encampment, do not leave an impression of organisation. There is obviously a headman and it is equally obvious that he has some authority—but that is about all. It is a deceptive impression. I do not mean by that that there is a firm organisation among the Gypsies, that Gypsy families are subject to discipline as we, in this age of bureaucratic regimentation, understand the word. There is nothing of that sort. It would be entirely foreign to the Gypsy temperament. But there is a social organisation, and I am quite convinced that the obvious presence of the headman has led to too much importance being attached to him by most of the investigators of Romani life from George Borrow onwards. Borrow, for example, writes much of Jasper Petulengro. He knew Petulengro well, and Petulengro was a headman and a man of substance and importance. Borrow accepted him as such, looked no further, and so unconsciously stressed too greatly his importance.

Jasper Petulengro was Ambrose Smith, the son of Mireli Smith. Mireli was herself a daughter of another Mireli Smith, whose second husband was John Chilcott, by whom she had a son, bearing the same name. Around these two children of old Mireli Smith was built up a clan that travelled East Anglia and engaged very largely in horse-dealing. The headmen were Ambrose Smith and John Chilcott. This clan, despite its sub-divisions (Ambrose Smith had his headquarters around Norwich and John Chilcott his around Woodbridge), was a single, closely-knit, social and economic unit, which on special occasions, such as funerals, would assemble as a whole and which would sometimes, as on the fringe of London, trade as a whole. Now, Mireli Smith, the younger, had six children, Ambrose and a younger son Faden (who seems never to have married), and four daughters, Laini, Elizabeth, Liti and Prudence. These formed one subdivision. The other was formed by John Chilcott and his four daughters, Union, Caroline, Florence and Shuri. Ambrose's four sisters all married : Laini to Tom Cooper, who was deported ; Elizabeth to Elijah Buckley ; Liti to Būi Brown ; and Prudence to Matt Barker, a gorgio horse-dealer. John Chilcott's four daughters also married : Union to Charles Lee ; Caroline to Tom Lee ; Florence to Wester Boswell ; and Shuri to Taiso Young. But when these eight women married they did not leave the clan. In every case their husbands came to join the clan, to live, travel, and work with them. It was, in fact, a typical example of a matrilineal and matrilocal society. And there are plenty of other examples in Gypsy history.

There was, for example, another East Anglian clan which migrated to Blackpool and settled there. This clan had its origin in another Ambrose Smith, the paternal uncle of the Ambrose Smith who was Borrow's Jasper Petulengro. This Ambrose Smith married Mireli Draper and had five daughters, Honor, Fēmi, Rachel, Moll and Athalia, who was nicknamed Happy. He also had three sons, but they need not concern us because they, with their father, were transported. The daughters married : Honor to her first cousin Frank Smith ; Fēmi to Sampson Robinson ; Rachel to Nixi Lovell ; Moll to Golden Hope ; and " Happy " to a man named Nicholson. The men joined their wives. Frank Smith and Sampson Robinson were the headmen of this clan, but there seems to be little doubt that in its early days at any rate the real force in the society was old Mireli Draper.

A third, very much larger, and, in Gypsydom at least, more famous organisation was the north country clan headed by " No Name " Heron and Taiso Boswell, who were cousins. Here again there were subdivisions, but the clan was a single social unit, at least during the lifetime of

" No Name " and Taiso, who were inseparable companions until their deaths at Tetford in 1831, where they
were struck by lightning. After this tragedy there does not
seem to have been any definite headman, and the whole
organisation was much looser, but it still remained a clan.
Matrimonial relationships in this clan are complicated by
the fact that most of the women married more than once
and because " No Name " went in for wives on a big scale.
But Thompson has worked them out as well as they can be
worked out. Taiso Boswell had only one wife, Sophia
Heron, who was the daughter of " No Name's " elder
brother. By her he had six daughters, Maria, Lucy, Seji,
Betsy, Dorīlia and Delēta. Maria first of all married David
Williams, but this was a purely temporary affair and he
later migrated to America. Her permanent husband was
Jack Gray. Lucy married Riley Boss ; Sēji, Joseph Smith ;
Betsy, Job Williams ; Dorīlia, Khulai Heron ; and Delēta,
Allen Boswell. " No Name's " adventures in matrimony
are not so simple. He had many wives, including his niece
Sophia, who became Taiso's wife, and he had some of
them at the same time. By his niece he had a daughter
whose name has been given as Sēji. By Rose Lovell he
had Eldorai, Eliza, Waddi, Amelia and Sarah. Then
there were two closely related women, Sibella Smith or
Boss and Seni Boss or Smith, and one of these bore him
two more daughters—Emanaia and Hannah. His two
permanent wives appear to have been Rose Lovell and
Sibella Smith, who was also called Boss. These daughters
all married and most of them more than once. Eldorai
married " Stumpy " Frank Heron. Eliza married first
Jack Gray, who later became the husband of Maria Boswell, and then his brother Oseri. Waddi married first
Jack Gray (apparently at the same time as he was married
to Maria) and later Oti Printer. Amelia married Piramus
Gray, another brother of the much-married Jack. Sarah
married first Wester Boswell (this was a temporary affair),
then Major Boswell (who later migrated to America), and
then Jack Lovell. Emanaia (who was also called Smith

and Boss) married " Big " Frank Heron. Hannah (who had the same aliases as her sister) married first "Big" Frank Heron and then " Kaki " Sam Boswell. Further complications in this astonishing family are caused by the daughter of " No Name " by his niece, for she lived first with Job and then with David Williams, and later with Jack Gray (who must, I fancy, have been an exceptionally attractive man), for he raised yet another family by Harriet Williams (who was Maria Boswell's daughter by her first marriage to David Williams), and did so at just about the same time as the family he had by Maria. I have not mentioned any of the sons of " No Name," for when they married it was with women outside the clan, and they left to join their wives' families. Similarly I have mentioned only one son of Taiso Boswell, Wester, for Ned married outside the clan and left to join his wife's people on doing so. Wester did the same thing after his temporary alliance with Sarah Heron. Similarly inside the clan " Big " Frank Heron, " Kaki " Sam Boswell and Major Boswell all, sooner or later, made permanent alliances with women outside the clan and on doing so left to join the families of their wives, leaving (as is the invariable Gypsy custom) their children behind them. Though the men drifted away either on their first marriage or on the acquisition of permanent wives, the husbands of all these women came into the clan. In the next generation relationships in this clan were much more stable, but I do not think there is any need to trace them further. Though numbers dropped fairly rapidly, owing to large scale emigration to America, the same rule held good. The men joined the people of their wives : the women brought their husbands into the clan. It was a matrilineal and matrilocal society just as much as was that of Ambrose Smith–John Chilcott and of Mireli Draper.

A similar state of affairs is to be found in the Welsh Locks. Mairik Lock, who was the eldest son of Henry Lock, married Mary Smith and had two sons and eight daughters. The two sons married, one a Draper and the other a gorgie woman named Dixon, and in each case left the clan. The eight daughters also married and in every case the husband joined the clan.

It is not so easy to find clear-cut examples of the sort I have given above for the south country Gypsies, the Gypsies of the south-west and west midlands, or even for the Welsh Gypsies. Study of these groups began too late for any such evidence to be collected. Yet even in these groups there is a strong suggestion of a loosely organised matrilineal society. No one would suggest that the famous Welsh Gypsy family of Woods was not a clan, but it was a clan of rather a different nature due to entirely different conditions. The Woods were in Wales long before any other Gypsies, and they came into Wales under the leadership of Abram Wood. They were cut off from all contact with other Gypsies for many years and so there was a great deal of inter-marriage and a number (surprisingly few all the same) of marriages with the Welsh gorgie. Even so, when contact was re-established and marriages took place, the matrilocal rule appears to have operated and husbands joined their wives' families.

In these matrilineal and matrilocal clans the only exception to the rule that husbands joined the families of their wives was the headman, who was generally, but not always, the eldest son. His wife joined him. But, even so, her property remained her own, and should she die childless or with infant children, her husband had no claim on her property, which returned to her family. Gypsy laws of inheritance are very complex and I do not pretend that I understand them—nor have I found a *Romano Rai* who does understand them fully. Generally speaking, the laws of inheritance excluded all paternal kindred and all women as possible heirs. Beyond that, there seems to have been a good deal of variation as between clan and clan, but that at least seems to have been a firm rule, and, though conditions have altered so greatly of recent years, and though the inheritance laws have altered to keep pace with economic conditions, it does seem that that law is not

yet entirely defunct. Money and stock-in-trade (and it
must be remembered that some Gypsies were and are
wealthy, judged even by modern gorgio standards) was
inherited by the eldest son, or, if no son arrived, by the
eldest grandson, who might, of course, be the son of a
daughter. But he must be grown-up. He could not
inherit if he was not grown-up. No doubt the age at
which manhood was attained varied a good deal from clan
to clan, but it was generally, if not always, younger than
under our own law. If there was no adult male in the
direct line the inheritance passed to the nearest maternal
kinsman of the deceased, a brother, an uncle, a nephew
or a cousin. There has in the past been considerable dispute as to the order of precedency between a brother and a
maternal uncle, and as to the merits of seniority and mere
age among nephews and cousins. But it is certain that
paternal kindred were excluded. The rule that barred
women from succeeding to an inheritance does not, however, appear to have been universal among British Gypsies.
Widows were always allowed to keep what was left of
travelling and domestic equipment after the funeral
destruction, even in those families that barred them as
successors. And among south country Gypsies and the
Gypsies of the Welsh border I think the law was somewhat
less stringent. When Prudence Buckland, the widow of
Sidnal Smith, died at Charlbury without issue she left a
farm and £1,500 in gold and her sister, Sēgul, inherited
them, despite the fact that there were nephews alive.
Furthermore, the fact that Prudence left this property
suggests that she came into possession of her husband's
property at his death. Amos Churen was very definite
that, should the husband die and there be no surviving son
or grandson of age, all the property went to the widow, and
Gerania Barney (who was born a Lee) bears out this
statement. Gerania also maintained that the sister of a
deceased woman had a better right to inheritance than
nephews or cousins and would inherit without opposition
(which is what happened in the case of Prudence Buck-

land), but neither she nor Amos would hear of any succession by paternal kindred. Should there be a son or grandson of age the inheritance passed to him without quibble and with it went the duty of supporting the widow. Neither in the north nor in the south was there any division of the inheritance, it being considered the duty of the heir to support so far as was necessary all those people previously dependent upon the deceased.

There are many examples in Gypsy lore of the working of these inheritance rules, and some of them have been collected by Thompson. I quote from a paper published by him one case from the Lawrence Boswell family : " Lias's paternal grandfather, Moses Boswell, had for his first wife a Saiëra Buckland, whose marriage gift included a sum of money and a pair of diamond-studded shoe buckles. She died young, leaving two sons, Sam and Nathan, who were little more than infants, and therefore debarred from inheriting. Moses intended to bury the buckles with her, but some uncles of hers arrived before the funeral, and, laying claim to them as well as to her private money, received both at his hands, for he did not dispute their right to them. What happened further, beyond a quarrel among these Buckland uncles as to what should be done with the inheritance, is not known ; nor can anyone say now exactly who the claimants were. Moses himself died in 1855, survived by Sam but not Nathan ; also by his second wife, Trēnit Heron, and most of her family, which ranged from Nelson, a married man of several years standing, to a girl of about fifteen. Sam, who shortly afterwards went to America, declined the inheritance because of the responsibility attached, and it passed to Nelson, with whom Trēnit travelled until her death many years later." There are many other instances to be found in the pages of the *Journal* and some interesting cases of dispute. One of these, which occurred in 1903, was between the widow of a childless man and a son of his elder brother, and was reported at the time in the Scottish papers, for it came into the Law Courts. It was brought by Eldorai Smith, who married her cousin William Lovell in New Jersey in 1868, " Gypsy fashion, by joining hands and promising each other before the rest of the tribe," against Christopher Lovell, the son of her husband's brother. Eldorai and William came back to Scotland in 1876 and lived in a van at Vinegar Hill, and it was here on July 2nd, 1903, that William died. He left goods valued at £357, and Christopher, who was the son of William's brother Cornelius and Eldorai's sister, Deloraifi, seized them. Eldorai brought the action for a decree declaratory of marriage and after one Dr. Thomas Mowat of Clydebank had deposed " from personal knowledge " that the Gypsy marriage custom was as Eldorai had stated, she was declared to have been legally married. She then got the goods back by threatening to prosecute her nephew for theft. It is, by the way, interesting to note that the papers of the time called her Mary Ann Smith or Lovell and not Eldorai. She was then fifty-two and obviously a woman of vigorous and determined temperament. Her brother, Shandres Smith, who talked about this case to Thompson, fully approved his sister's action, maintaining that when a man died everything went to his widow, except the money, which was divided equally between the sons and daughters. It seems to indicate some divergence of opinion between the families, the Smith side believing that the widow could inherit and the Lovell side believing that the goods should go to the nearest male relative on the maternal side. Christopher would be not this, however, for Shandres as brother would have precedence over a nephew. Nor can I believe that families as closely connected as these Smiths and Lovells could have different inheritance laws. Shandres's statement that the widow inherits over the heads of grown sons is not one for which I can find any independent support. And it is well to remember that when Gypsies appeal to gorgio law it is, as often as not, no more than an attempt to set aside Romani custom.

For Shandres's statement that the money was always divided equally between the sons and daughters there is a good deal of support, so long as it refers only to money actually in the possession of the deceased, that is, in the *vardo* or somewhere in the camp, at the time of death, and not to money that may be deposited in a bank. So long ago as 1821 a certain Absolom Smith died at Twyford, in Leicestershire, and each of his children, of whom several were daughters, is said to have received £100. Another account says that he left a gallon of sovereigns and that they were divided equally among his children. Certain it is that nowadays the rule that there shall be no division of inheritance does not include the money actually in the possession of the deceased at the time of death. At Helen Shevlin's funeral the money in the *vardo* was divided by her eldest son Cornelius with his brothers and sisters. The money in Urania Boswell's waggon was divided between her five children. And I know personally of the same thing happening in six recent cases, in none of which was there any holocaust after the burial.

The division of inheritance rule no longer applies universally, probably not even generally. Inheritance laws and practices are largely based upon conceptions of kinship and changes in the latter are always followed, though never very quickly, by changes in the former. English Gypsy ideas on kinship have changed considerably, for they will now trace relationship and descent through both parents just as we do. Even so, the English Gypsy, though he no longer practises matrilocal marriage (that custom has not entirely died out), though he will now recognise kinship and descent through both parents, though he will at death divide the inheritance, though he will accept paternal kindred as heirs to inheritance (in this connection I must point out that in one recent case of which I have personal knowledge, the direct line having failed, the inheritance passed to the maternal kindred though there were plenty of paternal kindred available, including the dead man's brother), remains matrilineal in outlook. Circumstances and economic conditions have forced and are forcing changes in his outlook and in his actions, but they cannot affect the

rooted custom of his race. Even to-day you will find
children taking the mother's name. Originally the whole
of our Gypsy stock was matrilineal, the mother was the sole
fount of kinship, and you do not get rid of the beliefs and
instincts of centuries in a hurry.

It is in the light of all this that we must consider the
headman. I do not suggest that he was a mere figurehead
or that he was a man without authority. Some headmen
wielded very great authority indeed—Abram Wood, for
example. But Abram Wood really was more of a king
than a headman. Nor can there be any doubt that
Ambrose Smith (Borrow's Petulengro) exercised great
authority. John Chilcott did also, and the same is true
of " No Name " Heron and Taiso Boswell, and, in Scotland, of the great Billy Marshall. And we know of other
headmen of great authority. Dick Heron was such a man,
a headman of great and very wide authority and one noteworthy in another way. He objected very much to his sons
and grandsons going away when they married, and it is
said of him that in an attempt to overcome this he organised
wife-getting expeditions. He would travel round the
country every now and again (so it is said) accompanied
by all the young men of the clan who were of marriageable
age and all of them ready equipped for married life even
down to the kettles and pans. When they came upon a
likely girl they just carried her off and discarded her with
as little ceremony if she did not prove satisfactory. I
imagine the tale is untrue. But there can be no doubt that
Dick Heron did try to found a paternal clan, and he failed
miserably. His sons and grandsons adhered to their wives'
families in the normal way. Another headman of considerable authority who failed in a similar way was Būi
Boswell. In the days when the clan system was in operation, portions were always splitting off from the main body
and founding smaller clans of their own. This was inevitable because if a clan got much too big it became unwieldy
and uneconomic. There are plenty of records of this
splitting off from the main body—the Locks who went into

Wales and were really Boswells are a good example—and no doubt the clan we commenced this chapter with, the Ambrose Smith–John Chilcott clan, was really a split from a much larger, more loosely organised society, and it in its turn split. The headmen of these break-away parties were always men of some force of character. Būi Boswell was one. He belongs to the huge Heron-Boswell clan, and he had ten daughters who were all very fond of him. He broke away from the main body and tried to found a maternal clan of his own. He failed because he treated his sons-in-law far too harshly. It is said that he tried to force them into submission by flogging them and starving them, that he would put the police on to them to bring them back if they left him, and that two of them, who failed to meet with his approval (both gorgios), were dis-misssed and their wives forced to accept the dismissal. He certainly did do this, and he certainly did put the police on to erring sons-in-law, and it is quite probable that he also flogged them. He was, in any case, a peculiar man. But he failed, and he failed because he exercised too much authority. Dick Heron failed for very much the same reason. There are plenty of other examples, but Abram Wood is the only one who made a real success of it.

Among English Gypsies (among most Gypsies for that matter) the mother is usually the main supporter of the family, and it is the women of the family who do the lion's share of the work. That, and the fact that the mother was originally the fount of all kinship, that the whole structure of society was matrilineal, gave to the women enormous power. The " clans " broke up in the end as they were always bound to do, and to-day there are no clans though the social structure is still vaguely discernible. But there is still the family, the group of two or three families, the women still do most of the work, the mother is still the *main* supporter of the family—and there is still a headman.

For George Borrow, Jasper Petulengro was the chief of the Gypsies. But that clan was founded by the two children of old Mireli Smith, and Ambrose Smith was the son of one of the founders. He stayed with his mother until she died. Can there be any doubt who was the real ruler of that sub-division ? For the matter of that, can there be any doubt what force it was that held those two divisions together ? Yet we hear nothing, or practically nothing, of Mireli Smith, the younger. We do know something of Mireli Draper, who was a woman of outstanding force of character, but we hear more of the two headmen. We hear nothing of the mothers of " No Name " and Taiso Boswell. But are we to suppose, therefore, they were of no importance—in a matrilineal society that gave rise to so huge a clan as that founded by the two cousins ? And when these old ladies died, the Mireli Smiths and the Mireli Drapers of Gypsydom, were there no women to take their places ?

The fact of the matter is that from George Borrow downwards we have paid far too much attention to the Gypsy men and far too little to the Gypsy women, far too much attention to Gypsy " kings " and Gypsy " chiefs " and far too little to Gypsy "queens." Indeed we have been inclined to take these Gypsy headmen at whatever valuation they set upon themselves for the benefit of the gorgios and to regard " Gypsy queen" as a title put on to add colour to fortune-telling and to bemuse servant girls. But whereas Gypsy chiefs may be common enough—they are often created for the benefit of the gorgios—and Gypsy kings come and go (generally in the columns of the daily Press) you hear very little about Gypsy queens. Nor in my experience can you get Gypsies to talk very much about their queens, and they just do not seem to know what the honour amounts to. But then the Gypsy will not talk about the kings he does not want to talk about, and the *Romane Raia* have yet a lot to find out from the Romanies and much that they will never find out. Personally I have no doubt that the title Gypsy chief, even when bestowed by Gypsies upon a Gypsy, does not amount to much. I am not so sure about Gypsy queens. There are not so many of them as one might suppose—I discount, of course,

the obvious fakes of the show grounds and pierheads—and
there is always a good deal of bother about the succession
when a queen dies, which is surely rather odd if the title
means nothing at all. Urania Boswell was " Queen of the
Gypsies." It was a title acknowledged by other Gypsies.
She was the wife, you will remember, of Levi Boswell, the
Gypsy Chief. Now on the headstone of Levi's grave you
will find this inscription :

In Loving Memory
of
Levi Boswell
The Gypsy Chief
Who passed away May 4th 1924
Aged 77 years.

A light is from our household gone,
A voice we loved is still,
A place is vacant in our home,
Which never will be filled.

And when Urania died, they added this :

Also of
Urania Boswell
(Gipsy Lee)
Beloved of the above
Who died 24 April, 1933
Aged 81 years
Reunited home at last.

No mention, you will notice, of any such title as
" Queen." Yet Urania was acknowledged as Queen, and
a good deal of care was taken, it would seem, over the
choice of her successor. But Levi is referred to as " The
Gypsy Chief," yet so far as I know there was no bother
about his successor and I do not even know if there was a
successor. It seems to me to be deliberately misleading.
And I am more than ever sure that there is more to a
Gypsy queen than the mere title.

Urania Boswell was Queen of the Gypsies, and by that
was meant not merely the Gypsies of Kent or Brighton or

of Southern England, but Queen of the Gypsies of England.
I do not think the title included the Gypsies of Wales, but
I am not sure that it does not imply a certain suzerainty.
Her successor was Morjiana Lee of Blackpool—a far cry
from Bromley. I do not know how the successor is chosen
(nor does anybody else outside the Gypsies themselves
and, I imagine, only a comparatively small circle of them),
and I do not know what reasons govern the choice any
more than I know what being a Queen of the Gypsies
implies in the way of duties and obligations. The Rev.
D. M. M. Bartlett, a *Romano Rai* of great experience, has
suggested that there are two elements in the choice that
appear to be more or less constant and of which the
second is by far the most important.

(1) Money or property, possessed either by the individual or the family.

(2) Family, and all that the word implies. Not necessarily direct descent, but the possession of blood in which
flows the richest blend of the real old families and is
unmixed with gorgio or mumper taint.

So far as (1) is concerned, Urania Boswell was wealthy
and was succeeded by the wealthy Morjiana Lee. And
Selina Lee, who was Reni's sister-in-law and who became
Queen of Kent and Sussex Gypsies when the title of Queen
of the Gypsies went to the north, was definitely very com-
fortably off and quite possibly wealthy. Helen Shevlin,
who was also a Queen (but I am not sure what she was
Queen of, nor do I know how she ranked with Urania
Boswell) was a very wealthy woman. She was succeeded
by Data Burton, who was not wealthy but was certainly
not poor.

So far as (2) is concerned, Urania Boswell was the
daughter of Abraham Lee and grand-daughter of Fighting
Zacki Lee who is said to have died in 1902 at the age of
128. Her great-grandparents included David Lee and
Sophy Stanley. There is no lack of good blood here, and
she married a Boswell. Her successor, Morjiana Lee, had
in her veins the blood of Woods, Lees and Coopers, was

the daughter of Alice Wood and Henry Lee, her grand-mothers were " Blind Nelly " Wood and Seni Cooper, and her great-grandparents included Jane Boswell and Valen-tine, the son of Abram Wood. This is indeed a royal lineage, as Bartlett points out. Helen Shevlin was a Price and descended from the true black blood of the Ingrams. Her successor, Data Burton, was born Ashela Price, the daughter of Kradok and the grand-daughter of Fred Price, and in her veins was Lock, Wood and possibly a dash of Ingram blood. At least as ancient and honourable a descent as one could wish.

I think Mr. Bartlett's second factor may be taken as proved and his first is probably constant. Does not the insistence on ancient lineage and unadulterated blood suggest that some importance is vested in this apparently nebulous title ? For myself, I am convinced that great importance is attached to the title and that it carries much weight and authority in ways which we have never dis-covered and quite probably never will discover.

I am also convinced that the *real* authority in any Gypsy camp is held by one of the women—probably the eldest— and in any Gypsy family by the mother. I am aware, of course, that this is not apparent on a casual visit to a Gypsy camp, that it is not noticeable even when one knows Gypsies fairly well. The apparent authority rests with the father, and, indeed, in all small or unimportant matters the authority is with him. But is it not an extraordinary thing that we do not know the name of a single Gypsy law-giver ? That the Gypsies have laws is beyond dispute. Just what they are we do not know, and we know only a few cases in which law has obviously operated, but it is evident that they exist. Yet the only English Gypsy name that can possibly be called that of a law-giver is Newsome Heron—and he apparently only legislated on card play-ing ! The reason surely is that Gypsy law, or such Gypsy law as still survives, is and always has been in the hands of the women, handed down from Queen to Queen, from mother to mother. The mother, let it be remembered, is

the main support of the family ; the society, let it be
remembered, is matrilineal and was until recently matrilocal ; and it is always the mother, or wife, who holds the
money, all of it, and lets her husband have whatever may
be necessary for business or pleasure. It is an old gorgio
saying that the one that pays the piper calls the tune. So
in all big matters, when any big decision has to be made,
when some big quarrel has to be settled, then the voice of
the mother is the final voice. You can find plenty of
examples of this in the literature—an excellent one is in
Miss Lyster's exquisite book—but they have never been
given their proper interpretation. And for this reason—
we have all been bemused by the swagger of the Romani
men. The Romani man is so very much the master, so
very proud of himself. It is easy, even when one has learnt
to discount much of the swagger, to be taken in. There is
no speech anywhere in the world so assertively masculine
as that of the true Romani man. But what the Romano
says and what he means are very different. The Romano
scarcely ever says what is in his heart. He usually says
that which is not. And so, though a great many gorgios
have written most understandingly about the Romano,
have known a great deal about him, very very few have
written understandingly about Romani women, and no
gorgio has yet understood a Romani woman—not even
Francis Hindes Groome, who married one.

VII

FORTUNE-TELLING

" Witches, warlocks and gypsies know ae the ither."—
OLD SCOTS SAYING.

THERE is an old rhyme about the Gypsies coming to
town which ends :

> And for every Gypsy woman old
> A maiden's fortune will be told.

Gypsies and fortune-telling ; the words go together in the
mind of the gorgio. Of course nobody admits belief in
what the Gypsy woman foretells. We are now an educated
people and above such foolish things. Superstition—
except among the poorer country folk who live too close
to the soil and the elements to be anything but superstitious
—is out of fashion in Britain to-day. Indeed I am frequently astonished at the vehemence with which people
(almost always townspeople) will deny holding even such
age-old and simple luck superstitions as bowing to the new
moon or stroking a black cat, while belief in the supernatural is either laughed at or hotly denied. Yet large
numbers of these very townspeople attend spiritualist
meetings that are conducted by fake mediums and are not
in the least deterred when their medium is exposed in the
courts. And still larger numbers—thousands upon thousands, and again mainly townspeople, hard, material folk—
turn first in their newspapers to the horoscopes. Men who
forecast the course of the war by the aid of the stars and
published their findings in the Sunday Press were more
implicitly believed than the General Staff, nor did really
bad blunders shake the faith of their followers. A paper
devoted entirely to forecasting the future has a large circu-
lation, and a visit to any bazaar should be sufficient to
convince anybody of the hold the astrology racket has on
this country. And still the Gypsy women tell fortunes as

they trade from door to door, nor do they appear to experience much difficulty in obtaining clients.

For as far back as we have any knowledge of the Gypsies they have been fortune-tellers. They have done more than any race on earth to spread belief in fortune-telling, in sorcery, in magical and sympathetic cures. Their women have always pretended to possess occult powers. And there can be no doubt at all that they have, by the exercise of their wits and much practice, acquired considerable skill in the art of reading character and even thought which, though it is more often than not allied to deceit, is yet in some measure true in itself. And it must be remembered that deceit and imposture alone could never have built up and supported a practice that has withstood the passage of centuries and the constant attacks of progress. There must also be some truth.

There are many forms of fortune-telling practised among Gypsies. Most are undoubtedly simply forms of deceit. Darklis Lee, talking to Miss Lyster of *dukkeriben*, said : " I only tells them a lot of *hokibens*. Now my sister can *dukker* proper. My sister was my mother's seventh daughter. She can make and unmake luck. Seventh daughters can see more nor we can." There is not a Gypsy woman living who will not tell you " a lot of *hokibens* " if you give her a chance. Ninety-nine per cent. of the " cross my hand with silver, pretty lady," is of this class, and it includes all the casual fortune-telling during door to door trade. Yet even in this casual trade the ability to read character, and sometimes thought, is astonishing. But it is not so uncanny as it might appear. Our characters are writ larger on our faces than we realise, and to those who live by their wits, are descended from generations of ancestors who lived by their wits and practised this very trade at the expense of the gorgio, and who make a habit (even though unconsciously) of studying faces as part of the daily business of life, our characters are sometimes dreadfully plain. It is never the palm of the hand (though the hand will often betray the calling of the owner) that is read, but the mouth and the eyes of the face behind it. Nor is the reading of thoughts so uncanny as it might seem. Life is pretty much the same for all human beings so far as desires are concerned. The range of thought and desire in the vast majority of men and women, and particularly young men and women, is very narrow. Indeed Leland, who was the first President of the Gypsy Lore Society, went so far as to list fourteen basic rules for fortune-telling. I give them here :

1. It is safe in most cases with middle-aged men to declare that they have had a lawsuit, or a great dispute as to property, which has given them a great deal of trouble. This must be impressively uttered. Emphasis and sinking the voice are of great assistance in fortune-telling. If the subject betray the least emotion, or admit it, promptly improve the occasion, express sympathy, and " work it up."

2. Declare that a great fortune, or something greatly to the advantage of the subject, or something which will gratify him, will soon come in his way, but that he must be keen to watch his opportunity and be bold and energetic.

3. He will have three great chances, or fortunes, in his life. If you *know* that he has inherited or made a fortune, or had a good appointment, you may say that he has already realised one of them. This seldom fails.

4. A lady of great wealth and beauty, who is of singularly sympathetic disposition, is in love with him, or ready to be, and it will depend on himself to secure his happiness. Or he will soon meet such a person when he shall least expect it.

5. " You had at one time great troubles with your relations (or friends). They treated you very unkindly." Or " They were prepared to do so, but your resolute conduct daunted them."

6. " You have been three times in great danger of death." Pronounce this very impressively. Everybody,

though it be a schoolboy, believes, or likes to believe, that he has encountered perils. This is infallible, or at least it takes in most people. If the subject can be induced to relate his hairbreadth escapes, you may foretell future perils.

7. " You have had an enemy who has caused you great trouble. But he, or she, it is well not to specify which till you find out the sex—will ere long go too far, and his or her effort to injure you will recoil on him or her." Or, briefly, " It is written that someone, by trying to wrong you, will incur terrible retribution." Or, " You have had enemies, but they are all destined to come to grief." Or, " You had an enemy but you outlived him."

8. " You got yourself once into great trouble by doing a good act.

9. " Your passions have thrice got you into great trouble. Once your inconsiderate anger (or pursuit of pleasure) involved you in great suffering which, in the end, was to your advantage." Or else, " This will come to pass : therefore be on your guard."

10. " You will soon meet with a person who will have a great influence on your future life if you cultivate his friendship. You will ere long meet someone who will fall in love with you if encouraged."

11. " You will find something very valuable if you keep your eyes open and watch closely. You have twice passed over a treasure and missed it, but you will have a third opportunity."

12. " You have done a great deal of good, or made the fortune or prosperity of persons who have been very ungrateful."

13. " You have been involved in several love affairs, but your conduct in all was really perfectly blameless."

14. " You have great capacity for something, and before long an occasion will present itself for you to exert it to your advantage."

Obviously Leland over-simplified the business. But even
with his fourteen rules (and it is easy to think of another
half-dozen that would be useful, to say the least of it) or
rather a combination of some of them varied to suit the
client, a convincing case could be made out by the veriest
novice. How much more convincing then when the teller
is dark, with compelling eyes and impressive voice, with
arresting gesture and strange dress. And how much more
convincing still when to those distinct assets are added a
little intuition and a great ability to decipher the character
that is written on all our faces. Little wonder that the
Gypsy woman going from door to door on her hawking
rounds has some success with fortune-telling. She must
often hit upon the truth, and if she does her fame will soon
spread. But, though there may be and very often is more
than a grain of truth in this type of fortune-telling, it
remains very largely a form of deceit, an easy way of picking up a little cash. It is a second string to the Gypsy bow,
a useful adjunct to the hawking, and it is not regarded as
any more than that by those that practise it.

To this class of fortune-telling belongs also the use of
cards. Nowadays cards are not used in this connection
very widely by British Gypsies (though I have known them
used more than once), but time was when a special pack
was used for this purpose. This is the *Tarot*. It is still
used by some Gypsies in Hungary and Eastern Europe,
and no doubt elsewhere, but I have never seen it used by
British Gypsies, though I have known British Gypsies who
knew some of the symbols. I have, however, seen it used
in England and have, in fact, had my fortune told by means
of it. This was in London in 1933, in Old Compton
Street, where for a short time some Greek Gypsies rented a
shop and did a pretty good business as phrenologists, fortune-tellers and, I suspect, one or two other things. It was
not a very satisfactory or convincing exhibition of fortune-
telling. The woman who did it got a good deal of my past
life correct and did not make a bad guess at one or two
of my thoughts and hopes (any door to door *diddikai* hawk-

ing Woolworth goods would have been as accurate I have no doubt), but in general she was pretty wide of the mark and my knowledge of a little Romani obviously unsettled her. She would not let me handle the cards, and did not herself appear to know much about them, but then nobody does know very much about them, though plenty of people have put forward any number of ideas.

The woman set out the cards in exactly the manner described by Mathers as long ago as 1888 and which, no doubt, she had learned by rote in her youth, but her reading of them, or rather her pretence of reading them, was not in the least convincing. She knew the purpose of the cards, and the manner in which they should be used, but she did not fully understand (or perhaps she was not trying) their meaning. She relied on reading my face. But then she was telling me a lot of *hokibens*.

Most Gypsy fortune-telling is just that—a lot of *hokibens* : an easy way of picking up cash from the gullible gorgio. It is used, however, as a cover for many things. There is more than one picture of a Gypsy woman reading the palm of a client, the while some other Gypsy (generally a child) picks the unfortunate pigeon's pocket. That practice is, perhaps, more frequent than one realises. I have, for example, had it tried on me on Epsom Downs on Derby Day. The youngster got nothing, for the simple reason that my approachable pockets rarely contain anything but scraps of paper, string and similar unmarketable oddments. But it is also used to cover bigger operations than picking pockets or petty pilfering. It is used, or rather was used (for I have not heard of the trick being practised in Britain of recent years), to cover the larger sort of fraud, in particular as a cover for, or a means of approach to, the *hokano baro*, the great trick. There are many forms of the *hokano baro*, but in essence they are all the same. It is the confidence trick. Whenever we read about the confidence trick it seems just too obvious for words, and we are always surprised that anybody can get taken in. Yet many a hardheaded business man has been defrauded by means of it, and it is practised regularly and frequently, and successfully, in every big city of the world. So with the *hokano baro;* described in cold print it seems altogether too obvious and we cannot believe that anybody could be so foolish as to get taken in. Cold print makes no allowance for the mystery, the fascination, the compelling eyes and the insidious hypnotic voice ; no allowance for the natural gullibility of man ; no allowance for the particular circumstances (they are never revealed anyway) that prompted the Gypsy to work the trick on that particular dupe. (We have, too, no right or reason to feel superior about those that are duped. Whole nations—our own included—have fallen for much the same sort of thing recently.)

Hokano baro is practised all over the world, with modifications to suit the country, and has been described by almost every writer on the Gypsies. In its standardised form it consists of three parts. Firstly, getting into the house of the dupe, or, if that is not essential, into his or her confidence (this is generally achieved by fortune-telling, but it may be done by means of offering cheap goods for sale or even by plain begging.) Secondly, the removal of the property. Thirdly, the binding of the victim by oath not to say anything about it for three or more weeks. Leland gives an imaginary example of the technique, which rings, I think, remarkably true. " The feat . . . is performed by inducing some woman of largely magnified faith to believe that there is hidden in her house a magic treasure, which can only be made ' to come to hand ' by depositing in the cellar another treasure, to which it will come by natural affinity and attraction. ' For gold, as you see, draws gold, my deari, and so if you ties up all your money in a pocket-handkerchief, an' leaves it, you'll find it doubled. An' wasn't there the Squire's lady—you know Mrs. Trefarlo, of course—and didn't she draw two hundred old gold guineas out of the ground where they'd laid in an old grave—and only one guinea she gave me for all my trouble ; an' I hope you'll do better than that for the poor old Gypsy, my deari——.' The gold and the spoons are all tied up—for, as the enchantress sagely observes, ' there may be silver too '—and she solemnly repeats over it magical rhymes, while the children, standing around in awe, listen to every word. It is a good subject for a picture. Sometimes the windows are closed, and candles lighted—to add to the effect. The bundle is left or buried in a certain place. The next day the Gypsy comes and sees how the charm is working. Could anyone look under her cloak, he might find another bundle precisely resembling the one containing the treasure. She looks at the precious deposit, repeats her rhyme again solemnly and departs, after charging the housewife that the bundle must not be touched, looked at or spoken of for three weeks. ' Every word you tell about it, my deari, will be a guinea gone away.' Sometimes she exacts an oath on the Bible, when she *chive o manzin apre tatti*—that nothing shall be said. . . . After three weeks another *Extraordinary Instance of Gross Credulity* appears in the country papers, and is perhaps repeated in a colossal London daily, with a reference to the absence of the schoolmaster. There is wailing and shame in the house —perhaps great suffering—for it may be that the savings of years, and bequeathed tankards, and marriage rings, and inherited jewellery, and mother's sovereigns have been swept away. The charm has worked."

That was written in 1890. I think Leland's Gypsy has altogether too grammatical a command of the English language, but some such scene as that described has, I am sure, happened many times in England in the past. The technique in Germany was but little different. Liebich, in his *Die Zigeuner*, published in 1863, says : " When a Gypsy has found some old peasant who has the reputation of being rich or very well-to-do he sets himself to work with utmost care to learn the disposition of his man with every possible detail as to his house and habits. And so some day, when all the rest of the family are in the fields, the Gypsy—man or woman—comes, and entering into a conversation, leads it to the subject of the house, remarking that it is a belief among his people that in it a treasure lies buried. He offers, if he may have permission to take it away, to give one-fourth, a third or a half its value. This all seems fair enough, but the peasant is greedy and wants more. The Gypsy, on his side, also assumes suspicion and distrust. He proves that he is a conjuror by performing some strange tricks—thus he takes an egg from under a hen, breaks it, and apparently brings out a small human skull or some strange object, and finally persuades the peasant to collect all his coin and other valuables in notes, gold and silver, into a bundle, cautioning him to hold them fast. He must go to bed and put the packet under his pillow, while he, the conjuror, finds the treasure. This done— probably in a darkened room—he takes a bundle of similar appearance which he has quickly prepared, and, under pretence of facilitating the operation and putting the man into a proper position, takes the original package and sub- stitutes another. Then the victim is cautioned that it is of the utmost importance for him to lie perfectly still." The technique, it will be seen, is very much the same.

The last recorded example of *hokano baro* that I know occurred as recently as 1937, but I suspect that a good many others, not recorded because the victim has been afraid to face the publicity, have occurred, just as many examples of the success of the gorgio confidence trick are never brought to light. The Gypsy, of course, uses his or her power of voice and eye and the astonishing quickness of hand with which the whole race is gifted to cover many forms of fraud, but these do not come under the heading of *hokano baro*, which must always be allied to some tale of the future or of prophetic vision into the past. Ringing the changes, Lord John Russell, and so forth are quite definitely in another category. But I am not so sure about an instance that occurred in Cardiff as recently as 1933. This was when a " Greek " Gypsy, named George Stirio, got into conversation with a commercial traveller in a café, talked to him with such lightning rapidity in Romani mixed with English that he reduced him to a sort of stupor and got him to hand over his wallet, which contained £36.

The Gypsy made some pretence of telling the man's fortune, handed him back the notes, and left the café. When the commercial traveller recovered sufficiently to count his money he found that £17 was missing. Stirio got six months hard labour for this feat. This is obviously not true *hokano baro*, but it springs I fancy from the same root. Earlier in the same year in South Wales another foreign Gypsy, a woman of huge height and no small girth, did well in the big stores under guise of fortune-telling, extracting money from men ; but here I fancy a mixture of intimidation and plain bustling occurred. There was a huge Gypsy woman in the New Forest in 1936 and again in 1938, and I have heard that she was in Cornwall in 1939. I saw her twice and she must have been nearer seven than six feet in height, and her weight around twenty stones. She was a " Greek," though she said she was born in Blackpool in the 'nineties. She certainly knew a great deal about horses, but her method of living was to get talking to some man in as public a place as possible, choosing a well-dressed man, and then by a mixture of begging and fortune-telling to make him feel too conspicuous, thus forcing money from him to get rid of her.

But when all the many forms of deception in the guise of fortune-telling have been taken into account there yet remains a considerable residue that is absolutely honest and uncannily accurate, and which can be explained, I think, only by postulating the gift of " second sight " in the tellers. Nowadays there is no belief among the majority of people in the fact of second sight. Plenty of people believe wholeheartedly in the ability of certain journalists to foretell the future because of their intimacy with the stars ; plenty of people believe wholeheartedly that one of the ancient Hebrew poets foresaw this present war and the course it would take ; plenty of people believe wholeheartedly in the prophecies of the Pyramids—indeed, I understand that there are some who order their whole lives by these prophecies. But very, very few of these people would credit any modern human being with the gift of second sight. Yet second sight is a fact that may not be gainsaid. It is a form of involuntary prophetic vision, either direct or symbolical. Its existence has been acknowledged almost from the time man began to record events. Mention of it, though not under this name, occurs in the *Odyssey*; occurrences of it are frequently recorded in Ancient Hebrew literature, it is mentioned in the *Argonautica* of Apollonais Rhodius, and in several of the Icelandic sagas, particularly in *Njala*. It is not a gift confined to any one people. Lapps and Red Indians, Zulus and Maoris have given proof of it to explorers and travellers and these things have been duly recorded. Eskimos, Hungarians, Russians, Spaniards, Arabs—all these people have instances of it. But, nowadays at any rate, it seems to be connected mainly—but this is due, of course, not to any especial physical or spiritual condition so much as to proximity—with Celtic peoples, with the Celts of Scotland, Ireland and Wales, and especially of Scotland and Western Ireland, the wild and mountainous regions. It was first recorded for Scotland by Ranulf Higden in his fourteenth-century *Polychronicon*, and the Rev. Kirk in his *The Secret Commonwealth of Elves, Fawns and Fairies*, originally published in 1691, has much more to say about it. It has never been common among the English, indeed it has always been so rare that those unfortunate enough to be so gifted have generally come to a sudden and sad ending at the hands of their prosaic brethren. But for Scotland and Ireland and Wales there have been many very authenticated cases of prophetic vision, and no Highland Scot, no true Irishman, no Welshman, in fact no Celt would dream of denying its occurrence, its frequent occurrence, and certainly none would be so foolish as to laugh at it. I am myself a full-blooded Celt. I do not claim to have second sight, and am indeed very thankful that I am not so gifted, but I must confess that I do experience at times premonitions that have proved, both for myself and others, uncannily accurate.

That many Gypsy women have had this gift of second

sight is, I think, beyond all question. Among them (to take a recent example) was Urania Boswell. In particular, she was able to foretell danger and death, but her prophecies (for the majority of which there is exceedingly good testimony) went far beyond that. In 1897 she foretold that " Queen Victoria would see the leaves fall four times before she went to her long rest " ; that " the King who comes after her will die long before my turn comes " ; that " after that the world will change—not all at once, but we'll live to see strange things, you and I. Men will fly like birds, and swim under the water in boats shaped like fishes. They'll sit by their own firesides and listen to voices and music a thousand miles away, same as if it was in the room." Do you remember Mother Shipton's famous prophecy ?

> Carriages without horses shall go,
> And accidents fill the world with woe :
> Iron on the water shall float
> As easily as a wooden boat,

and so on. Reni, with her foreknowledge of aeroplanes, submarines and wireless, at least deserves to rank with Mother Shipton. And, further, at Henley Regatta she warned Mr. Vanderbilt most urgently not to sail in the maiden voyage of the *Titanic*, which was then being built. In the following April the ship struck an iceberg and Vanderbilt and 1,502 other people were drowned. The Rev. D. M. M. Bartlett mentions three prophecies concerning her own family. In April she predicted that her son Levi would not live longer than the following February. He was buried on February 2nd at Bromley, Kent. She predicted correctly to the day the deaths of others also, including her brother's wife's brother. Just before her death in 1933 she foresaw the death of her brother Job in March, 1936, and on the Saturday before she herself died she said : " On the third day from now I shall die and on that day it will rain." She died, and it did. On the day previously she said that the missel-thrush would sing before her death. One perched in a tree close to the *vardo* and sang all Saturday. When she died it left. And actually in 1924 she said of herself : " I shall die in nine years and it will be cold." Again she did, and it was.

Urania Boswell told my fortune in 1928. I do not propose to set it all forth here—in any case it is not yet completed—but I can say, in all honesty, that so far at least it has all come true. Furthermore, some of the things she saw in 1928 seemed then to me to be utterly fantastic ; so much so that I remember laughing and her reply, " You will see, young man." Is it any wonder that I believe in the gift of second sight in Gypsy women ?

I have since, by the way, had my fortune told, spontaneously and without payment, by a young Gypsy woman. The two fortunes agree in almost every particular.

VIII

GYPSY MEDICINE

GYPSIES very rarely call in a doctor. They have to do so for a death nowadays, since the death cannot be registered without a doctor's certificate, and perhaps they use a doctor's services for a birth more frequently than they used to do, but for ordinary illness and ailments, for which the gorgio would summon medical assistance, they still rely for the most part upon their own knowledge or the knowledge of the old women among them. Gypsies all over the world, and English Gypsies are no exceptions, have always had a great reputation as healers ; nor is that reputation dead in the English countryside to-day. I know an old Gypsy woman, who travels Dorset and Hampshire, whose fame as a curer of warts is enormous—and deserved.

It is almost always the Gypsy woman who is the doctor, and she is usually a chemist as well. She has at her fingers' tips knowledge of remedies and prescriptions she learnt from her mother, her grandmother, her great-grandmother. Preserved in these remedies is the knowledge and experience of hundreds of years, and they are very jealously guarded, and handed on to the daughters when they are about to become mothers themselves. The Gypsies' knowledge of herbal remedies is very great, as great perhaps as that possessed by the Benedictine monks in mediæval times, and I cannot pretend to give a complete list of all the plants used by them, much less a complete catalogue of all their medicines. I do not know them, nor indeed a tenth of them ; nor, I am sure, does any gorgio. But in any case, every Gypsy woman has private concoctions of her own, which she alone knows and employs. But there are certain plants which are widely known (many of them are used regularly in English folk herbals) and Thompson has made a list of some of the plants used by midland Gypsies. I have been making a list myself for the past twenty years or so (collected rather aimlessly mainly from south and west country Gypsies, but with oddments from other parts of the country), and I think that the list I give here is the most complete yet published of the plants used by Gypsies. Where the plant occurs in Thompson's list I mention his name and the purpose for which he says it is used, adding information of my own only when it differs from his.

ADDER'S TONGUE (*Ophioglossum vulgatum*), also called Snake's Tongue and Serpent's Tongue. Crushed and boiled in olive oil it is used as a dressing for open wounds.

Most Gypsies to whom I have mentioned this have denied knowledge of it, but I have had it given me by three old women in widely separated districts.

AGARIC (*Polyporus officinalis*), used in small doses as a cure for diarrhœa.

AGRIMONY (*Agrimonia Eupatoria*), also called Sticklewort, Stickwort and Lockleburr, an infusion of leaves used to lower the temperature and cure coughs (Thompson). Very widely known as a cough cure, but I have not come across it being used to lower the temperature. One old woman told me it was good for the eyesight if poured into the eye.

ALDER (*Alaus glutinosa*), decoction of inner bark given for jaundice and ague (Thompson). I think this must be a concoction of the Derbyshire Boswells alone. I have come across it nowhere and can find it mentioned nowhere else.

AVENS (*Geum urbanum*), also called Clove Root, Colewort, Way Bennet, Wild Rye. The crushed root is used as a cure for diarrhœa, and a little in boiling water relieves sore throats.

BARBERRY (*Berberis vulgaris*), also called Holy Thorn. A weak infusion of the berries is good for kidney troubles.

BETTONY (*Stachys betonica*), the Wood Betony. An infusion of the leaves relieves stomach troubles : ointment made from juice of fresh leaves and unsalted lard removes the poison from stings and bites (Thompson).

BINDWEED (*Convolvulus arvensis*), the Lesser Bindweed.

An infusion of leaves or flowers expels worms (Thompson). Commonly used by Gypsies.

BISTORT (*Polygonum bistorta*), also called Adderswort, Easter Giant, Passion's Dock, Snakeward. A very common weed, particularly in the north, but I have only heard of its use once, when an old Gypsy woman (Martha Young) told me it was good for diphtheria.

BLACKBERRY (*Rubus fruticosus*), leaves smoked relieve internal inflammation and reduce fevers (Thompson).

BLADDER-CAMPION (*Silene cucubulus*), also called Round Campion and John's Plant, leaves applied externally as a poultice cure erysipelas (Thompson).

BLADDERWRACK (*Fuens vesiculosus*), also called Kelpware. The most familiar of our seaweeds. Used with hot water and sometimes in whisky as an embrocation. Very good for rheumatism.

BRACKEN (*Pteris aquilina*), decoction of sliced roots taken in wine expels worms (Thompson). Commonly used as a cure for constipation.

BROOKLIME (*Veronica beccabunga*), also called Water Pimpernel. The leaves are used for a poultice for piles, boils, etc.

BROOM (*Cytisus scoparius*), infusion of young shoots or leaves is good for kidney troubles (Thompson). One of the Grays also told Thompson that it expelled worms. Commonly used for kidney complaints by Gypsies.

BUCKBEAN (*Menyanthes trifoliata*), also called Marsh Trefoil and Bogbean, infusion of leaves remedies loss of appetite ; purifies the blood (Thompson).

BUCKTHORN ALDER (*Rhamans frangula*), also called Black Alder. The berries make a very powerful purgative. Once popular this is very rarely used nowadays. A decoction of the bark is used a good deal as a purgative, being mild in action.

BURDOCK (*Actium lappa*), also called Beggar's Burr, Cockle Buttons, Clote Burr, Fox's Cloth, Hardock, Lappa, Thorny Burr. Infusion of leaves or flowers, or better still of crushed seeds, relieves and will cure rheumatism

(Thompson). Commonly used as a cure for rheumatism. Some Gypsies carry the seeds in a little bag slung round the neck as a preventive of rheumatism.

CARROT (*Dancus corota*), this is the wild carrot common on chalk soil, also called Bee's Nest. An infusion of the leaves used for kidney troubles.

CELANDINE (*Chelidonium majus*), the juice is used as an outward application for corns and warts. It is very effective indeed.

CENTAURY (*Erythræa sentaurium*), also called Christ's Ladder, Fellwort, Feverwort, Ball-of-the-Earth. Infusion of leaves is good for jaundice (Thompson). The dried herb is used as a tea by many south country Gypsies and is regarded as a first-rate tonic, and very good for consumption.

CHAMOMILE (*Athemis nobilis*), also called Earth Apple, infusion of flowers or leaves cures flatulence (Thompson). Used as a tonic by many Gypsies and country women.

CHESTNUT (*Castanea vulgaris*), also called Sweet Chestnut. The powdered nuts are good for piles. Some Gypsies wear the nut in a little bag round their necks as a prevention of piles. The bag must never be made of silk.

CHICORY (*Cichorium intybus*), also called Wild Succory. A decoction of the root is good for jaundice.

CLIVERS (*Galium aperine*), also called Catchweed, Goose-grass, Love Man, Robin-run-by-the-Grass, Scratchweed. An infusion drunk very hot the last thing at night is the remedy for a cold in the head. It is also a very ancient remedy for cancer, but I have not met a Gypsy who remembered that.

COLTSFOOT (*Tussilago farfara*), also called Laughwort. Smoking dried leaves is beneficial for asthma and bronchitis, juice from fresh leaves is used in preparing ointment that heals ulcers, running sores and piles (Thompson). It is, of course, used largely in all herbal tobaccos. Drunk as a tea is good for curing coughs.

COMFREY (*Symphytum officinale*), also called Knitbone, Nipbone and Blackwort. Is used by many Gypsies to bind broken bones, and was known in this connection as long ago as the time of Pliny.

COUCH GRASS (*Agropyrum repens*), also called Dog-grass, Twitch-grass. A decoction in cold water excellent for reducing temperatures. Also given for gall-stones.

COWSLIP (*Primula veris*), infusion of dried flowers allays convulsions and lowers temperature (Thompson).

CUCKOO-PINT (*Arum maculatum*), also called Wake Robin, decoction of finely-sliced roots, or infusion of dry powdered flowers, relieves croup and bronchitis ; bruised leaves heal festering sores, gatherings and boils (Thomspon).

DAISY (*Bellis perannis*), juice from roots mixed with juice from ginger roots cures toothache (Thompson). This, I think, must be another Boswell remedy only. I have been unable to trace its use anywhere else.

DANDELION (*Taraxacum officinale*), leaves eaten in spring salads to purify the blood : juice from roots an ingredient of medicine used to treat jaundice, dropsy, liver and kidney troubles generally (Thompson). The juice from the stem is excellent for treating warts.

DOCK (*Rumex*), any of the common kinds but particularly *R. obtusifolius*, decoction of sliced roots taken in elderberry wine dispels spring rash (Thompson).

ELDER (*Sambucus nigra*), infusion of flowers or leaves, or failing these of bark, is a certain remedy for colic, fermentation in the stomach and internal inflammation (Thompson). The elder has always been greatly valued by herbalists and country peoples generally. Every bit of it from roots to flowers has its uses, and in addition to these given by Thompson, I have found it used for rheumatism, strained eyes, neuralgia, toothache and boils. Not always an infusion of flowers or leaves, of course.

EYEBRIGHT (*Euphrasia officinalis*), also called Euphrasy. Infusion of leaves taken internally cures coughs ; applied as a lotion it strengthens weak eyes and heals sore ones (Thompson). I have met Gypsies who smoked it mixed with Coltsfoot—and it is an ingredient of most herbal tobaccos—maintaining that it cured asthma and catarrh. Is widely used by Gypsies for eye troubles.

FEVERFEW (*Chrysanthemum partnenium*), also called Batchelors' Buttons and Flirtwort. Belongs to the Chamomile family and is often used by Gypsies in place of Chamomile.

FOXGLOVE (*Digitalis purpurea*), ointment made from fresh leaves cures eczema ; very weak infusion of dried leaves allays fevers (Thompson). I have never found foxglove used for either purpose by Gypsies. I imagine this might be confined to a few midland families.

GENTIAN (*Gentiana campestris*), also called Baldmony and Felwort. An infusion of root and herb relieves heartburn and flatulence.

GOLDEN ROD (*Solidago virganrea*), also called Aaron's Rod ; infusion of leaves used for treating gravel and stone, ointment made from fresh leaves heals wounds and sores (Thompson).

GROUND IVY (*Nepeta glachoma*), also called Alehoof, Cat's Foot, Devil's Candlesticks, Hale House, Horseshone, Thunder Vine. Infusion of leaves is a strong tonic, will cure ulcerated stomach (Thompson). An infusion of the dried herb is excellent for coughs : used with wood sage and made into a tea is good for colds : an ointment from the stems mixed with chickweed is used for sprains.

GROUNDSEL (*Semecis vulgaris*). Bruised stems and leaves applied externally as a poultice relieve colic and inflammation (Thompson). Is used as a poultice for sprains by some families, but is not used generally by Gypsies.

HAWKWEED (*Hieracium pilosella*), also called Mouse-ear. Infusion of leaves allays convulsions (Thompson). This must be a family medicine of the Derbyshire Boswells. I have never heard of its use among Gypsies.

HEMLOCK (GIANT) (*Conium maculatum*). Ointment made from fresh leaves reduces neck swellings and heals sores and ulcers (Thompson). I have not heard of this among Gypsies and fancy it must be another private medicine of the Derbyshire Boswells.

HENBANE (COMMON) (*Hyoxyamus night*). Very weak infusion of leaves is good for sharp pains in the head, spasms and sleeplessness : may be given with advantage to delirious patients (Thompson). Is commonly used as a cure for headaches and neuralgia by the Gypsies I know.

HONEYSUCKLE (*Lonicana periclymenum*), juice from berries cures sore throat and canker of the mouth : is used in an ointment for the treatment of ulcers, running sores and piles (Thompson). Juice from the berries is used for sore throat by Gypsies I know, but I have not come across it used in ointments.

HOP (*Humulus lupulus*), tops and flowers added in preparing medicine given to sufferers from jaundice, dropsy or liver or kidney complaints (Thompson). An ounce of hops to a pint of boiling water taken some time before meals is a good cure for loss of appetite. A poultice of the tops will relieve sciatica or lumbago. An infusion of the flowers will cure worms in children. Put hops into a muslin bag and use the bag as a pillow and you will cure insomnia.

HOREHOUND (*Marrubiam vulgare*), also called Madweed. An infusion of leaves cures coughs and colds : is a good tonic (Thompson).

HOREHOUND (BLACK) (*Ballota nigra*), also called Madweed, Gypsy Wort. Used as a tea is good for asthma and bronchitis. A good laxative for children.

JUNIPER (*Juniperus communis*). The juice of the berries in hot water is good for flatulence. The berries eaten by a person fasting will cure stones : ten berries a day for ten days is the treatment I was told.

LIME (*Tilia europæa*). Infusion of flowers allays convulsions : benefits those subject to epileptic fits (Thompson). Many Gypsies use it to cure biliousness.

LINSEED (*Linum usitatissimum*), also called Flax. Linseed tea drunk throughout pregnancy will ensure an easy birth.

LOOSESTRIFE (YELLOW) (*Lysimachia vulgaris*). Infusion of leaves cures diarrhœa (Thompson). I think another Derbyshire Boswell family medicine.

Marsh Mallow (*Althæa officinalis*), also called Wild Geranium. Bruised leaves heal sore eyes and neutralise the effect of stings and bites : infusion of leaves or sliced roots, with paregoric added, cures sore throats, coughs and colds (Thompson). Ointment made from crushed roots good for sore feet and varicose veins : a hot poultice of the leaves good for toothache.

Meadow-saffron (*Colchicum autumnale*). A very weak infusion of sliced roots is good for dropsy and gout (Thompson). This is a common Gypsy remedy for gout.

Meadow-sweet (*Spirea almaria*). Infusion of flowers or leaves allays internal inflammation : stimulates sluggish kidneys (Thompson).

Milkwort (*Polygala vulgaris*). Decoction of sliced roots cures inflammation of the lungs (Thompson). I have not come across this.

Mistletoe (*Viscum album*). Juice of berries much diluted, or infusion of leaves, benefits sufferers from epilepsy and St. Vitus's Dance (Thompson). I have only heard of the berries being used.

Mouse-ear Chickweed (*Cerestium vulgatum*), also called Robin-under-the-Hedge. Infusion of leaves cures coughs and colds (Thompson). This information was obtained from a Lock. I think it must be a private remedy.

Nettle (*Urtica dioica*). The common stinging nettle. Nettle tea clears the blood and is a good tonic : infusion of the seeds is good for consumptives : infusion of the leaves is beneficial to goitre.

Parsley (*Petroselinum sativum*). Leaves used in preparing medicine for the treatment of dropsy, jaundice and kidney and liver troubles (Thompson).

Parsley Piert (*Alchemilla arvensis*), also called Home Wort. Infusion of the dried herb is good for gravel and other bladder troubles.

Pellitory-of-the-Wall (*Parietaria officinalis*). Juice from leaves is an ingredient of ointment that cures ulcers, running sores and piles (Thompson). Infusion of the leaves allays all bladder troubles : infusion of leaves and wild carrot is good for dropsy : ointment made from crushed roots is good for piles. ⸱

PENNYROYAL (*Mentha pulegium*), also called Hop Mar-joram, Pudding Brass, Run-by-the-Ground. Infusion of leaves allays spasms (Thompson). Used as a tea is good for chills and colds : juice of the herb rubbed on the skin prevents bites from insects.

PEPPERMINT (*Mentha piperita*), also called Brandy Mint. Used as a tea is excellent for headaches : a drop of the juice on an aching tooth will relieve the pain.

PILEWORT (*Ranunculus flearia*), also called Lesser Celan-dine. The common country remedy for piles, hence the popular name. The usual Gypsy remedy for the same complaint (I have been assured by more than one Gypsy that by merely carrying a sprig or two in one's pocket a complete cure may be effected) being used as an ointment; an infusion taken four times a day for four days will effect a cure.

PLANTAIN (*Plantago major*), also called Ripple Grass, Way Bread. Bruised leaves stop bleeding and heal cuts (Thompson). This is the common Gypsy use for the plant : infusion of leaves is good for internal hæmorrhages (Thompson). This does not appear to be a usual Gypsy remedy, but most Gypsies seem to have heard of it. The leaves soaked in hot water and bound round a finger will quickly cure a whitlow or any other gathering. It does not seem to be generally known that the leaves of the plantain are every whit as good as, and personally I think better than, the leaves of the dock for relieving stings by nettles. The Gaelic word for plantain is *slanlus*, which means " the healing plant." Arigho has told me that to eat the root is a cure for adder bites.

POLYPODY (*Polypodium vulgare*), also called Adder's Tongue, Oak Fern, Wall Fern, Rock Polypody. The crushed root used as a poultice and applied to the seat of the pain is a good remedy for rheumatism. An old country name for the plant is Rheum-purging Polypody, which indicates that its properties have long been known to a wider circle. The name has long since died out.

SAINT JOHN'S WORT (*Hypericum perforatum*), also called Amber, Blessed, Hundred Holes. Is used by many Gypsies as a hairdressing, makes the hair grow. Infusion is good for catarrh : ointment excellent for deep cuts, sprains and burns.

SCABIOUS (*Scabious arvensis*). Infusion of leaves strengthens the lungs and will cure pleurisy (Thompson). Unknown to all Gypsies I know, but known to my tinker friend.

SCURVY-GRASS (*Cochlearia officinalis*) The fresh leaves eaten untreated are good for all skin complaints.

SHEPHERD'S PURSE (*Capsella bursa-pastoris*), also called Case Weed, Pick Purse, St. James's Wort. Infusion of leaves an ingredient of medicine used in the treatment of dropsy, jaundice and kidney and liver complaints (Thompson). Used as an ointment is good for erysipelas.

SOAPWORT (*Saponaria officinalis*), also called Fuller's Herb. A decoction of the root applied to a bruise or a black eye will quickly get rid of the discoloration : slices of the freshly dug root laid on the place have the same effect but are slower in action.

SOLOMON'S SEAL (*Polygonatum multiflorum*), also called Jacob's Ladder, Seal Wort, Our Lady's Seal. An ointment made from the leaves and applied to a bruise or a black eye will quickly get rid of the discoloration.

TANSY (*Tanacetum vulgare*), also called Buttons. Infusion of the flowers will expel worms : hot fomentations of the herb good for gout; if you wear a sprig of tansy inside your boots you will never get the ague. (This is also an old Hampshire farm labourers' superstition.) Thompson gives the same uses for tansy as he does for shepherd's purse.

THYME (WILD) (*Thymus serpyllum*). Gypsies regard this plant as very unlucky and will not bring it into their waggons or tents. But it may be used out of doors as a cure for whooping cough, boiled in water with a little sugar added and drunk cold.

TORMENTIL (*Potentilla tormentilla*). Infusion of leaves

cures diarrhœa (Thompson). Decoction of roots will stop internal hæmorrhage.

TRAVELLER's JOY (*Clematis vitalba*). Infusion of leaves is good for rheumatism (Thompson).

VIOLET (*Viola odorata*). A poultice of the leaves steeped in boiling water is good for cancerous growths : an infusion of the leaves will aid internal cancers and, I have been told, will even cure them.

WOOD SAGE (*Tenerium scorodonia*), also called Hind Heal, Dittany. Infusion of the leaves relieves fever.

Most Gypsies seem to have a preference for simples. Some, however, do produce medicines into which are introduced all sorts of ingredients. Thompson knew a female Boswell (of the Derbyshire family) who was an adept at this, and he gives one or two very interesting recipes she used. For example, the ointment she used for ulcers, running sores and piles was made by mixing goose fat or pig's fat with juice extracted from pellitory-of-the-wall and coltsfoot leaves, and from honeysuckle berries. For dropsy, jaundice and kidney and liver troubles generally she made up a medicine that included shepherd's purse and tansy leaves, dandelion roots, parsley, hops and caraway seeds. For a cold she recommended a medicine which included a pennyworth (pre-1914 values) each of oil of peppermint, aniseed, paregoric, antimonial wine, tincture of opium and black treacle, together with sugar and added to a quart of boiling water. I have never come across a Gypsy who was a chemist to this extent, though Fanny Barney was pretty thorough in her methods, I am told : she, however, died before I really began to take an interest in Gypsy medicine. I have come across pig's fat being used on several occasions, and on several more the flesh of frogs. One old Gypsy woman of my acquaintance—a woman who could cure warts apparently by the simple process of wishing them away—used frog's flesh in an ointment she compounded for curing piles, and the skin of a frog was dropped into more than one of the concoctions she recommended as a drink. She was also credited, but I could never find any evidence in support of the suggestion, with using dor-beetles crushed and mixed with root of avens as a cure for diarrhœa. But most of the Gypsies I have known have stuck stoutly to simples.

Gypsies regard all fungi with suspicion. They eat the giant puff-ball (*Hycoperdon borista*) fried in dripping and garnished with herbs and onions. I have eaten this and found it very good indeed, though it is regarded as rather poor fare by Gypsies. Perhaps the novelty appealed to me. They use the puff-ball in its dry state for staunching wounds —it makes a very good styptic—and also another fungus (*Polyporous igniarius*) which is sometimes called touchwood. But, generally speaking, Gypsies will not have anything to do with fungi, certainly not with those that grow in woods, and only occasionally have I found men who would eat even such well-known open varieties as the fair-ring mushroom (*Agaricus oreades*) and the blue-legs (*Agaricus personatus*). This is because so many fungi are poisonous, of course, and the Gypsy knows well, or at any rate used to know well, the uses of some of them as poisons.

Further to the remedies I have given here there are symbolic remedies. A Gypsy woman in the New Forest once assured me that the best way to get rid of warts was to catch a big black slug and impale it on a thorn bush ; as the slug died the wart would shrivel, and when the slug was dead the wart would fall off. Thompson records that a Gypsy troubled with ague caught a spider and put it into a little bag made of silk which he wore round his neck, and as the spider died the ague left him. Many other examples of this could be given, and of course there are also the charms to keep away illness. Tansy in the boots is one, a sprig of gorse in the pocket will keep away all fevers, the skin of a frog or an eel carried anywhere about one will prevent rheumatism and keep the bearer supple, and so on. But these things are not properly worth a place in an account of Gypsy medicine. And then there is the cure without any apparent treatment. This can only be done to others, never to oneself, and unbelievable as it

sounds it does occur. There is an old Gypsy woman who
travels Dorset and Hampshire who can get rid of warts in
this way. I have heard of her doing so on three occasions
and have talked to one of the men she cured. He had
hands covered in warts (his friends supported this statement : never seen worse hands, they said) and he could
not get rid of them though he had tried all the usual
methods. Someone told him about the Gypsy, and he went
to see her. He put on his Sunday best to do so, though he
cannot explain why. She held his hands for a moment and
looked at them, and then told him to go away. Very dis-
appointed, he said that he had hoped she would do something for him ; she replied that she would be back in a
fortnight and he could come and see her then. In a fortnight his warts had gone, and he has not had a wart since.
The woman would take no money and would not discuss
the matter at all. I do not pretend to be able to explain
this sort of thing : I do not pretend to understand it. I
give the facts. There is perhaps a better name for it than
medicine.

In addition to having some skill as doctors for human
ailments, Gypsies have a considerable reputation as animal
doctors and particularly for the doctoring of horses. All
British Gypsies are interested in horses and most of them
know something about doctoring animals, while some have
an enormous knowledge and skill. The best horse doctor
that I have known was a Stanley, though Arigho knew a
good deal, and I give some of their remedies here, together
with some collected by Thompson.

BROKEN-WIND (this is the common name for asthma in
horses). Thompson got information on this from two
Gypsies, a Lock and a Smith. The former advocated wood
tar and aniseed, wood tar and treacle, or a mixture of the
three ; the latter maintained that balls made from lard
and saltpetre were as good as anything else. Lock also
recommended an infusion of shag or twist tobacco, one
and a half pints of boiling water to an ounce of tobacco.
He had another remedy, which he told Thompson was a

very old remedy and was a certain cure for mares, though it might be dangerous to horses, for it might kill them if it failed to cure. This is an oil obtained by placing the entrails of a freshly-killed chicken or other young fowl in a bottle, and decomposing them out of contact with air by sealing the bottle up and then burying it in a warm midden for a fortnight or so. Stanley's remedy was wood tar and aniseed, and he never used or recommended anything else. Arigho favoured the same mixture. Neither of them had heard of the use of tobacco, but I have known other Gypsies who do use it. Stanley knew the old remedy mentioned by Lock and also regarded it as a cure for mares but very dangerous for horses, but he believed that you should only use young cockerels. Broken-wind is regarded by veterinary science as incurable. Stanley maintained that though he had never cured it he had so greatly lessened the inconvenience of the condition that the animal was to all intents and purposes cured. He strongly held that a broken-winded horse should never, no matter what the weather, be brought indoors.

Bog Spavin. This is a condition found most frequently in cart horses, and Clydesdales for some reason appear to be particularly addicted to it. It seems to occur generally in young horses that have been forced or overfed. Stanley, who had a considerable unofficial practice among farmers, recommended leaves of the common nettle boiled in water and applied as hot as possible if any lameness was present. If no lameness is evident he applied a good dressing of green tar.

Colic. Thompson has information from two Gypsies, a Smith and a Wharton, and from a potter family. The Smith remedy is a draught of warm ale containing sweet spirits of nitre and a little laudanum, the horse being well wrapped afterwards and kept without food for some time. Wharton favoured oil of turpentine and ground ginger made into balls with flour or meal. The potters believed in a purge of aloes and soap, to be followed by a dose of fennel oil in weak spirits. Stanley would have nothing to do with the laudanum, which, he declared, " don't do nothin' but hide it." His remedy is turpentine in linseed oil—two ounces of turpentine to one pint of oil—to be followed in a quarter of an hour by a quart of warm beer.

COUGHS. Stanley gave black treacle in warm water. But he would say " a *grai* don't cough : cough is simtims, *rai*," and he would look for the cause.

CRACKED HEELS. Thompson calls this complaint Greasy Heels, a Gypsy mishearing, I have always thought, of the common Grapy Heels, but it occurs, I think, in the *English Dialect Dictionary*. His information comes from the same Smith, who once cured an old and heavy-legged horse by poulticing with linseed until the discharge ceased, then washing with a solution of alum and copperas (green vitriol or crystallised ferrous sulphate) in order to clean and harden the wounds and the flesh around them, and finally by applying wood tar and some healing ointment. Sometimes with cracked heels there is fever, and for this Stanley gave a very strong infusion of agrimony leaves. He, too, poulticed with linseed, but he would never wash, using a wisp of hay to rub very gently any dirt away and afterwards applying an ointment he made from marsh mallow.

MANGE. Thompson's Smith believed that a cure could be effected by the external application of a salve made from lard, flowers of sulphur, and either snuff or powdered tobacco, and by dosing the animal every two or three days with " livers of antimony." Stanley recognised (perfectly correctly) three sorts of mange which he called mange, head and tail mange, and leg mange. He knew it was a condition caused by parasites—crabs he called them—and he knew that it was necessary not only to kill the adults but also the young after they had hatched and before they could lay eggs themselves. He used sulphur and lime in water (I am afraid I do not know the quantities, for I cannot find the note I made at the time) and he advised applications at intervals of five days. Four applications were generally sufficient.

QUITTOR. This is a disease of the foot that is most painful and can be very troublesome. It generally follows an injury to the foot. Among country horses it is uncommon, though I have seen it more than once, but I believe it is fairly common in towns. Stanley had a story that forty years or so ago, sometime in the 'nineties, when he was a young man, he was called in to look at two horses belonging to the railway company in a neighbouring town. The local veterinaries had been unable to do anything for them apparently, and someone had said that young Stanley was good with horses. (By the way, he called this disease Gitts or Gitters, the " g " being hard as in gold.) He was immensely proud of the fact that he had both horses working again very soon. His treatment was bread poultices applied cold, followed by a poultice of bruised plantain leaves, and liberal applications of cold water. He then used his marsh mallow ointment (when the inflammation had gone) and by continual applications of this got the animals back into working condition.

SPRAINS and SORES. Thompson says that one of the Herons used a liniment for sprains that contained methylated spirits, oil of turpentine and camphor ; and that one of the Boswells preferred to used marsh mallow ointment for all simple abrasions of the skin and slight wounds. Stanley also believed in methylated, oil of turpentine and camphor, and also used marsh mallow ointment (a great favourite of his for all sorts of things) for slight wounds. For burns and scalds he used carron oil.

STAGGERS. Thompson was told by one of the Locks that staggers is generally due to improper feeding having caused acute indigestion. He was perfectly right in that it is a stomach disorder, and his remedy of purging is in accord with the best veterinary practice. He used balls prepared from calomel, liquorice powder and treacle, and he would allow the animal no food and only warm water to drink for twelve hours. A Boswell remedy told to Thompson was balls made up of cream of tartar, ground ginger and castor oil. Stanley used liquorice powder ground ginger and castor oil in balls—a pretty powerful purgative I should say !—and would not allow the animal to eat for two days, but would give it all the warm water it required.   Arigho used aloes and warm water.   Amos Churen believed in liquorice powder, soap and black treacle.   Neither would allow the animal anything to eat for a day, but both believed in plenty of warm water to drink.

THRUSH.   (This is foot thrush : thrush in the mouth is called aptha.)   Thompson was told by Lock that " butter of antimony " (antimony trichloride) should be used to remove dead or decaying matter from the diseased parts. For dry thrush he used a solution of sal-ammoniac or blue-stone (blue vitriol or crystallised copper sulphate).   Thompson's Smith recommended white vitriol for the same purpose.   Stanley bathed with salt and water and afterwards dressed with his marsh mallow ointment mixed with charcoal, which he pressed into the bottom of the cleft with a stick.

THROMBI.   Stanley called this disease " warious swellin' " and it took me a long time to identify it.   It is not regarded as common in horses, but Stanley was evidently well acquainted with it, so it may be more common in Gypsy horses.   It is a stopping of the blood vessels and comes, as a rule, after a horse has made a long, quick journey and is left standing to rest.   On re-starting the animal is so lame in one of the hind legs that it can hardly move.   The vein becomes varicosed and the leg swells.   (Hence presumably " warious swellin'.")   I have never personally come across a case.   Stanley, who was fond of talking about it when on the subject of horses, believed in making the animal eat if possible and giving it regular doses of turpentine and the juice from juniper berries.   But the main cure is rest.

WORMS.   Thompson's Smith maintained that bay or laurel leaves, dried and powdered, and given at the rate of one a day in scalded bran, would almost always effect a cure within a fortnight or so.   He was told by a Gray that broom tops given in the same way were better, while his potter family would have nothing so mild and gave a " blue ball " two or three times a week, dosing with jalap between whiles. " Blue ball " is a composition containing quicksilver and is distinctly dangerous. Arigho, however, had the same idea as the potters. Stanley used broom tops in scalded bran.

The above is but a very short list of Gypsy remedies for ailments in horses. It would be possible to compile a very long list, for most Gypsies seem to have their own remedies for the various ailments common to horses, and those who fancy themselves as animal doctors also have remedies for ailments in cattle, pigs and sheep. There have been some very famous Gypsy animal doctors, and notably Constance Boss, who was the paternal grandmother of Borrow's Petulengro. Borrow maintained that she was 110 when she died. Thompson thinks this an exaggeration, but allows an age of 100 or thereabouts, believing that she was born about 1760 and died about 1860. She specialised as a bone-setter, and on one occasion begged a thoroughbred foal that had broken a foreleg and was going to be put down. She set the leg so thoroughly and nursed the youngster so well that later it won two races at Newmarket.

But with all this absolutely genuine and undeniably skilful doctoring, there is a certain amount of trickery. I have not dealt, and do not intend to deal, with the Gypsy as a " faker " of horseflesh. Suffice it to say that they are quite unsurpassed at the art, and many a broken-down nag has passed for a sprightly stepper or a good sound, strong animal with years of work before it on the day of sale. I have often heard it said that it is most unwise to buy a horse from a Gypsy. If you do not know the Gypsy it probably is. But I also know a farmer who will not buy a horse until it has been examined by a Gypsy friend of his. He has, he says, never been let down.

There is another side to Gypsy medicine. It is obvious that the people who have so great a knowledge of the medicinal properties of the various herbs of the country-

side will not be ignorant of the poisonous plants and their
properties. The Gypsy's knowledge of poisons was every
whit as profound as his knowledge of simples, and the fact
has long been known to gypsiologists and to toxicologists.
If you know your Borrow you will remember :

> The Rommany chi
> And his Rommany chal,
> Shall jaw Tasaulor
> To drab the bawler
> And dook the gry
> Of the farming rye.

And Borrow had good reason to know something of *drab*,
for you may remember he was poisoned and very nearly
killed by an old Gypsy woman who, not altogether without
reason I fancy, had taken a dislike to him. Yes, the
Gypsies did not hesitate to use their knowledge, but
poisoning was in the main confined to pigs. They would
then beg the body from the farmer and eat the flesh. I
think it may truly be said that the practice has long since
died out in this country—it is not yet dead on the Continent
—but the knowledge has not been entirely forgotten.

The most common poisonous plants of the British
countryside are : meadow-saffron, white hellebore, monk's
hood (aconite), foxglove, henbane, water hemlock or cow-
bane, hemlock-water dropwort, five-leaved water hemlock,
spotted hemlock, deadly nightshade, black nightshade,
woody nightshade or bittersweet, fool's parsley, yew (both
leaves and berries), potato tops and seeds, laburnum
(both seeds and bark) tobacco, and many species of fungi,
especially " warty red caps " (*Agaricus musicarius*) and
" brassy caps " (*Agaricus sulphureus*). All these poisons,
except possibly " warty red caps " in one form, belong to
the class known as " narcotics—irritants," and the first
symptom they produce is vomiting with severe internal
pains. After that they act as narcotics, causing uncon-
sciousness and, in severe cases, death.

One of the Boswells told Thompson that " warty red

caps "—that, by the way, is surely a Hampshire rather than a Derbyshire name ?—was the most powerful *drab* known to Gypsies, and that a few of them used to dry and powder it, though Thompson could not discover for what purpose.   The impression given by Thompson is that this was the ancient practice.   But I have actually had the stuff shown me by a Gypsy at Devizes Fair.   He carried it in an old silver tobacco box and obviously regarded it as a great treasure.   He assured me that it would kill anything, but he did not say how long it would take, and he told me that it was made from " warty red caps."   He was drunk at the time, or probably I should not have got the information ; and, of course, the fact that he was drunk does not make it certain that the information was accurate.   However, at St. Giles's Fair at Winchester a year later one of the Barneys told me that this man knew all about *drab*.   For what purpose it was used—the sample shown me was obviously old and more of a family heirloom than anything else—and what action it had was not told me.   It has been said, however, that the spores of one fungus when given in warm water attach themselves to the mucous membrane of the throat, causing all the symptoms of a phthisis and bringing about death in from two to three weeks.   This is referred to at least twice in toxicological literature, and it is definitely stated in one book that the spores are ground down to a fine brown powder.   (The powder I was shown was yellowish-brown in colour.)   It is further stated that after death the mushrooms soon disappear, leaving no trace whatever :   a very useful characteristic.

The favourite *drab* of the New Forest Gypsies used to be foxglove, which was prepared by boiling the leaves in water.   But they also used mustard in potatoes for killing pigs (a form of *drab* known to many Gypsies), and they knew all about monk's hood or aconite, one of the deadliest of our native poisons.   The method of using mustard was to put it into a potato—new or doughy bread was also used —after the centre had been removed, roll the potato in mud—and then throw it into the sty.   The pig having eaten the potato died pretty quickly. So far as I have been able to gather, aconite was used only for fowls, but I could not be sure about this. I think laburnum seeds were used for a more sinister purpose, since Gerania Lee (she has been dead these ten years so I may give her proper name : she was a Lee who married a gorgio soldier who took to the roads) was at some pains to assure me they looked just like peas. No doubt the south country Gypsies had at one time uses for most of the poisonous plants they came across, since they had not access, as had the Gypsies of the north, to mineral poisons, but I have no further information about the uses to which they put them and I fear that the lore has probably been lost for ever.

Borrow maintained that *drab* was bought by Gypsies in chemists' shops, and Thompson has shown that this was, in fact, the case at least for many East Anglian Gypsies. He obtained a sample—some twenty or so years ago now— and on analysis this proved to be barium carbonate. Now barium carbonate has long been recognised as a very effective rat poison by country people and particularly by professional rat-catchers, but it is not a scheduled poison and it can be bought by anyone and is stocked by most good chemists. Amos Churen knew of its use as *drab* by south country Gypsies, though he denied ever having used it himself, but then he originated in Wales or on the Welsh border and presumably knew about " raw " *drab*. The discovery that this *drab* was barium carbonate, obtained in its natural crystalline form, witherite, was made by Mr. John Myers as recently as 1909. He also discovered one of the sources of supply, a mine near Minsterley in Shropshire, and Thompson has since shown that the Gypsies of the Welsh border, Wales, the midlands and the north knew most of, if not all, the available sources of supply in the country. This was the stuff used by the majority of Gypsies for poisoning pigs and sheep, but mainly pigs, and it may well have been used fairly extensively by south country Gypsies, either bought in chemists' shops or procured from Welsh or midland Gypsies. Thompson even suggests that one Welsh Gypsy may have acted as a retailer of *drab*, and certainly the name water spar, which is another name for witherite, is not unknown in southern England. Though the stuff killed the pig, the flesh of the pig, though rather pink, was harmless to man. The entrails were thrown away and the head was left untouched, but the rest of the animal could be eaten. I think the practice was followed, probably, only in the hardest times. A Gypsy told Mr. Myers : " Many a poor Romanichal's family have been brought up by this *bar*." And Borrow in *The Romany Rye* makes a Gypsy say : " Had you tasted that pork, brother, you would have found that it was sweet and tasty, which ballura that is drabbed can hardly be expected to be. We have no reason to drab baulor at present, we have money and credit ; but necessity has no law. Our forefathers occasionally drabbed baulor ; some of our people may still do such a thing, but only from compulsion." That certainly suggests that it was used only as a last resort, but I am not absolutely certain that it was so. At least one family was quite renowned for its fondness for *mulo mas*, and this family was not always in the most straightened circumstances, indeed far from it. Even if the pig had been dead and buried a day or two Gypsies would dig it up and eat it, strange and horrible as it sounds. But that, I fancy, would only be done under the stress of real hunger, though it should be pointed out that certain Hungarian Gypsies have a fondness for carrion and will pass none by that is not too far gone.

Old Mrs. Hearne, an unpleasant lady not troubled with scruples and inspired by a genuine hatred for Borrow, undoubtedly used barium in her attempt to murder that gentleman. Borrow's *Lavengro*, and to a much greater extent his *Romany Rye*, are such a mixture of fiction and fact that it is not always possible to say which is which, but he gives a remarkably lucid description of his symptoms after eating Mrs. Hearne's cake, and with the exception of acute diarrhœa, which he does not mention, they are the symptoms of barium poisoning. Moreover, the place where the poisoning occurred would not have been very far from Minsterley, for we have a pretty accurate record of his movements at the time and even know the date, Saturday, June 11th, 1825, and the time, shortly after midday, when he was poisoned.

The Gypsies had other methods of securing meat when they needed it. One is recorded in *The Times* of November 14th, 1842, and is quoted by Myers. It describes how New Forest Gypsies crammed wool into a sheep's mouth thus causing its death by suffocation. They then begged the dead body, promising to return the skin to the owner. This method of getting meat is remembered by New Forest Gypsies to-day, but is not, of course, practised by them any longer. Another method was to break the neck of a lamb and then place its head through the bars of a gate or in the slats of a fence in such a way as to suggest that death was accidental.

Tinkers also used *drab*. So far as I know, but my information is very scanty and obtained only from one source, they confined their attentions to poultry. The method used was to squash yew berries, extracting the pips, and to give several pips in a small handful of grain. I have been assured, though I cannot vouch for the truth of it, that leghorns, and particularly " they black 'uns," will not take yew pips. I have had some experience as a poultry farmer and have found nothing to suggest that leghorns are any less foolish than other breeds of poultry.

IX

GYPSY WAGGONS

THE best known Gypsy possession is the caravan. Even
those who know nothing at all about Gypsies know that
they have caravans, and, indeed, the words Gypsy and
caravan are so closely connected in the mind of the average
Englishman as to be almost synonymous. And the caravan
is, of course, the most valuable possession of the Gypsy. It
is home, and in it he carries his most treasured belongings—
clothes, linen, china, a few photographs, perhaps medals
won by himself or his family in the last war. But no true
Gypsy ever talks of a caravan—unless he means one of
those luxurious edifices that in the piping days of peace
we used to see trailing along behind fast cars—he talks of
a waggon or a van. And the word *vardo* really means
living-waggon.

The typical *Romano vardo* is a comparatively recent introduction so far as this country is concerned. Nobody, so far
as I know, has written the history of the Gypsy living-
waggon, but I have an idea that it was in existence on the
Continent, and particularly in Hungary and Bohemia, long
before it came here. Dickens, in *The Old Curiosity Shop*, was
the first person, I think, to describe a waggon in England.
He called it a caravan, and his Mrs. Jarley's waggon was
obviously very similar in design and interior fittings to the
waggons we see on the road to-day. That was in 1840, and
there must have been waggons on the roads of Britain long
before that, for I think it very unlikely that the living-
waggon would have arrived all in one piece as it were.
It is much more probable that it was evolved, certainly so
far as interior fittings are concerned, bit by bit over a
period of years. But a standard in design, and in interior
fittings, was reached many years ago, for the modern
waggon differs but little—except that it is rarely built of
such well-seasoned wood—from those built at the beginning

of the century. The typical living-waggon is a one-roomed house on rather high wheels, with windows at the back and sides and a door and detachable steps at the front. There is a rack (known as the *cratch*) at the back for carrying domestic articles of various kinds, and underneath the waggon at the back there is built a cupboard (known as the pan-box) which serves both as larder and kitchen-cupboard. Inside the waggon, behind the door, are a coal-stove, with a chimney projecting through the roof, a cupboard and a locker-seat. On the other side there is a corner-cupboard for china, a chest of drawers in which is kept the family wardrobe and the family linen, and another locker. The whole of the back part is occupied by a two-berthed sleeping place. Naturally, just as there is some variation from waggon to waggon in external design, so all waggons are not fitted exactly in this way. But the variation inside is so slight that this description may truly serve as a standard.

So far as external design is concerned there are, according to Mr. Ferdinand Gerard Huth, the authority on this branch of Gypsy Lore, broadly speaking, four types of waggon now in use among British Gypsies. I say broadly speaking deliberately, because living-waggons are not mass-produced, and so no two waggons are exactly alike. But there are four easily recognisable types—the Reading waggon, the Leeds waggon, the Ledge waggon and the Burton or Showman's waggon. In addition, there was until fairly recently a fifth type called the Fen or Brush waggon, but I have not seen one for a good many years now.

The Reading waggon, so called because one of the best known builders lived in the Berkshire town, is a straight-sided waggon with the wheels outside the body. Reading was once a great winter resort for Gypsies, but in the hey-day of the great waggon builders, the Dunton family, Romanichals came from all over Britain to have waggons made for them. Reading waggons are usually about 10 feet 6 inches in length, but I have heard of one in Sussex that was 14 feet long. In width they are usually 6 feet at the bottom and 6 feet 6 inches at the eaves. There are a number of different types of Reading waggon—the variations on the basic design being related solely to the depth or otherwise of the purchaser's pockets. The better and more expensive ones are fitted with a skylight. Some are very ornate and some are very simple, but all are the same in having straight sides and outside wheels. Reading waggons were not, of course, built only by the Dunton family or only at Reading. Plenty of other makers also built this type of waggon and, in particular, excellent ones were made by a firm in Derbyshire.

The Leeds waggon is so called because the most famous builder of this type, one Bill Wright, lived near Leeds. It is also known as the bow or barrel-topped waggon because of its shape. The usual length is about 9 feet 6 inches and the usual width at the widest part of the barrel is 6 feet to 6 feet 2 inches. These waggons are very popular among north country Gypsies, but are not very often seen in the south country. I have heard an old Gypsy declare that a good Leeds waggon would outlive any other sort of waggon under any conditions. Leeds waggons are made in many other parts of the country, but the best builders still seem to be in Yorkshire, for I have heard a young west country Gypsy speak of them as " Yorkshire " waggons instead of Leeds waggons.

The Ledge waggon (some people call them Cottage waggons) is the type most commonly seen on the roads, for these waggons are made by all the recognised builders, and are not connected even by Gypsies with any particular place or any particular builder. In construction they come midway, as it were, between the Reading and the Leeds waggon. That is to say, they are not straight-sided and do not have outside wheels, they are not barrel-topped but have roofs very similar to those of the Reading waggon. The usual length is from 9 feet 6 inches to 10 feet, and the usual width 6 feet to 6 feet 2 inches at the widest part.

The Burton—presumably from Burton-on-Trent, but I
have found nothing to suggest that better waggons were
made there than anywhere else—or Showman's waggon is a
straight-sided waggon like the Reading, but the wheels are
placed underneath the body instead of outside it. There
are a good many other differences too, so that no one could
possibly mistake the one for the other. For one thing all
Burton waggons are made with a panelled or, less frequently, a rib and matchboard body, these latter sometimes with a panel about 4 inches wide running right
round the centre of the body. For another the roof is much
flatter than in the Reading waggon. Again, all Burton
waggons have pieces of carved wood attached to them
somewhere or other. In the panelled type these pieces of
ornate carving (which vary, of course, with the whim of
the individual builder) are screwed on to the panels, but
with the rib and matchboard type they are usually
attached only at the corners. The usual length is 10 feet
6 inches and the usual width 6 feet.

The last horse-drawn Fen or Brush waggon that I saw
was in Wiltshire and a good many years ago now. It was,
I imagine, the last of its kind, for I have not heard of one
since, and horse-drawn at least they may now be considered
extinct. That is a pity, for there can be no doubt at all that
they were by far the most picturesque of all waggons, but
they were never popular with true Gypsies, and were used,
as a rule, by *poshrats* or by people of dubious character who
had taken to the roads to earn a yet more dubious living.
The owner of the waggon I saw was not a Gypsy and could
lay claim to very little Gypsy blood. He earned a living
hawking brushes, baskets, pots and pans, and anything he
picked up on his travels, and for this sort of living, which
is not the true Gypsy way of doing things, the Fen or
Brush waggon was excellently adapted, for it had external
racks and cases for displaying wares for sale, and goods
could be carried on the roof, for a rail ran all round to
protect them. Motorised Brush waggons are still to be
seen in some remote country districts, but I think it may

safely be said that they are never owned by Gypsies, but usually by a shop in some country town. The name " Brush " is obviously derived from the type of goods most usually carried and displayed for sale. The name " Fen " seems to indicate an East Anglian origin for these waggons, but as far as I know there is no evidence to suggest that the original builder lived in the Fen country. The owner of the waggon I saw in Wiltshire, however, called it a Fen waggon.

In addition to the waggons there are two types of cart in use among British Gypsies. One, which may be built with two wheels or four wheels, is called the Pot cart : the other, which is two-wheeled, has not got, so far as I know, any particular name. These carts are used especially by travellers who live on the roads only during the spring, summer and autumn, and move into small houses for the winter. But they are also used in conjunction with the living-waggons in a variety of ways—for the children to sleep in, for example, or for goods to be carried in, or for short journeys when goods are taken for hawking or fire-wood is sold, and so on. In fact they are useful in many ways. The word cart, at least so far as the four-wheeled Pot cart is concerned, is rather misleading. " Cart " indicates a simple structure, and the four-wheeled Pot cart is anything but simple. Generally they are about 9 feet long and 4 feet wide across the floor. Some are made with open-work frame inside, but I have never seen one of this type. Those I have seen have had sides as solid as any farm cart, and I should imagine that those built with frame sides must be very draughty when the tilt is on. There is a projecting frame at the front of the cart under which is a shallow locker, the whole forming a seat, and slung at the back, and below the back rack, is the pan-box exactly as in a living-waggon. I believe that some of the two-wheeled Pot carts have also a pan-box, but I have not seen one so fitted. Both four- and two-wheeled Pot carts are fitted with a detachable frame, barrel-shaped as in the Leeds waggon. This frame is hooped and over these hoops a green proofed sheet is spread. The back is matchboard with, in the centre, a window that is hinged at the top and opens outward at the bottom. To the front of the green proofed sheet are attached curtains of the same material. I have never seen any interior fittings to these carts, but I believe some have such fittings and that one or two even go in for stoves. These carts are not wide enough for an adult to sleep in in any position but lengthways. There is, therefore, no fixed bed. The bedding is just laid down on the floor at night and rolled up and stowed away at the back during the day.

The other type of cart has a back rack, but no locker in the front and no pan-box at the rear. They are fitted with a detachable hoop frame over which is stretched a green or black tarpaulin sheet with curtain both at the back and the front. I have never seen any interior fittings, but I believe that some carts are fitted. Of this type of cart there are two sub-types, one a good deal narrower and shorter than the other. In these, which are definitely a poorer type, a few boards are laid across the back from one side to the other and on these boards the children sleep, while their parents sleep on the floor with their heads at the front of the cart and their feet underneath the boards which form their children's bed. The wider and longer cart, which is altogether superior (some of them have a matchboard back with a window) are wide enough for an adult to sleep across. In these carts the width is generally 6 feet and the height from the floor to the top of the tilt is usually about 5 feet 6 inches. These carts, moreover, have struts for their shafts, and there are also two struts at the back, so that at night the cart can be made absolutely level. I have never seen struts on the poorer type of cart and all sorts of ingenious methods are used for keeping them level, though the most usual seems to be to run the shafts into a thick hedge. I have seen the frames removed from the carts and used on the ground as tents (when they look not unlike igloos), for the ground makes a softer bed than the boards and, if the weather be dry, a sweeter bed, too, I have no doubt.

Sleeping arrangements in a living-waggon are naturally infinitely superior to those in a cart, and for comfort many of them could not be beaten by the best hotel in the world. The bed-place varies slightly with the type of waggon, but the principle is the same in all waggons. The bed-place, which occupies the whole of the rear of the waggon, consists of two berths, one above the other, and in a straight-sided waggon these are 6 feet long by 3 feet 10 inches to 4 feet wide. Naturally they are not so long, or at least the lower berth is not so long, in waggons that are not straight-sided. Across the front of the bed-place, that is across the front of the top berth, is a turned spindle rail about 6 inches wide. There is also a spindle rail enclosing a narrow shelf above the back window. Some bed-places, generally in the older waggons, have fixed bed-posts standing out about a foot from the side of the waggon and stretching from floor to ceiling, where they meet the arched roof-board. These posts are turned, and sometimes beautifully carved, from the top of the upper berth to the roof, but below they are square—and serve as the door-posts for the doors of the lower bed. If there are bed-posts there are almost always brightly coloured curtains tied back to them. The doors of the bottom berth are panelled and open outwards in this type of bed-place, but in some waggons the doors slide back behind a fixed panel. In this type there are, of course, no posts. Nowadays, for the young Gypsy woman is every whit as interested in her appearance as her more sophisticated sister of the town, mirror shutters are generally found as one of the fitments of the bed-place. In any van that is not straight-sided the length of the bottom bed is not sufficient for an adult—in many it does not exceed $4\frac{1}{2}$ feet, and so is really suitable only for small children. If adults have to use the bottom beds of this sort they lie parallel to the sides of the van with their feet stretching out towards the waggon door. The beds in these living-waggons are invariably comfortable. Only really good feather-beds are used as a rule and they are treated with the greatest care. Furthermore, the wealthier Gypsy women use the finest linen sheets (they are treasured family possessions which are not parted with under any circumstances to a gorgio, and only as a last resort to any other Gypsy, though sometimes they are destroyed in funeral pyres), and these sheets are as often as not bordered with wonderful crochet-work or the finest hand-made lace. Nowadays, of course, excellent quality eiderdowns are to be found in the living-waggons and wonderful bedspreads and quilts. Quite the finest patchwork quilt I have ever seen was in a living-waggon, and the owner's wife was engaged upon another which bid fair to rival it in every way. More than one Gypsy woman of my acquaintance has remarkable skill with the needle (it is a quality with which they are not generally credited) and does first-class work, but I do not know of any Gypsy woman who does such work for sale. Most Gypsy women take an infinite pride in their vans and go to infinite pains to keep their interiors as perfect as possible. Indeed I have seen very few slovenly waggons, no matter how slovenly their owners might appear. " House-proud " is not a characteristic of the gorgio alone. And yet no matter how fine the living-waggon or how comfortable the bed, in hot weather at least many Romani men and women prefer to sleep in the open underneath their vans. And I know one or two who though they own excellent waggons always sleep in a tent, or, if the weather is really fine, in the open.

Next to the bed in importance is the stove. I put the stove second in importance because most of the cooking is done in the open over a wood fire anyhow. In the older vans the type of stove is that known as the " Colchester " open grate. In this type of stove the case of the grate is made of sheet-iron with a brass front and blower to draw up the fire which slides down on brass side rods. The top of the case is conical, tapering up to the roof, where it joins the chimney pipe. In some of these stoves (the more recent ones) there is a small side oven and a trivet for the kettle. Above them is a curved mantelpiece with three brass rails to prevent things falling off. I have met old

Gypsies who swear by these stoves, but I have never met a Gypsy woman who prefers them to the " Hostess," which is the type found in all the more modern waggons. The " Colchester " on a windy day is not the cleanest of companions in the confined space of a living-waggon. In the modern waggons the boxed-in panelled fireplace, with tile-pattern enamelled iron plates surrounding it, and the " Hostess " range with its brass rail round the top and brass-fronted coal-box sliding underneath, is as clean as anyone could wish. These fireplaces are built in as fixtures. They have a brass-railed mantelpiece in the same way as the " Colchester," but behind the mantelpiece is an airing-cupboard with a door in the side of the fireplace. The chimney pipe passes through this cupboard —there is no fear of scorching clothes because it is enclosed in another pipe for the length of its passage through the cupboard—and so through the roof. The " Hostess " has indeed a number of advantages over the " Colchester," but the latter, despite its tendency to spread ash over everything, is undoubtedly more cheerful and more spiritually, if not physically, warming.

The rest of the furniture is composed of locker-seats, cupboards and a chest of drawers. The arrangement varies slightly with the type of van and even from van to van, but there are usually two lockers with comfortable upholstered seats, a square cupboard, a corner cupboard and a chest-of-drawers. Both the cupboards have two compartments, the top having glass doors and the bottom wooden panelled doors. In the square cupboard the two compartments are separated by a narrow drawer which is used for keeping knives, spoons, forks and so on. There is no drawer in the corner cupboard. The chests-of-drawers are usually level-fronted and have a polished table-top and sometimes an extra folding-leaf. Otherwise they are just like chests-of-drawers anywhere else—two small drawers at the top and three long ones underneath them—though in some of the waggons with narrower floor space (Ledge waggons for example) the bottom drawer is replaced by a narrow cupboard with a front that lets down on hinges, but is made to look like a drawer.

In the corner cupboard the Romani wife keeps her china —her plates and cups and so forth. These are always of very good china, much better than is to be found in the average English middle-class home. Some of this china is old, but the modern is usually of the best quality, and replacements are usually made from the best quality obtainable. Poor china is not a feature of the *Romano vardo*. So, too, with the china figures and brass candlesticks that adorn the mantelpiece. They are good. Often they are rare pieces of Staffordshire or Chelsea, but sometimes they are modern : if they are, the taste is impeccable and the china excellent. The same is true of the brass candlesticks. They are good, old and heavy. The brass production of Birmingham does not impress the Romani. Indeed the only furnishings in these living-waggons that I have seen that has not been of first-rate quality has been the linoleum on the floor. Usually that is good, too, and the rug or strip of carpet is always as good as the owner can afford, and some of the rugs are old and valuable, but in some waggons I have found linoleum that has obviously been bought on the principle that anything is good enough for the floor. Check linoleum is not popular, but I have recently seen a waggon, the property of a young couple just setting out on the hard road of the traveller, which was fitted up with cheerful check curtains and a strip of excellent check linoleum. The effect was most pleasing.

When new, the waggons are, of course, painted by the builders. As with farm carts and waggons, there are, or seem to be, certain stereotyped colours. But these wear off in time, and then the Gypsy artist comes into his own. True, many more vans than not remain unpainted and gradually increase in shabbiness until some excite wonder, wonder that they are still able to move over the roads and hold together. But some have owners with an artistic urge, and plenty of leisure in which to satisfy it, and the results are wonderful. I have seen a black van tastefully picked

out in red, a red van picked out in green with bright
yellow wheels, a red van picked out in black with yellow
and black wheels (red, yellow and black are just as truly
the Gypsy colours to-day as they were in Lord Lilford's
day), but sometimes the effect is bizarre in the extreme.
One traveller of my acquaintance just dabbed a spot of
paint on whenever he felt like it and had any paint. As he
also mended his van by nailing any odd bit of wood over
the affected part the result was interesting, if somewhat
unusual.

I have known one Gypsy artist who painted dragons on
the outside of his van. He had snakes wandering along
the shafts and lions and elephants on the half-door. This
sort of external decoration is most unusual, but there is a
great deal of outside decoration to the vans by means of
carving. This is really a study in itself and is a subject
about which, I fear, I know very little. Much of the
decorative work on the waggons is copied, of course, from
works of gorgio origin. But there is still much work about
which is of true Romani origin, and sometimes you will
still come across a Gypsy craftsman who has no need of
models. Then you may be sure that you are watching real
folk craft, that something, perhaps centuries old, is being
recreated before your eyes.

A special study could also be made of Gypsy harness, on
which subject I am again much indebted to Mr. Huth. The
type generally used by Gypsies is a van harness made with
plated or brass fittings. Plated fittings are more common
among Gypsies, but I think that brass induces a greater
pride in the owner. The bridle of a good set of harness
has a red patent-leather forehead-band with a chain front.
The ornaments on the blinkers (invariably shield-shaped)
and on other parts of the harness are usually engraved
with the owner's initials mounted on a piece of red patent-
leather, and another piece of red patent-leather, usually
scalloped, sticks out from the back of the blinkers. The
bridle is usually fitted with a stainless double-ring snaffle-
bit and bridoon chains. There is a throat strap that

unbuckles at both sides, and a bearing rein as well as driving reins. The ends of the straps thread into plated metal instead of leather runners. Generally the horse's collar is of the piped type and has a serge lining, and is topped with ornamental housing. The hames are fitted with short chain-tugs and have curled tops, and above the hame strap is another strap bearing a name plate. Most of these name plates are decorated with three galloping horses. The pad is the usual waggon type ornamented with shield-shaped bosses and half-round beading, both plated. The back-strap is fitted with very large leather tug-loops because the shafts of a *vardo* are usually pretty thick. The crupper often has two or three loin-straps faced with red patent-leather and ornamented with plated shields. The breeching is fitted with short chain tugs. All the strappings are stitched on the two edges. All the straps—back-strap, belly-band, etc.—unbuckle on both sides. The reason for this is that it is much more adjustable and so is more easily fitted to horses of any size, a very sensible provision where Gypsies are concerned. This sort of harness is made only by certain saddlers. There is a very good one, for example, at Thame in Oxfordshire.

Sometimes, however, one comes across remarkable brass fittings to Gypsy harness sets. Horse brasses are a subject of perennial interest, and every carter worth the name takes the greatest pride in his brasses if he has a good set. In these days of mechanisation they are not seen as often as they might be, but they are still remarkably hard to pick up from the collecting point of view. Some find their way to Gypsy sets and I have seen some very good ones on the road. Years ago it was the fashion for the nobility or great landed gentry to have their crest or monogram on their horse brasses. On the harness of a traveller in Dorset not long ago I saw the crest of one of our great ducal houses— on just a single piece. But my most astonishing find in this way was in Surrey, where on a very ordinary turn-out I found three brasses bearing the arms of some Indian Rajah. They were genuine, not Birmingham imitations, and they were old and worn. At some time they had adorned, I fancy, the royal elephants. When I asked the owner where he had got them he replied that when he knew what business it was of mine he would be "wery pleased to tell me," but as it was no business of mine he would be "wery pleased not to."

One horse is sufficient to draw a light waggon. When the van is heavy a pony is put on the off-side to help the horse. This pony is known as a "sider," and sometimes you will see a "sider" to an obviously light van when the horse is not as good as it might be. To keep the "sider" in position a short rope is run from its bridle to the tug ring on the hame of the horse. When two or more waggons are travelling in company they help one another up very steep hills by doubling, which is by taking the horse from one waggon and putting him in traces in front of the horse in the other. When the first waggon reaches the top of the hill both horses are taken out and walked back to fetch the second waggon. When climbing steep hills one of the boys, or if there is not a boy one of the women, walks behind the waggon carrying a block of wood fixed on to the end of a stick. When the horses stop to regain their wind the wheels are blocked up.

I have devoted a good deal of space to the Gypsy horse-drawn living-waggon because I have an idea that in the not-distant future it will have disappeared from the roads and lanes of Britain. Already, in too many places, they have become immoblised, the shafts are down, they are no more than shacks on wheels occupying year in and year out the same position on some patch of derelict ground. And somehow once the waggon becomes a fixture it loses all personality. It becomes a hovel, the field almost a rural slum. The Gypsy was never intended for a sedentary life, even a sedentary life in the open. An excellent example of this is to be seen—and it may be seen from the railway without any inconvenience—on the outskirts of Ash Vale in Surrey.

I shall regret the passing of the horse-drawn waggon. I

like its picturesqueness.   But it would be idle to pretend
that it is an essential part of the true Gypsy way of life.
It is a comparatively recent introduction.   It is now no
more than a symbol of the brief prosperity that came to the
British Romanies in the last century.

X

GYPSIES TO-DAY

GEORGE BORROW was of the opinion that he was studying a race that would soon die out. Leland, who followed after Borrow, was of the same opinion. When Borrow travelled the roads of Britain in the early years of the last century the Romani language was spoken grammatically by many, perhaps the majority of Gypsies. When Leland travelled the same roads in the latter half of the century the language was already becoming a jargon, and many of the customs and taboos were already falling into disuse or had already become so greatly modified as to be scarcely recognisable. The process has continued. Even in Wales, where Sampson a mere fifty years ago rediscovered the language spoken in all its perfection of vocabulary, construction and inflexion, speakers of pure Romani are to-day very few and far between. In England it has become altogether corrupted. Anglo-Romani is now no more than a jargon. Judging by the language alone it would seem that Borrow and Leland were right. They were, I think, utterly wrong.

Romani is the language of the Gypsies. It is the same language all over the world wherever Gypsies are to be found, and naturally it varies enormously from country to country. Some words are the same and have the same meaning everywhere (though the pronunciation may vary slightly) and in some countries the language is much more complete than in others, in some many more words of the native language have been incorporated than in others, in some the native language has almost replaced the mother tongue. This is what has happened in Britain. The inflexions have been lost, there is no longer any attempt at grammar or construction, a very large part of the vocabulary has been forgotten. I do not suppose that there is a single English Gypsy living who can speak pure

Romani and there are very, very few Welsh Gypsies left
who can do so. There are, indeed, very, very few to-day
who possesses any extensive vocabulary (I lay no claim to
being a Romani scholar, but I am too " deep " for many
of the English Gypsies I have met), but they cling passionately to those words they do know and they take care
that their children shall know them also. So you will find
that most English Gypsies talk a queer mixture of English
and Romani with the English predominating. If you
are a *mush* what *jins* the *chib* it is all right, but if you are not
it must be very confusing indeed. But, despite all this, it
would be a very great mistake to regard (as many do)
Romani in England as a dead language. It is not dead,
and, I am sure, it will never die. It is, on the other hand,
very much alive. It is in the blood of Gypsies, part of their
being, and it is never entirely forgotten. Sometimes a
word never commonly used, a word that might truly be
said to be forgotten, will come to the surface in some
sudden burst of excited speech or in the telling of a story.
Sometimes the word is not an English Romani word at
all. Thus, once in the New Forest I listened to a Lee
recounting the tale of a poaching expedition, a famous
adventure that had had more than its share of excitement.
He took his listeners step by step through the night and
then as he approached the climax he suddenly said
" *Disilo*." I asked him what it meant. " Day comes," he
said impatiently, and went on with the tale. I had never
heard that word from any English Gypsy. But it is used
sometimes among Balkan Gypsies and means just what it
meant to this Hampshire Lee. The excitement of the
story had acted like some great volcanic disturbance in his
mind and thrown up to the surface a word long since forgotten, one which maybe he had heard in childhood from
his grandfather or perhaps from some wandering stranger,
but a word not forgotten absolutely. Yet when I asked
him a week or two later did he know the word, *Disilo*, he
said no, and was obviously astounded to hear that he had
ever used it. So, too, I have heard the word *shil* used for

" a whistle " (it comes from the same part of the world), *mindtsi* used for " a virgin " (I do not know where this comes from) and *gabor* used for " how much." These are certainly not Anglo-Romani words, but I do not think that their occurrence among New Forest Gypsies need occasion much surprise. Foreign Gypsies are by no means as uncommon as all that in England—I have myself come across " Greek," " Roumanian " and " Russian " Gypsies in southern England (a band of " Roumanian " Gypsies spent some time in the New Forest in 1923)—and some of their words would stick if there was any intercourse with their English cousins. In the same way, words that are not Romani at all (*mindtsi* may be one for all I know) sometimes come bubbling to the surface. I have heard *balow* used for a " broken nose " by a Stanley. And twice I have heard Moroccan or Arabic words (I do not know which), used by English Gypsies. Once in a quarrel between two of the Barneys, husband and wife, the woman in a furious rage hurled a plate at her husband shouting " *Balec*, you bloody toad." It was obvious enough what she meant. Afterwards I asked her what it meant, but she had already forgotten or would not remember. But anyone who has been in Morocco will know what *Balec* means : it means " Make way." This Gypsy woman meant " get out of my sight." The other word was also used by the same woman. It was near Winchester, and she was referring to a church-yard in the neighbourhood that has a slightly unsavoury reputation with the country folk as a haunt of ghosts. " It's *horm*," she said, " it's *horm*." I understand that the word cannot be translated exactly into English, but it means roughly something that is holy in a supernatural way and must only be visited or touched by the initiated. Now this woman, to my knowledge, has never been out of England, never even as far as Chichester on the one side or Wey-mouth on the other, so how she got hold of these two words is beyond guessing. But she spent a good deal of time in Southampton as a girl and perhaps picked them up from some visiting Arab sailor. Anyway, there they were, deep

down in her subconscious mind, and I should not be at all
surprised to find her children using them one day. In the
same way I have heard Romani children using soldier's
Hindustani quite naturally, picked up no doubt from
parents or other Gypsies who served in the British forces
abroad in the last war. So, too, you will find queer forms of
Romani used sometimes by English Gypsies. Again in the
New Forest I have heard, frequently too, *prala* for brother,
though I have never heard it anywhere else. Amos Churen
always used *kongry* for a match, and *kari* for a hat—words
I have never heard used by anyone else—and David
Burton always talked of a policeman as a *yokmush*, which is
sensible enough since it means " eye-man," but a word I
have never heard used in that connection by any other
Gypsy. I have, however, heard it used by a small boy
to describe a night-watchman for the Hampshire County
Council Highways Department. This lad used to make
use of the watchman's brazier and was very friendly with
him, always calling him *yokmush*. Children, I have found,
are often " deeper " than their parents and will use words
quite naturally that their parents do not know or have
forgotten, or at any rate appear to have forgotten, for you
can never be certain. You can never be certain just how
much Romani an English Gypsy does know. The poorest
speaker may remember some word or words long since forgotten, or never known, by those who speak the language
comparatively well, and I always have the idea that the
modern English Gypsy can speak his language a good deal
better than he is going to let the mere gorgio know. I
cannot, therefore, agree with those who maintain that
Romani in England is a dead language. It may for everyday use become even more of a jargon than it is at present,
but it will, I am sure, always remain very much alive in
the minds of the Romani folk. And certainly I cannot
agree with those who see in the growth of jargon signs of
the passing of the Gypsy race in England. If it is a sign
of anything it is a sign of adaptability, and that is surely a
sign of strength. For in the same period as the Gypsies

have been in England the English language has altered
almost beyond recognition. The spoken language of to-
day is as far from Tudor English as Tudor English was
from Chaucerian English. Language undergoes evolution
just as everything else does.

Nor can the passing of the old Gypsy customs, the old
Gypsy dress, the old Gypsy occupations be regarded as
proof of the passing of the Gypsy. Our own dress, our
own customs, or own occupations have changed no less
drastically in the last 400 years. It would be foolish to
pretend that the Englishman of to-day is the same as the
Englishman of Henry VII's day : but he is still an
Englishman. It would be idle to pretend that the Gypsy
of to-day is the same as the Gypsy of 400 years ago, but he
is still a Gypsy. And taking it all in all, his way of life
has altered less than that of any other people in Europe.
Shiftless and happy-go-lucky as he is, inveterate wanderer
as he is, he is yet the most conservative being on earth.
And this applies with equal force to his methods of earning
a living.

The ways in which Gypsies earn a living are legion. No
less than 135 are listed in the Index to the Old Series of
the *Journal* of the Gypsy Lore Society, and this number
could probably be doubled or trebled without undue
difficulty. It is true that that list covers Gypsy occupations all over the world, and that quite a lot of them have
never been followed by British Gypsies, while some of
them, snake-charming for example, have probably never
been followed by more than a few individuals. But it does
indicate a certain versatility. And the Gypsy is a most
versatile person. Horse-dealing between the two great
wars was not always as paying a business as it used to be,
but there was a very good trade to be done in second-
hand motor-cars. I knew one Gypsy who traded in cars
of uncertain age and unwilling performance. He was
quite as successful a car-doctor as his father had been a
horse-doctor, and was as successful in buying and selling
old cars as his father had been in buying and selling

horses. A true Gypsy can make a living out of anything—
or nothing. It is not, therefore, surprising to find so
extensive a list of occupations. But it would be a mistake
—certainly so far as British, and probably so far as any
Gypsies are concerned—to regard many of these occupations as typical of Gypsies. Most of those mentioned in
literature as being followed by Gypsies are no more than
temporary aids to a living. The normal occupations of the
Gypsies, whether British or not, are very few.

Naturally, these normal occupations vary according to
the country in which the people concerned have made a
home. Music, for example, is part of the Gypsy's life.
Most English Gypsies are passionately fond of music, and
not a few of them are excellent performers. But music
among British Gypsies has never become a full-time occupation. There have been a few whole-time Welsh Gypsy
musicians, both harpers and fiddlers (John Roberts was
Telynor Cymru, Harper of Wales, the highest honour), and
the fiddle has often been used by English and Scots Gypsies
and by Irish tinkers to earn a few shillings, but for the
British Gypsy in general music has remained a relaxation.
In Hungary a large proportion of the orchestras are composed of Gypsies, and many are entirely Gypsy in personnel.
Similarly, there are not, so far as I know, any British
families of coppersmiths or silversmiths or blacksmiths,
although I know of more than one man who could turn
his hands to such trades and make a decent showing provided no complicated work was required. Nor do I know
of a British Gypsy bear-leader, though bear-leading certainly deserves to rank as a regular Gypsy occupation. No
longer do we see the dancing bear on the English roads.
There were still some when I was a child, and I can
remember two well, one because I touched the bear and
the other because the man had a long feather in his black
hat. Neither, I feel pretty certain, was English. I can
also remember a man who had two trained monkeys that
wore little red coats and collected the money earned by
the man's fiddling, and a woman who danced with a tam-

bourine. I do not think these could have been English
Gypsies either, but the occupations are normal enough for
Balkan Gypsies.

Some occupations are, however, common to Gypsies all
over the world, and of these fortune-telling and horse-
dealing are the most popular, the various forms of the
smith's art and music coming next. And to these should
be added, though I do not know that they are ever whole-
time occupations, begging and poaching. All Gypsies do
not beg, by no means all, but all Gypsies are really accomplished beggars ; all Gypsies do not poach, by no means
all, but all Gypsies know more than a little about poaching.
These are the staple Gypsy occupations (perhaps I should
not include poaching as a staple occupation, it being
largely a matter of opportunity and being common to more
countrymen than the average landowner realises). The
others—acrobats and jugglers, knife-grinders and cobblers,
flower-sellers and street musicians, and dancers and
griddlers (a " griddler " is a man or woman who sings in
the street), and so on through all the manifold ways of
turning an honest penny—are temporary occupations for
the majority of Gypsies, though there are one or two
families of Gypsy acrobats and jugglers and knife-grinders.
Even these, however, are not at a loss when it comes to
dealing with a horse, nor are their women nonplussed when
it comes to a bit of *dukkeriben*. There was a Scamp who
travelled a restricted area of Kent with a knife-grinding
machine and had a very good side-line in horses, while one
of his daughters made the most of Canterbury Cricket Week
in the fortune-telling line. And then most Gypsies are
hawkers. Some hawk what they make, but most hawk
stuff they have bought on the cheap.

The actual occupations that I have personally come
across among British Gypsies in the past twenty years or
so (I have come across many others among Gypsies abroad)
make a varied enough list. These are some of them :
Punch and Judy showman, skittle-alley proprietor, dancing
marionette man, chimney sweep, basket maker, beehive

maker, clothes-peg maker, china mender, knife and
scissors grinder, umbrella mender, wild birds' egg collector
(he sold his finds to a wealthy man in London), kettle and
general pots and pans mender, acrobat, jockey, bare-back
rider in a circus (it is a mistake to suppose that many
Gypsies join the circus : the circus is an entirely separate
world, alike only in that it is also nomadic), blacksmith,
rat-catcher, mole-catcher, horse-dealer, cattle-dealer,
farmer, horse-doctor, herb-gatherer, mason, chairmaker,
singer, fiddler, house-painter, palmist, phrenologist, café
proprietor, chucker-out at cinema, herbalist (quite different from herb-gatherer), fortune-telling (using a crystal
only), rabbit-catcher, fisherman, professional wrestler,
pawnbroker, and professional boxer. In every case these
men were full-blooded or nearly full-blooded Gypsies, with
the exception of the pawnbroker, who lived in Portsmouth
and from whom I bought some very good carpets. I was
never sure about the pawnbroker. He had very fair hair
and very blue eyes—but so have lots of Gypsies : the
Grays, for instance, are a very fair family—and he dressed
like a business man, but he spoke a good deal of Romani
rather well, and his wife and his children looked very Gypsy.
Also he shook hands like a Gypsy. The house-painter was
quite definitely a full-blooded Gypsy—a Loveridge from
Dorset—who had married a gorgie from Glasgow who was
maid-servant at a big house near Ferndown. He returned
with her to Glasgow, for she would not take to the roads
and he was very much in love with her. He hated towns
and loathed house-painting, but he stuck Glasgow till a
bomb in the blitz killed him.

Gypsies are naturally handy with their fists, and there
have been many famous Gypsy boxers. In the old bare-
knuckle days the Gypsy was a power in the British professional ring. The following Champions of England under
Prize Ring Rules were Gypsies : Tom Smith (the feather-
weight champion of 1844), Hooper the Tinman (who was
middle-weight champion in 1790 and whose real name was
William Cooper), Posh Price (a middle-weight champion of

the early nineteenth century, whose real name was Amos
Price), Tom Sayers (who was heavy-weight champion of
England in 1857 and who fought the famous battle with
Heenan)—Joe Goss is also supposed to have been a Gypsy,
but the name is not a Romani name. Goss, however, went
the round of the fairs with a booth and undoubtedly had
a Romani wife name Helen Gray—and, of course, Jem
Mace, the most famous of them all and a true champion of
the world. With the coming of the gloves there have been
fewer Gypsies in the British ring, but some of them have
done remarkably well. Digger Stanley won a world's
championship and Gypsy Daniels an English championship. There was more than a little Gypsy blood in Joe
Bowker, Pedlar Palmer (whose mother was a London-side
Lee) and Joe Beckett. Peerless Jem Driscoll is commonly
regarded as a Welshman as he came from South Wales.
He had not got, so far as I know, a single drop of Welsh
blood in him. He came of a travelling Irish tinker family
and a Romani mother named Taylor or Jones. He learned
his boxing in travelling booths run by a Gypsy named
Boswell who travelled South Wales, the west country and
the midlands. Jem could *rakker Romanes* with the best of
them, and I remember well the pleased smile on his face
when I wished him *Kushto Bok* the night he fought his last
fight, a grand but tragic effort, against Charles Ledoux.
Quite recently one Charlie Hickman showed for a few
fights promise of bringing the Gypsy to the fore in the heavy-
weight ring again, but he soon faded away after a few good
fights, and the last I heard of him he was touring the fair
grounds of the midlands. The normal Gypsy method of
fighting—head on chest and elbows held well into the ribs
—was no doubt excellent for the old bare-knuckle prize
ring, but it has considerable drawbacks for the ring of to-
day, which may be one of the reasons for the lack of Gypsy
champions of recent years.

The Gypsy is by no means averse to a fight, is indeed
inclined to be quarrelsome when *motto*, and is certainly
not a physical coward. But no one could rightfully call the

average Gypsy a tough. His appearance is deceptive.
The Irish tinker is a tough, though his appearance is also,
as often as not, deceptive. He is by nature a fighter, and
he fights with a cold fury and a fixed desire to maim that is
rather frightening. When the travelling Irish first invaded
Wales and the Welsh border counties they came into rough
contact with the Gypsies, and the Gypsies very definitely
had the worst of it. So much so, in fact, that they would
move camp rather than risk a fight, unless they were in
greatly superior numbers. All that was long ago, and the
Irish tinker, with the passage of time, and influenced, perhaps, by the English climate and certainly by marriage
with Welsh and English (and Romani), has softened, if he
has not entirely disappeared. But the memory lingers in
the Gypsy mind. In the same way the Irishmen of Liverpool have softened considerably since the days of Dr.
Sampson's Shelta explorations, but their reputation is not
altogether dead.

To-day an Irish tinker, as opposed to an Irish tramp, is
a rarity on the roads of England, and almost a rarity in
Wales. I have known only one, and he only in his old age, a
mellowed, humorous, generous man. I am, therefore, not
at all qualified to write about Irish tinkers and, maybe,
James was a different fellow when the blood was hot in his
veins. I can write of him only as I have found him, kindly
and courteous. Mind you, I am not saying he has not his
faults. It depends how you look on these things. His
language is not always fit for a drawing-room ; indeed it
has shocked more than one English tramp into silence. He
has, in fact, the largest store of round, mighty and extraordinary oaths that I have ever heard, a command of the
picturesque in swearing that must, I am sure, be un-
rivalled in the British Isles. Yes, but he has, too, a
magnificent command of the traditional tales of Irish folk-
lore, a great love of poetry, and the soul of a poet. He
plays the fiddle divinely. He has never, I am sure, stolen
money or clothes or personal property. But he is an
inveterate and highly skilled poacher. He does not, how-

ever, poach to sell. He regards that as a low form of crime. He poaches to eat : not for James the paying of butchers' or fishmongers' bills. And he poaches only when he must eat (which is, of course, regularly !) and then only sufficient for his needs. He does this—not from any altruistic reason—but solely because it takes less time and is therefore less risky. He does not poach for sport.

His equipment is simple : a catapult, a very long whip with a very short handle, a net or two, a pair of highly trained dogs and his hands. He hardly ever sets a snare, though he knows how to as well as any man : snares take time to fill, and James likes to be quick. The reason for his success, of course, is his uncanny knowledge of the ways of birds and animals. He knows more about the ways of the wild creatures of the countryside than any other man I have known, and far, far more than any gamekeeper I have met. But then he has lived all his life in the open, cheek by jowl, day and night, with the wild creatures of the countryside, and he is a naturally observant man with a great love for birds and animals.

I have described in an earlier book how I have seen him bring down a roosting pheasant with his long whip, and so silently that he has a moment later got the next on the roost by the same method. That is a feat requiring great knowledge not only of how to use a whip but of woodcraft. It is no easy job to approach roosting pheasants without disturbing them, or disturbing something that will disturb them. And I have seen him take a hare in its form with his bare hands, just walk up to it in broad daylight. It may sound easy or incredible : it depends upon how much you know of the way of hares. I should have said it was impossible had I not seen it done. James assures me that it is easy, and I now know how to do it (more or less !), but I am not going to put temptation in your way. I have also seen him take rabbits with his catapult—by no means an easy feat for a crack shot—but his catapult is reserved as a rule for birds, and his method for rabbits and hares is the net and his dogs.

His dogs are trained to a pitch I have not yet encountered in any other dogs anywhere, though I have heard rumours of a Dorset farm labourer who, if the jade does not lie, has a better pair. The dogs are a pure-bred greyhound and a greyhound x collie. They seem to know exactly what their master means by every word and every gesture, and they know exactly what to do when the night's work is over. They never accompany him home, and they always return home separately and by devious routes. I understand that the Dorset man can get his dogs to meet him at a given spot, and though this may sound incredible I do not believe that it is beyond the ability of a good trainer with intelligent dogs. James's dogs are not up to that standard, but they are not fools. They know better than to follow at master's heels. They know exactly what to do should a policeman or a gamekeeper appear : they vanish—but they will be waiting in hedge or ditch further along the road. Nor does James ever talk to them. His orders are given by signs and occasionally by whistle, but as often as not the dogs know what is required of them and have no need of orders. And they know better than to follow master home : the night's work finished the three separate, each finding its own way home. These dogs are much, much more intelligent and much better and steadier than the best of Field Trial Champions, and I have watched most of the Field Trial Champions of the last ten years or so.

Taking rabbits with a net and the aid of two intelligent dogs is an easy business, particularly if you do not want many rabbits. And rabbits are easy things to conceal ; a man can carry four, two down each trouser leg, one in front of the leg and one behind, and swing along without an appreciable sign of his additional burden. Taking hares with just two dogs, a net and a man is an altogether different business. The net is fixed at the gateway to the field and the man stands by to do the necessary so soon as the animal is in the net. The difficulty comes in training the dogs to turn the hare into the net, for hares are conservative animals and have their own exits and entrances to the fields they live in. This means that there must be some reconnaissance beforehand to find the hare's way in and way out. It is the way out that matters—hares will invariably leave a field if they have their own way by the same exit, but they are not so particular about the way of their return as a rule. It might seem that the obvious thing to do is to net this exit, and this is done when the exit is in a good place for the man's own getaway. But the occasions on which it is are remarkably few—the exit is usually in a corner, and a corner is an awkward place to be caught in. So the net is set at the gate. Then one dog is placed at the hare's exit (where he will wait patiently, knowing full well what he has to do) and the other dog is taken round the field to the side opposite the exit and as nearly as possible at the furthermost extremity consistent with this from the gate. The man then returns to the gate and when he is ready gives a low whistle. The dog at the exit remains steady, but the other enters the field and puts up the hare. The hare goes for its exit, finds it barred, turns and is instantly between two fires and it does not take two good dogs long to turn it into the gate. Here another difficult point arises, for it is not easy to train two excited dogs not to follow the hare into the net and kill it. The man must do the killing : it saves the net. James's dogs are adept at this business, and James kills a hare with remarkable speed and efficiency, generally before it has time to utter a scream. This, too, is important, for the scream of a hare carries a long way on a still night.

There have been many famous Gypsy fishermen, and Welsh Gypsies, in particular, have earned great renown both as anglers and takers of fish by less conventional methods. It was James, however, who taught me how to take fish from the streams without aid of rod and line, with the hands alone. A nefarious business I admit, but an exciting one. He had two methods, one for use at night and one for use in daylight. At night you use a torch. A torch shining into the water at night seems to have a fatal fascination for fish. You put the light right down to the water, holding the torch in your left hand. In due course, and generally very soon, a fish will come up to have a look at the light and will hang in the water, almost standing on its tail, as close to the light as it can get. You use your right hand as a scoop, coming úp under the fish in one quick movement. I have seen five sizeable fish taken from the water in as many minutes by this method. It is as easy as that—after a great deal of practice. The daylight method is known in England as " tickling," but by Arigho as guddling. I do not consider James to be a real expert at this very difficult science (it is quite as difficult as catching an educated Test trout on a fly !), for I have seen the real experts, the men who work the hill streams of Wales and the burns and becks of the Border, but he is a very passable imitation of an expert and he does not go without fish when he wants fish for supper.

You must always start guddling at the downstream end of the water you intend to work. The reason for this is that if you startle your fish and fail to take it, it will be off downstream in a flash, frightening all the other fish and ruining your chances for the day. Having selected your water you must next locate your trout. You do this by finding some likely stone and feeling under it for the fish. Once you know your water it is easy to find fish, for there are favourite lies, and if you take a fish from one you can be quite certain that there will be another fish in the same place on the following day, and if you take that one, another the day after. Having found your fish you rub your fingers gently along its tummy. The first touch of your hand on the fish is the most dangerous moment, more often than not it is at the first touch that you lose the fish. Once you have started to rub you are fairly safe, for fish for some unknown reason seem to like having their tummies rubbed (it is not only trout that do : I practised on golden orfe in a garden pond), and if you are not clumsy or too quick you should get the fish. You work your hand gradually up its body with your thumb and forefinger on each side until you have reached the point where you can thrust thumb and forefinger into the gills. That accomplished the fish cannot escape and you lift it out and kill it. You can, of course, lift the fish out of the water without doing this gill business if the fish is small and you do not want to hurt it. I have lifted many a golden orfe so. But, as you will not be guddling for fun but for food (and, of course, I hope you will not be guddling at all, for I am at heart a law-abiding citizen), it is better to take no chances and to go for his gills. I have experienced many thrills in my lifetime, but there is no thrill to compare with that which comes when first your hand touches a big trout under a stone.

Gypsy crafts are getting fewer with every passing year. Mass production has almost extinguished the Gypsy basket makers, beehive makers and tinsmiths. There is little point in having a kettle repaired when Woolworths or Timothy Whites will produce a new one for as little or less money. So, too, with the beehive makers and the basket makers. The wandering tinsmith, the tinker, is part of Gypsy history, going back pretty well as far as the Gypsy race. The craft of the tinsmith can truly be called a Gypsy craft. But beehive-making and basket-making, in Britain at any rate, are not truly Gypsy crafts. They are British rural crafts that have been adopted by Gypsies. I do not know if there is a single Gypsy beehive-maker left in Britain to-day, though in Charles Kingsley's time several families of them (Lees, Smiths, and Gregories) used to camp on Hartford-bridge Flats in the neighbourhood of Eversley, and Levi Carey and his family used to pursue this craft well into the second decade of the present century. A few Gypsy basket-makers still survive, but they are disappearing fast, and so for that matter is basket-making as a British rural craft. I do not know any Gypsy basket-maker well, and I know very little about Gypsy basket-making, but I do not think that any Gypsy basket-maker has ever equalled in skill either of construction or design the work of British rural craftsmen. Certainly I have never seen a Gypsy basket to compare with the work turned out by the basket-makers of Deerhurst or Thame or Micheldever or Burley. I do not think that Gypsy basket-makers have ever evolved a design of their own, and even their very considerable knowledge of natural dyes is not Romani knowledge, but the old folk knowledge of the English countryside now largely forgotten by country folk. Even the word commonly used by Gypsy basket-makers for rushes, " junkers," is not a Gypsy word but a distortion of the Latin *Juncus*, a rush : it is not even a Gypsy distortion, for it is the word commonly used by the older Hampshire and Gloucestershire farm labourers.   No, basket-making is not a true Gypsy craft, but one of the old village crafts adopted by certain Gypsies.   Like most of our village craft it is almost extinct, and it is, therefore, the greater pity that it is also dying out among Gypsies.

I have blamed mass-production for the extinction of these individual crafts.   I should have blamed mass-production and the internal combustion engine. Before the Industrial Revolution, which brought a wholesale migration of rural craftsmen into urban factories, basket-making was a whole-time occupation in many English villages : a whole-time occupation because it involved not only the manufacture of baskets, but the ownership or tenancy of withy or osier beds, their cultivation (a specialised and technical job), and the cutting, sorting, stacking and so forth of the rods, jobs which also required specialised knowledge.   I believe that at Deerhurst, where a few baskets are still made (though basket-making is now no more than a spare-time occupation), one or two of the villagers still own osier beds, but if this is so the old specialised cultivation has certainly not been maintained.   There is, unfortunately, no reason why it should be.

Mass-production sounded the death-knell of rural craftsmanship, but it was the internal combustion engine which drove the nails into its coffin.   There can be no craftsmanship without apprenticeship.   The internal combustion

engine effectively killed apprenticeship, already sorely
wounded by mass-production. The internal combustion
engine has been described as the greatest invention of
modern times. Undoubtedly it is, for it has done more to
alter the mode of life of *homo sapiens* than any other invention in history. But greatest is not synonymous with best.
The good that has been accomplished by the internal combustion engine has been far outweighed by the evil, and
this is particularly true of the countryside. So between the
two great gods of modern life, mass-production and the
internal combustion engine, the countryside and the
country crafts have been squashed to death. It is a
matter of opinion whether or no the towns have been
improved.

Basket-making, as I have tried to indicate, was a highly
specialised job, requiring technical knowledge of quite a
number of things beyond the actual manufacture. The
first and all-important condition of any craft is a complete
understanding of the materials that are to be used. Now,
there are some thirty-five different sorts of osiers suitable
for basket-making and there are, in addition, a good many
rushes suitable for weaving, and there are—or at any rate
there were—a great many different sorts of baskets for
which there was a steady demand : fruit baskets, errand
boy baskets, coal and wood baskets, travelling hampers,
wicker pots, publican's bottles, chaff baskets, lobster pots,
eel traps, various sorts of bird traps and so on. All that
was not learnt in a day or a year. It was, in fact, a profession to which a boy was apprenticed and in which he
remained for the course of his working life. And it was a
profession which demanded, particularly, a fixed abode,
for the osier beds which were its life-blood needed constant
care and attention, having their cycles which must be
observed. You do not see cultivated osier beds in Britain
nowadays, or very few, and for just the same reason, the
decline of woodwork generally, of hurdles and besoms and
so forth, the cultivation of birch, hazel and alder woods has
declined or ceased. It is for this reason that basket-making

is not truly a Gypsy craft. Spending a lifetime in one place, cultivating seduously one small patch of osier bed, learning all the different forms of osier and the uses to which they can be put, these things are quite foreign to the nature of the Gypsy. He is a nomad : he must move. Basket-making is, in essence, a sedentary craft. So the Gypsy basket-makers have been, in the main, itinerant handymen, excellent copyists, but not true craftsmen. Yet, even so, they hold—the few of them that are left—the remnants of a great English tradition and the last vestiges of one branch of English rural lore. The many years in which we have put quantity and cheapness before quality and durability have killed most of the English rural crafts. If it is difficult to find a basket-maker nowadays, it is almost equally difficult to find a good thatcher, or stone-roofer, or bodger. Yet the demand has not entirely ceased. It is true there is not the demand there once was for good baskets. Almost anything will do nowadays : look at any shopping crowd, and you will find the women carrying every sort of mass-produced monstrosity. But there is still some small demand for good work and this is met by the few surviving basket-makers. For, let there be no mistake about this, the Gypsy basket-maker, even though he cannot be called a craftsman in the full sense of the word, is an artist, usually in love with his job quite apart from regarding it as one of several means of livelihood, and does go to great pains to produce really good work. Inevitably he suffers in comparison with the sedentary craftsman in that he must pick up his material where and how he can, instead of cultivating his own over a lifetime ; inevitably he suffers in that basket-making, though it may be his main, is not his sole means of livelihood, but in comparison with most of the stuff to be seen about to-day the work he produces is excellent indeed.

Probably the Gypsy basket-maker is doomed to extinction like the Gypsy tinker and beehive maker. Yet in England there will always be sensible people who prefer quality to quantity, and for them there will always be men to produce. The Gypsy, volatile and shiftless as he is, is yet tenacious. The rural craftsman may be doomed, but the Gypsy will remain, and in him will remain also some, a faint shadow perhaps, but yet some of the old traditional lore and skill of rural England.

Happily one of the oldest of Gypsy crafts is still going strong, in southern England anyway. This is the making of clothes-pegs. The Gypsy still makes better clothes-pegs than anybody else, and he still makes them in just the same way as his forefathers did many years ago. Walter Raymond, in his *English Country Life*, describes a visit he made about 1905 to a family of Gypsy peg-makers encamped in Somerset in the neighbourhood of the Quantock Hills. His book was originally published in 1910 by T. N. Foulis, and a memorial edition was published in 1934 by J. M. Dent and Sons. I have the permission of Messrs. Dent to quote from the chapter on the Gypsy peg-maker in the 1910 edition. The occasion on which it was written is sufficiently long ago to make comparison with modern practice valuable.

When Raymond came on the camp it was late in the evening. It was a small camp : no waggon, just a high two-wheeled cart and two small tents, " neither covering a much greater space than an old-fashioned gig umbrella." At the time of Raymond's arrival only a man was in the camp and he made the author welcome at the fire. " The man sat down on the opposite side. Beside him was a heap of biscuit tins and canisters of all sorts and sizes, and with a pair of long pincers he held them in the fire, melted the solder, and burnt off the paper labels, spread them abroad, and then with a handful of moss and earth, polished the flattened metal.

" ' I suppose you ask at the houses for the empty tins ? '

" ' Most often at the shops. We sell more clothes-pegs in towns to the shops. There is no call for them in the villages. They don't use many there. . . . They've got all they want. Pegs last for years. Besides they dry more on the hedgerows than they do on the line. But take a town now, with gardens shut in by walls—they must have a line there. But then they don't want when we call. They buy at the shops there."

" ' What do you charge for them ? '

" ' A shilling a gross to the shops.'

" ' How long does it take to make a gross ? '

" ' Three gross a day is good work,' said he ; ' but we are up before all the stars are in.' "

Raymond's Gypsy speaks English rather too well perhaps, but what he said then holds good to-day. Gypsies still get most of their tins from the shops (though rubbish tips are by no means neglected) and the method of treating them is just the same, even to the polishing of them with a handful of moss and earth. You can clean old tins—and knives, too, for that matter—better that way than you can with a rag. And still Gypsies sell rather to the shops than to the houses, and in towns rather than in villages. Furthermore, the output is just about the same to-day as it was forty years ago. Three gross in the day was good work then ; a good peg-maker to-day will make about four dozen an hour. Forty-eight pegs an hour makes peg-making sound easy. And, if you should watch a good peg-maker at work (like all experts he will not appear to be hurrying at all), it looks easy enough. But if you try it—and I have—you will find that it is not at all easy.

Raymond noticed in front of one of the tents a stick that had been driven into the ground. It was about 2 inches in diameter and stood about 1 foot high. The Gypsy noticed his interest.

" ' That's to cut off the clothes-pegs on,' said he. He sat down on a bag, which I think was to serve as a mattress, drew a sheath knife, took a willow wand already peeled, and measured the length by means of a piece of hazel cut half through at the right distance and split down to the cut. Then he hammered the knife through the willow, using the stake as a block. He chucked the little 5-inch

piece upon a heap of hundreds of others which he had cut
off during the day. ' But they must be dry, and there has
been no sun to-day,' said he.

"However, to show me he hammered on the little ring
of biscuit tin which prevents the split from going too far
under pressure of a clothes-line. Here was the article
complete."

The system is still the same. The tools have not altered.
A peg-maker needs very few tools—a pair of pincers, a
hammer, a stake and a knife and some nails to hold the
strip of tin fast to the peg. One nail per peg is generally
sufficient (the more nails you have the greater the risk of
splitting the wood), but some peg-makers do not use nails
at all, merely twisting the ends of the tin strip tight by
means of the pliers. The stake—it is called a stale, a stool,
a block, and a table in different parts of the country—is
made from any bit of sound wood, though beech is
probably the most popular, and is generally about a foot
high, since that is the most comfortable height for a man
sitting down. All peg-makers work sitting down. It is,
they maintain, essential to good peg-making to be comfortable. The knife, too, can be any sort of knife. Raymond's Gypsy used a sheath knife, many use old table
knives cut down to half their length and sharpened to a
degree unknown in unmutilated table knives, and some
use ordinary boy-scout folding knives. The one essential
thing is that the knife should be sharp. This is for peeling
the wands, and I think that this operation (the first in the
whole process) is the most difficult for the gorgio to master.
Most of us are right-handed, and it is our instinct to hold
the knife in the right hand and to move it against the wood
which we would hold for preference in our left hand. The
Gypsy peg-maker always holds the knife in his left hand,
and moves the wood against the knife. He does not move
the knife, and he does not move the wood up and down
against the knife, but round and round. That is the secret
of stripping the willows—all really good pegs are made of
willow—and it is by no means an easy one to master.

Indeed, only one factor in the craft of peg-making has changed since Raymond wrote—the price. The Gypsy now gets, or should get, threepence to fourpence a dozen instead of a shilling a gross, which is better—though still not very much—for a trade that is purely a summer trade, since the wood must be dry.

Peg-making is not necessarily a one-man job. Nearly always it is, I think, the man who makes the pegs and the woman who takes them with her when she goes *bikk'ning*, and certainly the man never hawks them. But I know one south country family who all combine in the making of pegs. It is an industry with them, and they have reduced it to a fine art in which each member of the family is a specialist, a cog in one great peg-making machine.

The family consists of Mavky and his wife Orlenda (I have not always in this book used the correct names of living Gypsies, for obvious reasons. Mavky, however, is the correct name of this man. It is a name I have never come across anywhere else, either among Gypsies or gorgie, here or abroad. I think it must be Mafeking, misheard by the parents), his son Daniel and his daughter Alice, his brother Isaac and his wife Miranda and their daughter Defiance. Mavky would sit at the head of the line and round off the sticks. He is the quickest man at this job that I have ever seen, the stick twirling round almost as if it was machine driven and the bark coming off in nice curling strips. Next to him sits his wife with a stake between her outstretched legs, a peg knife in her left hand and a hammer in her right. She sits on the right hand of her husband, picks up his sticks with her left hand (which also holds the knife), places them on the stake and with one sharp blow of her hammer chops them into neat and uncannily accurate 5-inch lengths. (I once measured fifty consecutive choppings done by her. Thirty-nine measured exactly 5 inches, six were just over 5 inches, but not $5\frac{1}{4}$ inches, five were just under 5 inches but over $4\frac{3}{4}$ inches.) Next to her sits Daniel, armed with a pair of pliers and a pile of strips of tin. He binds the peg, using no nails and working at a pace which, though it cannot keep pace with his mother, is quick enough not to cause a time-lag in the line. Nex to him sits Alice—the most silent Gypsy girl I ever met—who picks up the bound pegs and splits each one as neatly as maybe and almost without looking. (Alice's great interest in life is not peg-making, but birds. She knows birds intimately, and wild birds seem to come to her instinctively.) Next to Alice sits Miranda, who shapes the bottom of each peg with some quick cuts before passing it on to her husband, who puts the finishing touches to the job by making the inside bevels. As he drops the pegs, his daughter Defiance, aged nine, picks them up and ties them in bundles of a dozen, arranging them neatly in big hawking baskets. The order of peg making in this family has always been the same whenever I have watched it, but Mavky tells me that it is often altered, that every member of the family, except little Defiance, can undertake any of the jobs. The output is relatively enormous. Much of it is hawked from door to door by Orlenda, Miranda and Alice (though Alice is not good at hawking because she will not talk enough), but at least three big shops take large quantities from time to time, paying threepence a dozen. "A bloody price," says Mavky, "but it's safe, if you understand me, brother."

Another feature of Gypsy life that has been greatly stressed from time to time is the *patteran*, properly the *patrin*. Borrow, of course, brought it to the knowledge of the general public, and the word caught on. It has been over-romanticised by many writers on Gypsies, and it has been astonishingly mis-used by some novelists. In a recent novel by a well-known writer the word has been used to indicate Gypsy talk, presumably the Romani language, the author being apparently under the impression that it is the word from which we get the stage term " patter " ! The *patrin* is, of course, the sign left on the road by Gypsies to indicate which way they have taken. It may be a few leaves, or a stick or two, or a handful of grass, but it is arranged in such a way as to leave a perfectly clear message for those that follow after. The most common form is a cross, thus †, the long arm pointing the way taken. The *patrin* is common to Gypsies all over the world, but has naturally undergone certain local or national developments. In England to-day it is not, I think, much used, certainly to nothing like the same extent as it used to be, and I do not know that there has been much local development away from the ordinary, except among south country Gypsies, and particularly those of Hampshire and the New Forest. Here, development at one time attained an extraordinary degree, and though this has not been maintained at the full it is still very much more complex than anywhere else in Britain. Here, for example, bent sticks are used to indicate travellers on foot, straight sticks to indicate travellers with vans. These sticks are placed a little way from the directional signs. Then branched twigs, or a sprig of heather, or a spray of gorse is laid down to indicate a family with children, and so on. The Gypsy is an extremely observant person and an expert at what is usually termed woodcraft. The *patrin* thus means much more to him than it would to a gorgio. The Gypsy coming upon these signs will know more or less when they were put down and knowing roughly how fast people travel will know pretty well how far ahead his friends are and where he is likely to meet them. At the same time the *patrin* of these New Forest and Hampshire Gypsies varies very much from family to family, so that some of the information contained in the signs is possible of interpretation only by members of the family. All the same, the various family patrins do get fairly well known. When with Amos Churen I have more than once come across *patrins* by the wayside, and he has stopped and examined them and then said : " Dey is Patemans," or Lees or Barneys or Stanleys as the case may be.

Similarly, Gypsies read signs in hedgerows and field and lane, or in an evacuated camp, which we would pass over as being of no significance. One of the main essentials when *pooving* the *grai*—that is putting a horse, without having first obtained permission of the farmer, into a field to graze at night—is to be certain that there is no stock already in the field. It is waste of time walking all over a field in the dark, for you might do so and yet miss stock in it. But if you have not already reconnoitred the ground in daylight you must walk round the field to make sure that there are no gaps in the hedges and that there is only the one gate (for obvious reasons fields with good gates leading on to a lane or a road are to be preferred to any others), and while you are doing this (never walk along a hedge in the dark, that is most unwise ; always walk a yard or so out into the field) you look out for dung. If there are, or have been, horses in the field you will not have to walk far before you find some. Horses are most particular where they excrete and usually choose the borders of the ground they graze. Moreover, a horse will not graze around his droppings, so the grass will be longer there. Cows are not so particular, and you may have to search a while longer for their droppings. A study of the weather during the day, however, will help. Cows always come into the lee of a hedge if it is raining, and generally, but not always, graze into the wind. When you have found the dung, you examine it. If it is warm you have no need to give the field further consideration. But it may be cold and yet fresh enough for the field to be occupied. Fresh dung—that is dung dropped within the last hour or so—crumbles in a certain way.

So, too, examination of an evacuated camp will tell you a lot about the people who have left it. The ashes will tell you within a few hours when they left : the state of the grass how many people were in the camp : the area covered, how they travelled. The position of tents will give you a pretty fair indication of the composition of the party. And all this, coupled with a look at the first *patrin* left by them, will give you almost as much information about them as you can want.

Roadside signs are not, of course, confined to Gypsies. The tramps of the English roads, like the tramps of America, use signs and are very fond of chalk marks on the gate-posts of houses. These marks tell the next man along the road almost all he wants or needs to know about the inhabitants of the house. I, too, have found out quite a lot about some of my neighbours from the signs I have found from time to time on their gate-posts. Tramps also use signs to indicate the way. I found the tramps' camp near Market Harborough and the one near Four Marks in Hampshire by following their signs in the hedges. Tramps have their own lingo, too. It is a queer mixture of back slang, rhyming slang, cant, and Shakespearian English, with a word or two of Romani and Shelta inserted every now and then. In the years immediately before the war a new and most undesirable type was invading the roads of Britain—the young women who " rode the lorries." They, too, had a lingo of their own, compounded of all the usual elements, together with lorry slang and Americanese from the films. I have not had the opportunity of learning it, but what I did pick up was certainly colourful.

Tramps often look filthy. If they travel the workhouses —and most tramps travel round and round the workhouses in a very restricted area—they are pretty clean, for work-houses are particular and thorough. Gypsies also look dirty more often than not, but those that I have known have been most particular about their personal cleanliness. Appearances are deceptive. The clothes are old and shabby, and this, coupled with a dark or weatherbeaten appearance, a lithe walk, flashing eyes and a suggestion of swagger, has given the Gypsy a reputation for roughness and toughness. That the Gypsy is tough I would not for one moment deny. He is certainly not rough. I have found them a gentle and naturally courteous people. They are very highly strung, and easily roused to anger : they are apt to fight when so roused (and when drunk very apt to fight), but the fire dies down as quickly as it is born. They do not like the gorgio (and they have reasons for their

dislike), but if they take to you they are astonishingly
friendly and amazingly loyal and generous. If they do not
take to you they are the most unapproachable people on
earth. They have an all-abiding love of children. Gypsy
children are the happiest (and most spoilt) children in the
world. They are very kind to their animals. They have
other characteristics too. They cheat, beg, steal—but I
do not think they steal more than gorgios, and major crime
is almost unknown among them. But no Gypsy has ever
attempted to steal from me. They lie as readily, more
readily, than they tell the truth. They are an unstable
people, living entirely for the moment. But many of their
faults are due to persecution—there is much persecution of
them in England, the land of the free, for Gypsies do not
make good bureaucrats—and I, personally, have not
found them any worse than many a gorgio and very much
better than some. They have their good points and their
bad. They are, in fact, very much as you and me—but they
are also foreigners.

Are they dying out in Britain ? Borrow thought so a
hundred years ago, and Leland thought so fifty years ago.
I think not. They have changed since Borrow's day, since
Leland's day, and they will change yet more. But they are,
I think, very firmly established and very vital. They have
in the past fifty years received a considerable influx of new
blood from foreign Gypsies (the arrival of foreign Gypsies
in this country is usually noticed, but their departure is very
rarely recorded, and many remain and are absorbed) and
they have shown themselves extremely adaptable. The
great revolution that has occurred in Britain in the last
hundred years—the enclosures, the spread of industrialisa-
tion, mass production, the motor car—these things, if any,
should have destroyed the British Gypsies. They have not.
The brief prosperity enjoyed by the Romani race in
Britain in the last century did them untold harm. Modern
conditions, industrialism and the sixpenny bazaar have
destroyed that prosperity, have reduced the Gypsies again
to poverty, and at the same time have saved them. There

cannot be the slightest doubt that tents and ponies, not living-waggons and a team of piebalds, are the true possessions of the Gypsies. The further they get away from them, the quicker they lose the characteristics of their race. Modern conditions are forcing them to return to the old, their true, way of life.

XI

VALEDICTORY

Looking back, I think that there can be no doubt that the most important date in the recent history of the Gypsies of Britain, perhaps the most important date in all their long history in this country, was the day in November 1947 when the Report of the New Forest Committee was published. The Committee was appointed in April 1946 " to investigate the state and condition of the New Forest and, having due regard to existing rights and interests, to recommend such measures as they consider desirable and necessary for adjusting the Forest to modern requirements". During the course of their investigations they visited the Gypsy compounds and, in their Report, commented upon them.

The compound system was started in 1926. Under this system seven areas were set aside where Gypsies could camp without hindrance or interference so long as they obeyed the by-laws. There was no restriction on movement between one area and another. Prior to 1926 Gypsies used to camp in small family groups anywhere in the Forest. They were not supposed to stay in the same place for more than forty-eight hours. Most understood the law well enough and would move on at the right intervals, near enough, travelling a regular circuit. You would know, pretty well to the day, when Joseph and Lavinia Cooper would turn up on the outskirts of Burley. Give or take a couple of days, it would be just about six weeks from their previous visit. Two days later they would be gone; leaving no trace of their presence, save only the small black patch that had been their camp-fire. There was then little or no harassment by the police.

After the institution of the compound system in 1926 all this changed. It was not the Gypsies or the police who had changed, but rather the climate. No one seems

to know why the compound system was instituted. No
one seems to know why it was thought necessary to interfere
with a minority way of life which had been part of the
New Forest scene for some four hundred years. Certainly
there was no incident, no accumulation of incidents, to
which one can attribute it. And certainly there was no
general outcry by the residents in the Forest against the
Gypsies and their ways, as seems to be widely believed.
I do not recall any general hostility to the Gypsies—which
is not to say that they were widely loved—and certainly
no New Forest pub would refuse to serve one. Now, almost
four decades later, I have heard it said that the Gypsies
brought it on themselves by leaving litter around, and by
their thieving ways. I have no recollection of Gypsy litter
and I can find no mention of it in any of the many books
about the New Forest written prior to 1926. (The litter
then, as now, was left by visitors at holiday times.) As to
their thieving ways, it is true there were losses. There
was some poaching, and holly was taken at Christmas time,
and daffodils at the time of their flowering. Occasionally
a chicken disappeared and invariably it was the Gypsy
who was blamed, never a fox. But these things had always
occurred and no one hitherto had thought of putting the
Gypsies into compounds because of them.

Now there was a change of climate. For the first time
there was a lack of understanding of the Gypsy way of life,
a complete lack of sympathy with it. Not among the
Commoners for they had lived with Gypsies on their door-
steps for generations, knew all about them and how to deal
with them, accepted them as part of the Forest way of life.
And not among the old-established gentry of the Forest
nor among the old-established villagers and tradesmen:
these, too, knew all about the Gypsies and how to deal with
them. But among a new type which settled in the New
Forest after the end of the First World War: the newly
wealthy. These were townspeople, wholly urban or
suburban in outlook. To them it was an affront that a
group of men and women, with no visible means of support,

should be able to wander freely in the Forest, to camp freely, while they had had to pay hard cash for the privilege of living there. And probably there was also a feeling that Gypsies let the " tone " of the place down. Be that as it may the newcomers did not approve and they were wealthy. Money talks loudly in Britain. Into the compounds went the Gypsies.

An official system came into being, which had to be observed. Gypsies could camp in any of the seven areas set aside for them and could stay within any of these areas for as long as they wished. They could move freely from area to area. What they could not do was camp outside the areas. So long as the Gypsies remained within their areas no one would interfere with them. And, since it was no more than a day's journey from one compound to another, there was no reason for them ever to camp outside a compound and, therefore, no reason why they should ever suffer harassment. To the urban bureaucratic mind this was a most reasonable arrangement, one to which no one, surely, could raise any objection. And, indeed, at the time, no doubt it was genuinely thought that the compound system would not interfere with the Gypsy way of life and would confer a benefit upon them by ensuring that, no matter how much some people might object to their presence, no one could harass them so long as they observed the by-laws.

In practice, the compound system interfered with the rhythm of the Gypsy way of life, which was nomadic. Sleeping in a compound, going out for the day and returning at night, is not the same thing at all. It interfered in another way as well. The Gypsy is the least gregarious of people. His is the family as opposed to the community way of life. It is only on special occasions—such as Appleby Fair, to take the best known example—that Gypsies gather together. Then they will be delighted to see old friends, to exchange gossip and news, to trade, to make merry. But for the rest of the time, the family group keeps to itself. The compound system put an end to that and led, rapidly, to bickering and trouble between families.

Even more important, the compound system did not allow for making a living in the age-old manner. In the 1920s, the old Gypsy crafts—those of tinsmith, china-mender, knife-grinder, clothes-peg maker, basket-weaver—still flourished and the women could still combine selling at the door with begging and dukkering. These are all individual skills. Their profitable exploitation depends upon confidence built up between Gypsy and client and, from their very nature, a reasonable interval between visits. Hence, the regular circuit. If a knife or scissors, or when at the end of the season garden shears or the lawn-mower needed sharpening, one got into the habit of saying " Ned Shevlin will be round shortly " and putting the tool on one side to await his coming, knowing from experience that he would do a very good job on the spot for a modest fee. In addition to his private clients Ned Shevlin worked for a couple of the local ironmongers. Many a resident in the territory he travelled, who would never have dreamed of entrusting his tools to a Gypsy, preferring to take them to the local ironmonger for " professional " attention, nevertheless had them sharpened by Ned Shevlin. Almost all the business of the Lees, who were peg-makers, was done with shops. Indeed, they had contracts with two shops in Bournemouth. Jem Stanley, a horse-dealer, also travelled a large territory—well into Dorset on the one hand, up to Winchester on the other—but the size of this territory was at least partly due to the fact that he had a great reputation as a horse-doctor. There were, indeed, farmers who would pass word for Stanley rather than go to their local vet. And of course the women, travelling with their husbands, lost no opportunity for hawking and fortune-telling, so helping to maintain the family.

The compound system at the outset brought all this to a halt. It was no longer possible for the Gypsy to maintain his regular circuit and so his business suffered. Ned Shevlin, for example, having to return to a compound each

night, simply could not get round in the normal way and
often had not the time to do the job properly. He would
not collect tools and take them to a compound to do the
work there; nor would the Lees make pegs in a compound.
It is unlikely that either ever tried. They knew that there
would be too much interference from other Gypsies and
their children: offering to help or criticising or just wanting
to gossip. Faced with the compound system, some packed
up and moved out of the New Forest altogether. Joseph
and Lavinia Cooper went off into mid-Dorset and the
Barneys to the Winchester area. Jem Stanley bought a
smallholding on the very frontier of the Forest and, with
this as base, continued to travel much as usual. Most of
the rest settled down to make the best of things, gradually
stretching the law. It was not too difficult, they found, to
camp away from the compounds and avoid detection.
And there can be no doubt that the police, who knew
most of the Gypsies very well from pre-compound days
when they had given little or no trouble, often turned a
blind eye. Be that as it may, ten years after the institution
of the compound system the compounds were being used
by the Gypsies as a matter of convenience rather than of
necessity and there were a number of Gypsy families camping in the Forest. So long as they did not make their presence too obvious, so long as they did not camp in full view
of the public, no one seemed to mind very much.

During the Second World War the New Forest Gypsies
were rounded up and put into five compounds. No one
who knew the Forest and the situation would deny that
this was necessary. Quite apart from the aerodromes the
New Forest was used for many purposes during the war
and it simply was not feasible to have the Gypsies wandering about. But it is very doubtful if anyone anticipated
that the five compounds would be maintained after the
war. Most people in the Forest, when the compounds
were filled, took it for granted that when the war was over
the position so far as the Gypsies were concerned would
return to the immediate pre-war situation. Few realised

then that a harsher, less tolerant, world was to be born of the Second World War.

These five compounds were visited by the three gentlemen who formed the New Forest Committee of 1947 and this is what they had to say:

> " While the standard of living throughout the country is steadily being raised, a group is allowed to live in the Forest which has hardly reached the standard of the Stone Age. The gypsies, it is true, have not been heard in their own defence, but we have visited their camps and we should hesitate to describe them in detail. Even the picturesque element which appeals to the imagination of their defenders is here entirely lacking. Whatever may have been the case in earlier times, those of today show little of the true Romany strain and a very few only maintain the old Romany way of life with its comparatively high standards. "

I have quoted that passage many many times. Whenever I read it my gorge rises.

I beg you to read it again. It is not what one expects to find in a Government White Paper. British Government White Papers have an enviable reputation for thoroughness and impartiality. At least so far as the Gypsies are concerned, this one is evidence of a shameful departure from the normal high standard.

" The gypsies, it is true, have not been heard in their own defence. " That is a shocking sentence to find in a Government White Paper. It is not just that the Gypsies were given no chance to speak. It is not just that nobody was called upon to speak for them. What is peculiarly shocking is the use of the words " in their own defence. " Immediately, everything is slanted against the Gypsies. They are guilty of something: they are on trial. They are guilty of living in appalling conditions: and one is given the impression that it is their own fault that they are doing so. No mention is made in the passage quoted that the Gypsies were herded into the compounds. And you have to read the Report very carefully to discover that the compounds either had no water at all or a wholly inadequate supply, and that no sanitary arrangements whatsoever were provided. Of course, the conditions were appalling: how could they be otherwise. But nowhere in this Report will you find any blame attached to the authorities.

And then, consider the next sentence: " Even the picturesque element which appeals to the imagination of their defenders is here entirely lacking." One could hardly expect to find the picturesque in a small compound with no water and no sanitation! But, of course, the purpose of this sentence is to dismiss those with some knowledge of Gypsies, those who have some contact with them on a friendly basis, as romantic sentimentalists unworthy to give evidence before the Committee. Now, there were some with knowledge of Gypsies in the neighbourhood. Augustus John, a great authority, lived on the frontier of the Forest within the boundaries of the Ringwood and Fordingbridge Rural District Council, a Council which joined with the New Forest Rural District Council in submitting a memorandum on the subject to the Minister of Health. No one who knew John could possibly have called him a sentimentalist, and those who know his portraits of Gypsies will agree that he saw something more than the picturesque. Of course, it must be remembered that he would have made a somewhat disturbing witness: he could be very blunt of speech. I myself gave evidence to the Committee on another aspect of Forest life. Though the members of the Committee must have been aware of my interest in Gypsies, they did not avail themselves of the opportunity of my presence. I was not asked any questions about them. I suppose that I was dismissed as a biased sentimentalist, one bemused by the picturesque.

But, much more important, people whose work brought them into contact with Gypsies were not called upon. In the memorandum submitted by the Rural District Councils to the Minister of Health you will find this.

" The parents of children attending the elementary schools resent the fact that their children have to be in close contact with the gypsy children. Their influence is bad, even when their numbers are small in comparison to other children, and in one school the number of gypsy children roughly equals or exceeds the number of other children attending that school.

Notwithstanding any educationist's theory on the subject, the mixing of these children in their present state is very much resented by the parents of other children."

Note the curt dismissal of the educationist; the patronising use of the word " theory ". It is only the parents of other children who have their feet on the ground. (Yet it would seem that these parents have little or no faith in their own children. It is never suggested that their influence might be to the good!) The point about schooling and Gypsy children is also made in the main Report of the Committee: " The gypsy children have to go to school and in some cases may outnumber the children of the local inhabitants." This is a good deal less precise than the Memorandum attached to the Report: " in some cases " rather than " in one school "—less easy to lay a finger on and at the same time rather more disturbing. One is somehow, with no figures mentioned, given the impression of large numbers upsetting the balance. To put the record straight: the total Gypsy population in the Forest at the time was 411—men, women, and children living in the five compounds.

However, let us return to the witnesses one would have expected to be called to speak but who were not. We have just read how the presence of Gypsy children in village schools was greatly resented by the parents of other children. On so problematic a subject one would expect to find at least one of those most closely concerned, a schoolteacher for instance, giving evidence before the Committee. At the end of their Report the Committee

publish a list of the witnesses who appeared before them.
There is no village schoolteacher among them. It would
not have been difficult to find two schoolteachers at any
rate, with personal experience of Gypsy children in their
classes, who would have been pleased to speak up for them.
Their absence forces one to the conclusion that nobody
wanted to listen to those who were prepared to speak up
for the Gypsies.

Now, as I have said, there were 411 people in the five
compounds. Not all, as a matter of fact, were Gypsies.
Some were townspeople with no drop of Gypsy blood in
their veins, who had been bombed out of Southampton,
among them a Hindu girl. But do not let us quibble about
race. So far as officialdom was concerned (which after
all, was all that mattered), those in the compounds were
Gypsies and a dangerous problem for the rest of the Forest.

And what should be the solution to this problem? Let
me quote from the Report of the Committee again:

> " The simple solution is to remove all the gypsies as
> soon as possible to some place at least five miles distant
> from the perambulation of the Forest. This was advoca-
> ted by all the witnesses who spoke on the subject, though
> they feared that so drastic a measure might not be
> practicable. With this we must reluctantly agree, but
> we remain of the opinon that the Forest compounds can
> no longer be tolerated."

" This was advocated by all the witnesses who spoke on the
subject." We are not told who they were. And, as we
have seen, those who might have put in a word for the
Gypsies were not given the opportunity to do so. What
officialdom would dearly have liked to do was to push the
Gypsies on to some other Local Authority but, of course,
it knew that no other Local Authority would have stood
for that. So, despite the Committee's opinion, the compounds remained. What is so remarkable about this
Report is that there was never any suggestion that the
Gypsies should be allowed to resume their ancient custom

of camping where they wished on the open Forest. There was never any realisation that the solitary camp of a Gypsy family, moved every forty-eight hours, constituted no danger, was more sanitary, and infinitely healthier in every way than the compound.

All this happened almost thirty years ago. The position now, at least so far as Gypsies in England and Wales are concerned, is entirely different. It may well be asked, therefore, why I should devote so much space to this Report now, when so much has happened since it was published. I do so because almost everything that has happened since, again so far as Gypsies in England and Wales are concerned, stems directly, though now the route may sometimes be a little fudged by the passage of time, from this Report of the New Forest Committee 1947.

This was the first Government-sponsored Report for a great many years to have mentioned Gypsies and the first in which it was made abundantly plain that officialdom regarded them as a serious problem, even as a latent menace to society. It was the first Report which adopted a hostile attitude and made no attempt to conceal the fact. " Villages near the compounds," says the Committee, " suffer something more than inconvenience from these undesirable neighbours." What do you do with undesirable neighbours, who are incapable of defending themselves? You get rid of them, if you possibly can. The Report, though it may well have done so unwittingly, set the tone for officialdom for years to come.

But it also did something else. It aroused interest in the compounds. But for that colourful phrase about the Stone Age, the compounds would have remained unknown beyond the Forest and to many within it. But the Press could not resist the Stone Age. Pretty well every national Daily, and most of the leading provincials, quoted from the Stone Age passage. Before the publication of the Report many, indeed most, of the middle-class residents in the Forest had no idea that the compounds were there. Most of them, in all probability, would never have known, because few, if any, would have bothered to buy and read the Report. Government White Papers do not make compulsive reading. But they did read their newspapers. As a result some went to see for themselves, and, in a few of those, conscience stirred.

The effect of the 1947 Report, therefore, reached far beyond the Forest. In June of the following year I had lunch with Tom Williams, then Minister of Agriculture and Fisheries, at his invitation. We had enjoyed—I, at least, had greatly enjoyed—a friendly acquaintance over a considerable number of years and, particularly during the early years of my editorship of *The Field*, had often had a chat over a snack. But he was not then a Minister. Ministers rarely have time for social luncheons with the editors of glossy magazines, so I was considerably surprised (and honoured) to be invited and more surprised still to find that I was his only guest. He wanted to know about Gypsies. We had never talked about them before, but invariably about those aspects of country life with which the editor of *The Field* is expected to be familiar, and I had no idea that he knew that I knew anything about Gypsies or was even interested in them. Of course, he knew about the compounds in the New Forest. He could not help but know, since, as Minister of Agriculture and Fisheries, it was to him that the Report of the New Forest Committee had been presented by the then Chairman of the Forestry Commission, Lord Robinson. But not once, during the course of that luncheon, was there so much as a mention of them. His shrewd searching questions, for this turned out to be more an interrogation than a conversation, were all concerned with Gypsies as people—as poor people. Tom Williams himself had started life as a coal-miner and knew well what poverty and hardship mean to those who suffer them. Though the compounds were never mentioned, I am sure that he was genuinely disturbed that there should be people in such a plight. But, of course, there was nothing that he could do about it at that time. He was a member of a reforming Government—there were those who called it a revolutionary Government and in the best sense it was just that—and times were still very difficult with the aftermath of war and the problems posed by shortages of every kind. Of these problems the plight of the Gypsies was, in Ministerial eyes, one of the least pressing. So, in the immediate post-war years, they were ignored at the highest level.

Nevertheless, there they were, and their presence was increasingly made known to more and more people. The problems they posed might not yet be acknowledged by Central Government, but they could not be ignored by Local Government. Furthermore, again largely due to that colourful phrase about the Stone Age, Gypsies were now, as never before, news: always good for a paragraph in the Local Press and sometimes, when all else failed, even in the National Press. And, since the news item was almost invariably concerned with some incident involving Gypsies and Local Authority in which the Gypsies inevitably came off the worse, it often proved an embarrassment to the Local Authority because it tended to arouse sympathy for the Gypsies.

In fact, of course, it was not the Gypsies that posed the problems. No Gypsy had the slightest idea that he him-self was making difficulties. For the most part he was completely bewildered by events. All he was trying to do was to live as his fathers had lived, and as he had been taught to live when a small boy. He just did not under-stand what was happening. Nor, for that matter, did anyone else. What was happening was that the pattern of life everywhere in the world was changing. And by far the most important feature of this changing pattern was speed. In the last resort it has been speed that, in England, has wrecked the Gypsy way of life.

But this was not immediately apparent: at least, it was not immediately apparent to me. In the early post-war years, I saw no reason why the Gypsy should not continue to lead a reasonably carefree nomadic life. In the intro-duction to the original edition of this book I wrote: " The

Gypsy, despite the unremitting attentions of the police, is still free. You know real freedom, real liberty, the moment you put foot on the road with the men and women who live on the road, the moment you sit, legs a-dangle, on the foot-board of a waggon, a good horse in front of you and fortune-knows-what around the corner." That was written from personal experience gained between the wars. I could see no reason why, after 1945, the Gypsy should not resume that way of life. There were still horses, there were still green lanes and by-ways, there were still fortunes to be told and pegs to be hawked. Of course, the police would chivvy. But that was part of the price you paid and, in my experience, it had not, generally speaking, been too high a price. So I took it more or less for granted that the old way of living would be resumed. And by a great many Gypsies it was. But the tempo was different. Of course, everyone knew that the war had changed the world and that the process of change would continue. But I do not believe that anyone foresaw the speed with which it would occur. Certainly, even as late as 1950, I did not appreciate how greatly conditions had altered. I was, I admit, living in cloud-cuckooland.

One day, after lunch at my Club, Hugh Dalton, then Minister of Town and Country Planning, who had been lunching with another member, came and sat down beside me. I knew him by sight, of course, but I was more than a little taken aback to find that he knew who I was. (I found out afterwards that he did not: he had asked a fellow member, and then said that he would prefer to introduce himself—a wily old boy.) He started to talk about Gypsies: and we had quite a long conversation. Well, as had been the case with Tom Williams, it was not so much a conversation as an interrogation; Dalton asking the questions. And, though it was almost immediately apparent that he knew absolutely nothing about Gypsies, the questions were shrewd and probing. He was seeking information—which he could have obtained from plenty of people (and no doubt did)—but I think that he must

also have wanted opinion: anyway, he got it. Towards
the end he asked if I thought that an enquiry into conditions of life for Gypsies would be helpful. Thinking of
Gypsies as nomads (which was the natural thing for me to
do in those days) I said that I thought that any sort of
official enquiry into Gypsies and their way of life would be
the very last thing they would want. But I added that
I thought that an enquiry into conditions for Gypsies
living in compounds was long overdue. I was, of course,
thinking of the compounds in the New Forest. He made
no comment. Indeed, I do not recall that he made a single
original contribution to what he would, no doubt, have
described as a conversation. And when he went away, I
was left wondering what on earth it had all been in aid of.
I had not realised at the time, for *Hansard* has never formed
part of my daily reading, that he was already being pressed
by Norman Dodds, then the Member for Dartford (later
the Member for Erith and Crayford, when the Dartford
constituency was carved up), for an enquiry into a particularly large, and locally very unpopular, Gypsy camp in
his constituency. I neither heard from nor set eyes on
Dalton again. But later I was asked if I would be prepared to assist in a survey of the Gypsies of Kent, which
was to be undertaken by the Kent County Council at the
request of the Minister of Town and Country Planning.
Naturally, I said that I would; and later I had a meeting
with Mr. Adams, who was organising the survey. Unfortunately, for a variety of reasons, I was able to attend
only one meeting at Maidstone. But that occasion was to
open my eyes in no uncertain fashion.

As a result, I visited Corkes Meadow several times. It
was the conditions in this Gypsy settlement which so disturbed Norman Dodds and started him on the crusade
which was to end only with his death in 1965. The conditions on Corkes Meadow were truly appalling, but essentially they were no worse, indeed basically they were rather
better, than those in the New Forest compounds. It
should always be remembered that Corkes Meadow was

not a State-owned compound into which unfortunates
were herded willy-nilly: the owner of Corkes Meadow was,
in fact, doing a kindness in providing a place for unfortunate people when no one else gave them a thought; a
kind thought, at anyrate. It was the numbers in the settlement that made Corkes Meadow so dreadful; that, and
the situation of the site itself. At least, the New Forest
compounds were in the New Forest: there was clean air
around, there were trees to look at and birds to listen to
and, if you were clever enough and had dogs fast enough,
maybe even a deer to poach every now and again. But
Corkes Meadow was over-powered by a gas-holder and,
if it was not a rubbish tip itself, it was not far off one: and
all around were the brick dwellings of the fortunate, and
the cold hostility of their inhabitants. It was the urban
situation, the harsh contrast between dwelling and dump,
that made Corkes Meadow so terrible.

Before I went to Corkes Meadow I had been told, and
indeed had read in a National newspaper, that it was a
Gypsy encampment. Of course, it was nothing of the
sort. I do not claim to have met everyone living on Corkes
Meadow, but I met very few Romanies and I doubt if I
missed any. There were a good many other travellers,
but there were also, as in the New Forest compounds, some
of the flotsam of war, the bombed out and the dispossessed.
All these were lumped together as " Gypsies " in the public
mind. I make the point now, because it is important, and
will be returned to later.

Also as a result of that Maidstone meeting, I met a *poshrat* (half-blood) who, as is the case with the majority of
posh-rats, in my experience, was more Romani than the
Romani. Nat's father was a Romani horse-dealer: his
mother had been a domestic servant in a noble household,
her father the head keeper on the same estate. Nat himself was a singularly intelligent man, who still spoke some
inflected Romanes and who understood very well what
was happening to his people. Through him, in the course
of three or four visits, I met a number of Kentish Gypsies,

all still travelling or trying to travel. From each one I heard the same tale of harassment by the police, the same sorry saga of " move on ". More than one remarked on the difference from pre-war days. One old man, *tacho kalo* and a good Romanes speaker (unusual in southern England nowadays), said to me, so sadly that I shall never forget it: " It was quiet then, *prala*. The *gavvers* (policemen) knew me and the farmers knew me. I had friends." It was not until then that I really understood how intolerant England had become.

I do not think that there is a single explanation for this intolerance. One reason, undoubtedly, lies in the vast and rapid increase of the bureaucracy, with its passion for form filling and filing. Bureaucracy is by definition the enemy of non-conformity. But I am sure that the " march of progress " which, with the ending of the war, broke into a canter and soon into a headlong gallop, played its part. I do not believe that anyone, hand on heart, can honestly say that he foresaw the effect that this was to have on the lives and minds of men. We have seen some of the results—addiction to drugs, the increase in nervous disorders and mental instability due to the speed and pressure of life, vast unemployment and social unrest, the readier resort to violence—and no one can say where these trends will end. But of one thing there can be no doubt. The effect on the Gypsy way of life has been wholly disastrous.

One important aspect of the post-war march of progress has been the increase in the standard of living enjoyed by the " settled " population. I am convinced that this was one of the chief causes of intolerance, for it was accompanied by a petty sharp snobbery and by a grim determination to " keep up with the Joneses ", no matter what. Consider. In my childhood the country dwelling was lit by oil-lamp—gas was strictly for the towns—and personal transport was by horse-and-carriage, pony-and-trap, or bicycle. For that matter, my first home as a married man was lit by oil-lamps, had no running water—we drew from a well where, in summer, we kept the butter: it made an

excellent refrigerator—and no sanitation. We used an
earth closet. Now, this was not because we lived in the
country; miles from anywhere. The village was within
easy reach of a large town and only a mile off the turnpike.
It was simply because no public services came to the village: no main water, no main drainage, no gas, no electricity. And this was mid-way between the wars. It will
be realised that, so far as the basic amenities were concerned, our way of life was not so very different from that
of the Gypsies. In that respect, at least, no vast gulf
separated us. (If you have to draw your water from a well,
slowly, bucket after bucket, then heat it in a copper, then
transfer it to a bath, and afterwards bale out the bath, let
me assure you that you think twice before taking on the
task. Even after I had a hand-pump put in, and a drain
from the bath to a soak-away, it was still hard work;
twenty minutes pumping for a bath and, of course, you
then had to fill up the tank again, another twenty minutes;
so you were still inclined to give the question of having a
bath very careful consideration. In fact, I doubt if the
hand-pump made any difference to our bath rate.) This
is not to say that the Gypsies were liked by the village as
a whole. There was no mixing, though this was probably
as much by desire of the Gypsies as of the villagers. But
certainly the Gypsies were not regarded with contempt, as
inferior beings; on the contrary, their women were regarded by the majority of the village women with a certain
measure of awe, and certainly they were not regarded as a
dirty people. Later main water and gas reached the village
and, later still, " th'lectric." But this made no difference
to the general tolerant attitude of the village towards the
Gypsies: the old primitive, days were too close and well
remembered.

Now, I am sure that this was the general attitude of
country folk towards Gypsies in the years between the
wars. If you read Patrick McEvoy's *The Gorse and the
Briar*, which is about Wiltshire Gypsies in the thirties, you
cannot but come to the conclusion that life for Gypsies

then, if hard, was peaceful enough. There was not continual harassment. And that was broadly true of rural
England as a whole. The complaints about Gypsies and
the harassment of them by the police occurred for the most
part in the vicinity of towns. Towards the end of the
period, however, life was beginning to become much more
difficult for Gypsies in the vicinity of villages in the " stock-
broker belt " of south-east England, in Buckinghamshire
and Surrey. In other words the complaints, then, came
mainly from the well-to-do middle-class.

This became much more noticeable after the war. There
was a good deal more money about, a generally higher
standard of living. More professional and business men,
townsmen at heart, bought homes in the country or acquired week-end cottages. The commuter belt stretched ever
further out from the big cities and the towns reached out
to swallow up the villages in their immediate neighbourhood. (The village I have just been talking about has
been swallowed up by the town: it retains its name but has
lost its identity. It has also lost its Gypsies: none now
visits the neighbourhood.) This is progress, of course, and
one must not complain; must not mourn the loss of good
farmland. But what it amounts to is that in many parts of
the country, and year by year more greedily (especially
in southern and south-eastern England), suburbia absorbs
the villages within commuter range of the cities. And
with suburbia come surburban ways of life and values:
everything for the sake of smartness, a faith in appearances,
pretentiousness. The rural village becomes pseudo-rural.
And, in the place of the old rhythms, since the values are
urban rather than rural, there is speed: not merely as
manifested by the rush to get the breadwinner on to the
train in the morning, but also that engendered by competition: the speed necessary to keep up with the Joneses who
are moving ever faster (hire purchase assisted) to catch up
with the Smiths who are themselves moving pretty briskly
to keep up with someone or other. It is the face value that
matters, not the real value. And that is not the ethos

of the true village.   If a Gypsy family appears on the edge
of this sort of society, it is lowering the tone of the neighbourhood and at once a complaint is made to the police.
Invariably, the Gypsies are moved on, and kept moving.
And even the police are different.   No longer is it the
village gavver on a bike, the gavver who almost certainly
knew the Gypsies and, if he had to move them on, was
probably quite content just to see them round the corner.
Now, it is a couple of coppers in a car: not the same thing
at all.

Dominic Reeve's *Smoke in the Lanes* and *No Place Like
Home* show clearly, often painfully clearly, the effect of this
sort of harassment on those who experience it.   Born of
personal experience, these two books vividly describe
conditions during the decade immediately after the war.
They should be compared with Patrick McEvoy's *The
Gorse and the Briar*, also born of personal experience which,
as already mentioned, describes conditions during the
decade immediately preceding the war.   If anyone needs
proof that a harsher, less tolerant, England emerged after
1945, then these books, at least so far as Gypsies are concerned, provide it.

According to the survey, *Gypsies and Other Travellers*
undertaken in 1965 and 1966 by the Ministry of Housing
and Local Government and the Welsh Office, the most
common complaints against travelling folk were

" that unsightly scrap metal was littered wherever the
travellers camped, and that their domestic litter was
a danger to health; that they used the fields as lavatories
and were generally dirty; that they begged water from
householders and intimidated those not giving it readily;
that they littered the hedges with drying washing; that
they allowed their horses to destroy crops and were not
averse to stealing."

Except for the accusation that they allowed their horses to
destroy crops, these are, surely, the complaints of town-bred
people.   By way of contrast, here is what Ralph Wightman,

country-born and country-bred, generations of whose family have farmed the same land in Dorset, has to say. I quote, with permission, from his book *Abiding Things*:

" One class of people who know all the old rights of way are the gypsies. In the fenced lanes their horses pick a sparse living from the grass between the ruts and from the hedge banks. They very seldom do any real harm, and they are better than most campers as far as litter is concerned. The wood they take from the hedges is usually dead stuff for fires, although they may cut some useful hazel rods for making clothes-pegs. The gypsies' trade must have suffered a lot from modern progress. Plastic clothes-pegs are replacing wooden ones and washing machines with spin driers make any sort of peg unnecessary. Farmers need far less thatching spars now that combine harvesters have cut out corn-stacks, and plastic sheets are used instead of thatch. Potatoes are planted and lifted by machine. Sugar beet is placed accurately in lines and hand hoeing is reduced to a minimum. Even hops are stripped from the bines mechanically, and every year sees less need for the seasonal piece-work which kept the whole gypsy family employed from March until Christmas. I shall miss the sight of their fire in the twilight, with a very pleasant smell of stew and the incredible array of gaudy washing hanging on the bushes to dry. Somehow, I think they will last for my time. As long as there is a grassy lane there will be gypsy caravans, silent, lean dogs and shaggy horses. If hoof prints appear in the meadow overnight it might be true that those horses broke in accidentally. In any case it isn't worth getting up in the small hours to catch them; they will be back in the lane before dawn."

Of course, Wightman had often had dealings with Gypsies between the wars, and knew them well. And he belonged to a more tolerant age. But he was born on a farm, spent the greater part of his life in agricultual practice, almost the whole of it within a few hundred yards of this same farmhouse (he was the younger son and first his brother, and later his nephew, actually farmed the farm on which he was born) and he would not have taken a kindly view of anyone who did damage to farm crops or hedgerows. If any Gypsy had ever put a horse into crops on the Wightman farm, or any farm for that matter, his condemnation would have been pungently forthright. The fact, of course, is that no Gypsy would be such a blind fool as to allow a horse into crops.

" Not averse to stealing." This complaint—really, it is a smear rather than a complaint—is simply not supported by the facts. Statistics are available and some have been published. Serious thefts are unlikely to be the work of Gypsies or other travellers, but there is, of course, some petty thieving. It might, perhaps, be described as not uncommon: stealing daffodils from gardens, that sort of thing. But, as Dr. Howard, author of the *Report on Gypsies and Other Travellers in Hampshire*, has pointed out, they will not do this if they know the owner of the garden. Gypsies, in fact, have an astonishingly high reputation for honesty. In 1950 (when there was still a fairly large nomadic Gypsy population), of seventy police authorities who had Gypsies or other travellers in their areas, only twenty reported that they suspected them of criminal offences, all of which were petty thefts and poaching. The other fifty police authorities did not suspect the Gypsies or other travellers in their areas of any criminal offences. Of course, Gypsies poach. I do not know that they do any more poaching than the average farm labourer or working countryman. I do know that they are very skilful and that they never poach more than they need but merely to eat. They are much more humane, because much more knowledgeable, than the car poachers from the towns.

And so to the question of hedges littered with drying washing; does it not strike you as odd that a " generally dirty " people should do so much? Wightman admits that he would miss seeing it. Obviously, it never offended him,

country bred. The offence is to the suburban countryman,
to the woman who normally hangs her washing on a line
in full view of her neighbours and thinks nothing of it and
who, if she goes camping, happily dries her washing on
the bushes. The complaint would seem to come down to
this, that it is Gypsy washing, not nice suburban laundry.
With one notable exception—scrap metal, which will be
considered in greater detail later—the complaint basically
is always not of what the Gypsy does, but of what he is,
a nomad.   It is nomadism that is disliked.

But the all-out attack on the Gypsy way of life did not,
of course, spring solely from the complaints of those of the
settled population who were enjoying a higher standard of
living in new semi-rural surroundings. They might, and
many did, complain to the police of Gypsies in the neighbourhood, and those who did were delighted to see the
objects of their complaint moved on. But that, so far as
the settled population was concerned, was as far as it
went; they were contented so long as the Gypsies were
moved on. Nevertheless, particularly in southern and
south-eastern England, this complaining did help to
establish an atmosphere hostile to Gypsies. The actual
attack came from the Town Hall or from the Council
Offices. Undoubtedly, in certain areas, it was aided by
the hostile atmosphere engendered by the higher standard
of living. But that said, it must also be stated that, often,
it sprang from the best of motives.

In the New Forest, for example, the Ringwood and
Fordingbridge Rural District Council very early started
on a policy of resettlement, moving families from the compounds to council house accomodation. And the New
Forest Rural District Council soon followed suit. There
can be no doubt that a certain amount of pressure was
brought to bear on both Councils by those New Forest
residents who had visited the compounds and been horrified by the conditions, but it must be said that the majority
of councillors were just as horrified. At the same time,
there was some criticism from outside the Forest that the

people in the compounds were given no alternative. True, they were not given the choice of resuming a nomadic way of life. But, in fact, in the conditions that then prevailed this would not have been possible within the perambulation of the Forest; and it is certain that not one family in the compounds would have considered for one moment the possibility of a nomadic life outside its confines. It must be remembered that the Councils were dealing with a more or less captive community. They really were concerned to do their best for the Gypsies, and their chief aim was to get rid of the compounds as soon as possible. Anything, in their eyes, was better; and in this there can be no question but that they were right. Unfortunately, this sometimes meant that the happiness of those to be resettled became a secondary consideration. Sven Berlin, who knew the Shave Green compound very well indeed, has described it vividly in his book *Dromengro*, and has touched on the effect of resettlement on some of those involved. There can be no doubt that there was a good deal of unhappiness among some of the older people, who were wholly unsuited to house life. But there was not nearly so much as there might have been, because most of the really elderly, those who had known the old nomadic life in the golden years before the First World War, died before the compounds were finally eliminated. For the process of resettlement was a lengthy one, due in some measure to a good deal of administrative muddle at higher levels. But now there are no compounds and all their residents have apparently been resettled more or less satisfactorily. This was a difficult operation and, of course, it left wounds and soreness of spirit in some. But altogether, in the Forest, it was accomplished with a degree of humanity which, when one considers what happened in some parts of the country, was wholly admirable.

I do not intend to give a blow-by-blow version of what happened elsewhere in the country. Admirable accounts by Angus M. Fraser are available and these are listed in the bibliography. It is intriguing, if profitless, to wonder what might have happened had not the Labour Government's Ministry of Town and Country Planning been succeeded by the Conservative Government's Ministry of Housing and Local Government in 1951. Perhaps it was as a result of the change that the already mentioned survey requested by Hugh Dalton, *Gypsies and Other Travellers in Kent* by James W. R. Adams, was never published. Be that as it may: that it was not published was a great pity. It was an excellent and informative survey which would surely have been of value to County Councils and Local Authorities elsewhere. Another result of the change of Government was that the Minister of Housing and Local Government, then Harold Macmillan, was naturally less inclined to lend an ear to the pleadings and protestations of Norman Dodds, a member of the Opposition, and much less inclined to involve his Ministry in the Gypsy problem. And this, too, was a pity, for it initiated a long period of " passing the buck ", which did no one, least of all Gypsies and other travellers, any good. Local Authorities maintained that the problem was essentially a national one which could not be solved without Government intervention. The Ministry maintained that there was no national problem, but merely some minor local difficulties and that these were matters for the Local Authorities themselves. In this highly unsatisfactory situation those Local Authorities with a Gypsy problem reverted to the words of the Report of the New Forest Committee 1947—" the simple solution is to remove all the gypsies as soon as possible to some place . . . "—and tried to solve their problem by pushing it on to a neighbouring Authority, increasing the harassment of the Gypsies by turning them off their camping grounds and continually moving them on in the hope that they would go away and stay away. Of course, they did not, because they could not. The neighbouring Authority took good care to see to that.

If the situation for the Gypsies had been bad in the immediately post-war Attlee Government, with its emphasis on planning and control (which, of course, meant a huge increase in the bureaucracy), at least that Government, from the very nature of the soil from which it sprang, had sympathy with the poor and the oppressed. The very fact that Hugh Dalton initiated a pilot survey of Gypsies is evidence of that. The situation became much worse for the Gypsies when a Conservative Government was returned to power in 1951. I do not suggest that this was the result of a deliberate act of policy on the part of that Government. It was not. As I have said, the Conservatives made it plain that they had no intention of becoming involved with any Gypsy problem. But that policy of non-involvement was sufficient. There can be no questioning the fact that, because of it, the atmosphere became colder and harsher for the Gypsies.

From 1951 onwards much greater use was made of Acts of Parliament by Local Authorities with a Gypsy problem on their doorstep; of such Acts as the Commons Act 1899, the Public Health Act 1936, the Town and Country Planning Act 1947 and, later, the Highways Act 1959. I do not recall the Commons Act 1899 having being invoked against Gypsies by a Local Authority between the wars and I do not think—at any rate, I have been unable to find a record of such an event—that the Public Health Act 1936 was used against nomadic Gypsies up to the out-break of war in 1939. From 1951 onwards the Public Health Act 1936 and the Town and Country Planning Act 1947 (and I feel sure that this was not the deliberate intention of the framers of that Act) have been used on any number of occasions by different Local Authorities to prevent Gypsies from setting up camps or for turning them off already established camping grounds. And, if for some reason or other the Acts were not used, then the police would exercise " informal persuasion " and residents in the area would be encouraged to refuse Gypsies water.

As things got worse—and there were some very bad cases, *vide* Angus M. Fraser—the Press took more and more notice, and this publicity began to worry the Local Authorities concerned. From now on, time after time, we find a distinction being drawn by the Local Authority between the " true Romani " and the people being harassed. Always the implication was that the " true Romani " would be welcomed, but that the people being turned off or moved on, so far from being " true Romanies ", were a menace to health, to property, to the public amenities. We are back with the New Forest Committee 1947: " the true Romany strain . . . the old Romany way of life with its comparatively high standards." But the three gentlemen who formed that New Forest Committee had no more than book-knowledge of Romani characteristics. They are condemned by their own words when, speaking of the compounds, they say that the people living in them " show little of the true Romany strain." Priscilla Wells lived in the Shave Green compound, and in the whole of Britain it would have been difficult to find one with more of the Romani. However, remembering the conditions in the Shave Green compound, perhaps one should not blame the three for not recognising this. But I do not believe for one moment that any one of them would have recognised the " a true Romani " even under the best of conditions. And I feel fairly confident that the number of Local Authorities able to recognise one could be " counted on the fingers of one badly mutilated hand."

So let us consider for a moment the " true Romani." Normally, as I have already pointed out, with the exception of showmen and tramps, all travelling folk, whether on the road, or in encampments such as the New Forest compounds or Corkes Meadow, are lumped together as " Gypsies." It is only when the going begins to get a bit hot, when there are signs that public sympathy might swing, albeit ever so slightly, towards the harassed, that officialdom produces the " true Romani " story. In fact, of course, there are many different types of " traveller ": Romani, diddikai, mumper, pikie, tinker, and so on. It used not to be very difficult to distinguish between them—the village policeman of the twenties and thirties knew well enough which was which—and the distinctions are certainly still acknowledged by the travelling folk themselves, though by no means to the same extent as they were between the wars. The original edition of this book was about Romanies, about a people following a certain way of life and adhering to certain age-old customs, the " true Romani." I think that to-day " true Romani " is often taken to mean a person with none but Romani blood in his veins. There is no such person in Britain and there has not been for a very very long time; perhaps there never was. The Romani blood has always been mixed in some measure with that of the local gorgio population.

Even the " royal " family of Wood, the descendants of Abram Wood, had some Welsh blood in their veins. Inevitably, when you come to think of it. Abram Wood and his followers (and there were not many of them) were the first Gypsies to enter Wales and for many years they were cut off from all contact with other Gypsies. The astonishing thing was that there was so little marriage with the Welsh in the early days. But, of course, marriage with the Welsh did occur off and on throughout the years. There was fresh Welsh blood, not all that far back, in Manfri Wood, who died recently.

And then, consider the Wells family. One day before the war (it would have been about 1935) I was having a cup of tea with Priscilla Wells in her *vardo*, which was drawn up at one of her regular stopping places, off the gravel track at Puck Pits, in the New Forest. (In those days the Wells family had a regular beat round the Forest. Priscilla Wells had a fantastic knowledge of plants and did a really good trade in herbs and herbal medicines, which she prepared herself.) I forget now what we were talking about and why what occurred did occur, but I remember the incident as clearly as if it were yesterday. She said, in a far-away voice, more as though she was talking to herself than to me: " Once we wuz the highest in the land, my *Rai*. An' all dis," waving her hand at the Forest

around, " wuz Wells land, I tell'ee." It was a strange
thing to say. Walking back, down through Oakley
Inclosure towards my mother's home, and thinking about
it, the penny dropped. Priscilla Wells had experienced a
deep stirring of family memory; she had been recounting,
not quite accurately, an episode in English history. Charles
II inherited all the virtues (which were many) of the
Stuarts, but also all their vices. He had a hungry eye for
a pretty girl and he was also by far the most spendthrift of
all the Stuarts. One girl who caught his eye and captured
his fancy was named Frances Wells. We find her petition-
ing the King " to bestow upon her and her children for
twenty-one years the morefall trees in three walks of the
New Forest " and she also wanted seven or eight acres and
ten or twelve trees " wherewith to build her a house."
Charles referred this petition to the Lord Treasurer, who
strongly disapproved and wrote upon the margin: " I
conceive this an unfit way to gratify this petitioner." But
the following year we find one Winifred Wells granted for
her own use the King's Coppice at Fawley and New
Coppice and Iron's Hill Coppice at Brockenhurst. This
time the King ignored the Lord Treasurer and issued a
Royal Warrant on his own account. Here, surely, we have
the beginnings of the New Forest Gypsy family of Wells.
If only one could unravel it all, trace it all back to that
Frances Winifred Wells, what a fascinating story it would
make. For of its truth there can be no doubt. This was
not something Priscilla Wells learned from a book. She
was illiterate, as were all her family; as had been all her
family, we may be sure, for generations back. And we may
be sure, too, that she did not pick up this story from some
foot-loose scholar with an interest in the mistresses of the
Stuart Kings. This was family memory, family tradition,
handed down through the centuries.

So, there is no " true Romani " in the pure-blood sense.
(And, indeed, a High Court ruling of 1967 defined a Gypsy,
for legal purposes, as a person without fixed abode who
leads a nomadic life dwelling in tents or other shelters or

caravans or other vehicles; that is to say, a class of person
and not a member of a particular race.) But, if there is
no " true Romani " in the pure-blood sense, there is a
" true Romani " way of life, for I refuse to believe that it
is wholly dead and gone: as one might well believe if one
took all the complaints at their face value. For example,
that they use " the fields as lavatories." That conjures up
a nauseating picture. And I have no doubt that it is, too
often, a true picture. But read that extract from Ralph
Wightman's *Abiding Things* (which was published as
recently as 1962) again. There is no mention of the fields
or fenced lanes being used as lavatories. Of course, they
were so used—somewhere has to be used as a lavatory—
but there was no sign that they were so used. Wightman's
gypsies followed the " true Romani " way of life: they
buried their faeces.

Such a way of life, it must be remembered, was a leisurely one, allied to the horse-drawn *vardo* and the seasonal
rhythm of the countryside. It is the lorry that has made
the difference. Although there is still a " true Romani "
way of life, few people nowadays have a chance to notice
it. The trouble is that Local Authorities, while paying
lip-service to the " true Romani ", hinting that he would
always be welcome because of his high standards, take
good care to see to it that he is given no opportunity of
stopping long enough to prove that he is one. Now, it
is easy enough to blame the Local Authority for this—just
as it is all too easy to get starry-eyed about the virtues of
the " true Romani "—but the Local Authority often has
a great deal to put up with from its ratepayers, who are
quick to complain of " undesirable travellers"' The
" traveller " moves, or is moved, on; the ratepayer is
always there. So far as the Local Authority is concerned
the priority is obvious. And so, one after another, traditional stopping places have been closed down.

As might have been expected, it was in Kent, the first
county to carry out a survey of Gypsies within its borders,
that the first step was taken to try to find a solution to

what was becoming an increasingly explosive problem. So in 1959 the West Ashford Rural District Council took the historic step of providing a camping site for Gypsies. (In passing, it is worthy of note that, in general, Rural District Councils and Parish Councils have been more farsighted and adventurous in their approach to the Gypsy problem than have County Councils and infinitely more so than have Urban and Borough Councils. Ringwood and Fordingbridge Rural District Council and the New Forest Rural District Council were, I believe, the first Councils in Britain to undertake the resettlement of gypsies in council houses as part of a definite policy and it was the Hampshire Association of Parish Councils, not the Hampshire County Council, that commissioned Dr. Howard's *Report on Gypsies and Other Travellers in Hampshire*.) But to return to the West Ashford Rural District Council's pioneering step, it came about like this. Because of a number of complaints from local residents, the Local Authority decided to evict some Gypsies from Hothfield Common, a recognised beauty spot. Gypsies had been stopping on Hothfield Common for years past, though never in large numbers; not more than one or two families, one or two horse-drawn *vardos* at a time, and then only occasionally for a night, for forty-eight hours at most. During that time there had been no complaints, or none that had been deemed worthy of official action. But now there were more Gypsies, with lorries and caravans in place of horse-drawn *vardos*, and they stayed put. So the Council decided to evict them and to close the common to them in future. And then someone pointed out that because so many of the traditional stopping-places had been closed, those that were still open were filled and that these Gypsies really had nowhere else to go. Most Councils at that time, faced with a similar situation, would undoubtedly have said that that was no concern of theirs and would have carried on with the eviction. West Ashford Rural District Council, to their eternal credit, decided to offer the Gypsies an alternative site at a shallow, disused quarry about a mile from the village of Great Chart. In this quarry the Council proposed to accommodate twelve caravans. Kent County Council were approached and gladly gave planning permission for a period of seven years. But there was violent opposition from many of the residents of Great Chart and from landowners in the neighbourhood. So a two-day public enquiry was held at Ashford in December 1959. At this meeting it was argued on behalf of the objectors that this was a national problem and that the burden should be borne by the Government and not by the Local Authority. The Kent County Council's Planning Officer, on the other hand, warmly welcomed the proposal and suggested that it was a matter for shame that, since the pilot survey of 1951-2, the county had done nothing to help Gypsies and other travellers. Kent is a county which, like Yorkshire, commands a strong local patriotism and pride, and this remark obviously affected a lot of people. But it was the West Ashford Rural District Council's firm belief that the scheme they proposed might give a lead to the rest of the country that clinched it. Kent led with the first county survey of Gypsies and now Kent would lead with the first approved site. So the Minister of Housing and Local Government gave his consent in May 1960. The site was given main water, an ablutions block, a cesspool, hard standings and a lorry park. A rent was charged for each caravan and five shillings a week was charged for each lorry. One of the Gypsies was appointed resident warden to exercise overall control and was charged no rent in return. About a year later the Clerk of the West Ashford R. D. C. reported that, despite the original fears of the local residents, he had received no complaints about the conduct of the " travellers " (the word " gypsy " had been dropped) and that the rents had been paid promptly. If the village had a complaint, it concerned the number of Gypsy children in the village school; the Gypsy complaint concerned the pools of water which formed in the quarry in wet weather. But this was a grumble rather than a complaint. They knew they had been treated well and they were genuinely grateful. A number of other Local Authorities showed interest in the West Ashford experiment; among them the Eton Rural District Council. The Buckinghamshire County Council had previously shown themselves to be unsympathetic to the idea of providing sites for Gypsies, stating flatly that " the establishment of a site or sites would not serve any useful purpose " and suggesting that problems posed by gypsies were really a matter for the police. Eton R.D.C. having studied the West Ashford experiment, were convinced that a site provided and run by the Local Authority was the only logical answer. They, therefore, established a site for thirty-two families at Iver. This, too, despite local misgivings, proved to be a success.

Elsewhere things did not move so smoothly. In 1961 the North Mimms Ratepayers Association forced the abandonment of plans for a site for six families on the outskirts of North Mimms, on land offered by Lord Salisbury to the Barbara Cartland-Onslow Romany Fund. The aim of this Fund was to establish a number of small sites, each to accommodate not more than six caravans, in different parts of Hertfordshire, so that nomadic Gypsies might be able to move about the county knowing that they could stop at certain places without fear of harassment. It was thought that small sites would not arouse local hostility: particularly as they were to be transit sites. Permanent residence was not visualised. But the very idea that there might possibly be as many as six Gypsy families stopping in the neighbourhood from time to time proved altogether too much for the ultra-respectable residents of North Mimms. In this case the Local Authority was not involved, at least not officially. It was the Ratepayers Association that was offended. This was an example of local pressure at its most formidable.

But other, more insidious, and in their wider implications more sinister, forms of pressure were exercised as well. On December 1st of the same year, 1961, Gypsies who had been living in a disused gravel pit at Corfe

Mullen in Dorset, suddenly found the pit closed to them by the owner. The owner admitted that he had no quarrel with them. He said that they did not bother him and that they had caused no trouble locally. And, indeed, there seem to have been no local complaints about them. His reason for evicting them? That he was " fed up with the Police and County Council badgering me to move them."

Shortly before the Corfe Mullen episode, the Gypsy problem had been debated for some five hours in the House of Commons. This was the result of a fluke. Norman Dodds had been lucky in the ballot for the right to introduce a Private Member's motion, and he naturally seized upon the opportunity to bring the plight of Gypsies and other travellers before the House. He pleaded for a national census and survey of the Gypsy population and for Government leadership. Most of the back bench speakers supported this plea. But Mr. Geoffrey Rippon, then Joint Parliamentary Secretary to the Ministry of Housing and Local Government, rejected a census (because of the difficulties of identification!) and maintained that the Gypsy problem was primarily a matter for local action. At the same time he offered a ray of hope for those who believed that the Government should take a more active part: " We shall certainly play our part in the Ministry in trying to co-ordinate more effectively what the county councils and the local authorities are beginning to seek to do." That sentence merits careful study. It is a master-piece of equivocation.

This debate received much wider publicity in the National Press than is usually the case with Private Members' motions; and this did help to alert the public. For example, but for this debate, it is doubtful if the Corfe Mullen episode would have received any publicity at all. Nevertheless, the Gypsy problem, despite the efforts of Norman Dodds, would almost certainly have sunk back into obscurity, but for the Darenth Woods affair. About 300 Gypsies and other travellers lived in Darenth Woods, which was a Church property near Dartford in Kent. In 1961 the Church Commissioners sold Darenth Woods to Darenth Parish Council, which made no secret of the fact that it wanted the property for the express purpose of evicting the inhabitants; but before the sale, the Church Commissioners told the Parish Council that they wished prior arrangements to be made for the proper accommodation of the Gypsies elsewhere. None were made. After the sale, when eviction was imminent, the Commissioners, though they now had no legal standing, expressed the hope that no hasty action would be taken. In January 1962 the notices to quit were issued. On eviction day, as a gesture of solidarity, Norman Dodds moved into Darenth Woods. The Parish Council applied for a High Court injunction restraining him from trespass; but his action had some effect, for eviction was delayed for a while. But, on 20th January, the eviction order was enforced and the Gypsies were taken, by lorry, their caravans towed by tractors, to the verge of the A2, a mile or so away; and there they were dumped. As the Chairman of the Dartford Rural District Council Planning Committee said at the time: "Once we get them on the main road, they become the police's problem, not ours." That was all he cared about.

Four days before the eviction from Darenth Woods, Norman Dodds had a meeting with Dr. Charles Hill, then the Minister of Housing and Local Government, who undertook to urge Local Authorities to provide sites for Gypsies and other travellers where needed. I think there can be little doubt that the arrival of 300 gypsies from Darenth Woods on the verge of the A2, one of the busiest trunk roads in Britain, hastened the issue of the circular of 8th February 1962 (which is reprinted in full in *Gypsies and Other Travellers*) and also influenced its views, which are much more forthrightly expressed than is usual in Ministry circulars. But it must be admitted that, nationwide, this circular had but little effect. I think that it would be true to say that the majority of County Councils and Local Authorities had for long taken the view that what was needed was a national plan co-ordinated by the Government. This circular, in many ways a notable document, did not mention a national plan. In that respect it did not differ from the Government's previous attitude. What it did do was to urge Local Authorities to do something a bit more quickly than hitherto. In general, it may be said that Local Authorities were unimpressed. Indeed, of the sixty-two County Councils in England and Wales, thirty-nine decided that there was no need to do anything at all. A few of the remainder recognised that there was a need to establish sites for Gypsies, but found local feeling so hostile that they dared not proceed. The few already doing something found it impossible to move more quickly.

Yet, there were the Gypsies literally dumped on the verge of the A2. And most of them were there for months. So more and more people saw them there and felt sorry for them. Offers to accommodate varying numbers came from several landowners in different parts of Kent; but always there was local opposition, too strong to overcome. And, of course, these dumped Gypsies were not only living in appalling conditions—quite apart from everything else (or the lack of it), the noise must have been terrible—most of them were no longer able to earn a living, certainly not one sufficient to enable them to keep their families. After the eviction, the amount of National Assistance paid to these Gypsies had to be increased sevenfold. Then, too, the Ministry of Transport was involved, for this was a trunk road. The Ministry drew the attention of the Dartford Rural District Council to the dangers inherent in having a Gypsy encampment on the verge. The Council took no notice. There was nothing more the Ministry could do except take action against the Gypsies themselves; and it was evident that any action of that sort would arouse a storm of protest. So the Minister found himself powerless. In the House of Commons, Mr. John Hay, then Parliamentary Secretary to the Minister of Transport, admitted that it was a disgraceful situation,

but found himself unable to offer any suggestion for over-
coming it.

This left the ball firmly in the Kent County Council's
court. Now, as we have seen, the Kent County Council
had been most progressive and far-sighted in the matter of
the Gypsy problem generally. They had undertaken the
pilot survey; they had given their blessing to the West
Ashford experiment, which, at this time, was almost two
years old and proving a great success. And elsewhere in
the county a number of Councils had housed a considerable
number of Gypsies with so little fuss that most people did
not even know that it had happened. The Darenth Woods
affair was, therefore, a really bitter blow. The Kent
County Council faced up to the situation, realised that
sites had simply got to be found and undertook to meet the
net cost incurred by any District Council in setting up and
maintaining a site. This brought the offer of a derelict
gun site at Cobham from a local builder. Strood Rural
District Council refused planning permission for the
Cobham gun site, but shortly afterwards offered to establish a camp at Meopham for some of those stranded on the
verge of the A2. It was stressed, however, that it would
take some considerable time to prepare such a camp.
Meanwhile an appeal had been lodged against the refusal
of planning permission for the Cobham site. At the public
enquiry the Kent County Council Planning Officer supported the action of the Rural District Council in refusing
permission, but the Minister of Housing and Local Government overruled both Councils and granted permission for
the site to be used for two years by not more than fifty
caravans.

There can be no doubt that the very bad publicity that
the plight of the Gypsies on the verge of the A2 was getting
in the Press and elsewhere influenced the minister's
decision. The situation was deteriorating with the passage
of time and the need to remove the families was becoming
increasingly urgent; it seems probable that the somewhat
leisurely approach of the Strood Rural District Council

also helped him to decide. This was the first time that a
Minister had given a decision against a Local Authority
in a matter involving Gypsies. His ruling came as a
severe shock to the County Council and, indeed, to Councils everywhere, for the inference was obvious. If Local
Authorities did not bestir themselves, then the Minister
might well grant planning permission to private individuals
willing to provide sites on their own land, ignoring the
opinion of the Local Authority as to the suitability of the
site. This had happend at Cobham and the implication
was not lost on Local Authorities up and down the country. There was suddenly quite a bustle in Council Planning Offices, especially in the Home Counties where
awareness of the A2 crisis was at its sharpest.

The Ministry of Housing and Local Government, appre-
ciating this uneasiness, did its best to keep the pot sim-
mering, urging Councils to provide sites with all possible speed. The County Councils, and especially the
Kent County Council, were only too anxious to provide
sites. But whenever a District Council put forward plans
it came up against strong and well-organised opposition,
able to advance any number of reasons why the site in
question was unsuitable. It was too far from a school, it
was too near a village, it was too far from a police station,
and so on. In one case, in Kent, one of the grounds for
opposition was that the site was too close to game preserves!
Among the objectors on this occasion was Mr. John Wells,
Conservative M.P. for Maidstone, in whose constituency
the proposed site lay. In the same year (1963) Mr. Wells
introduced a short Bill in the House of Commons entitled
the Gipsy Camps (Compensation) Bill, the aim of which
was to " provide compensation for owners of property
near to gipsy camps provided or controlled by local authorities." Compensation for damage to land, buildings,
crops and other vegetation, chattels and livestock was
envisaged. When introducing his Bill, Mr. Wells said
that its purpose was to " enable local authorities to proceed
even more willingly and rapidly towards the establishment

of these important camps." The Bill got no further than its First Reading, and it is mentioned here only because it shows so clearly the prejudices with which Local Authorities had to contend when proposing a site for Gypsies.

Mr. Wells, you will notice, admitted that the camps were important. What he was trying to do, he suggested, was to help in their more rapid establishment. But read again the list of things for which compensation was envisaged in his Bill: damage to land, to buildings, to crops and so on. Can it seriously be supposed that such a list would aid a Local Authority in establishing a camp? Would you welcome such neighbours? Mr. Wells knew about the West Ashford Rural District Council's camp at Great Chart and he must have known that there had been no complaints about damage to land or buildings, crops or livestock, by the Gypsies. At the time when he introduced his Bill there was no Gypsy camp in his constituency, although a public enquiry into a proposed site at Marden was pending. Planning permission for this site was granted in May 1963. Whatever conclusions one draws from such facts, I think one can safely say this, that, viewing the Gypsy problem dispassionately, from a safe distance, almost everyone agrees that the continual moving-on policy is no solution and that the solution lies in small camps. But when it is suggested to these people that a camp should be established in their area, they immediately rise up in arms, outraged at the very idea that their neighbourhood should be so polluted.

And so, progress towards strategically sited camps was very, very slow. It could not be otherwise, for always there was opposition, particularly in the Home Counties, to every proposition. But it must be admitted that Local Authorities themselves also contributed in some measure to this slow rate of progress. It was in the mind of every one of them that, by establishing a camp, it might multiply its own problems by attracting Gypsies from other, less favoured, areas. I believe that this fear did cause the abandonment of one project in Kent. In fact, the likelihood of attracting Gypsies from distant parts was minimal.

From the point of view of the Gypsies, the Local Authoritiy camp could, and in those districts where such camps existed, usually did, add to the troubles of those Gypsies not in them. At the public enquiry into the West Ashford R.D.C.'s plan for a camp at Great Chart, counsel for the Rural District Council made the point that if the application for planning permission was granted it would enable the Council to move on other Gypsies with a clear, or at least a clearer, conscience. And certainly harassment by moving-on increased considerably at this time, though not, I believe, in the area under the control of West Ashford. The Highways Act 1959, especially Section 124, was increasingly used by some Authorities and the Caravan Sites and Control of Development Act 1960 proved a real boon to others.

This Act was born of an investigation by Sir Arton Wilson (commissioned by the Minister of Housing and Local Government in November 1958) into "the nature and extent of the problem which arises in connection with caravans used as residential accommodation." The need for this enquiry arose from the rapid growth of commercial caravan sites, the owners of which were thought by some to be taking (as some no doubt were) a pecuniary advantage of the housing shortage. It was never intended that Gypsies should be included in the investigation and this was later confirmed in the House of Commons, where it was stated that it was concerned with "caravan-living by ordinary people, rather then the special problem of gypsies and vagrants." The Caravan Sites and Development Act 1960 put an end to Section 269 of the Public Health Act 1936. Under the latter, licences could be granted either to the caravan-dweller or to the controller of the site; but under the new Act no land could be used as a caravan site unless the landowner held a licence from the Local Authority. However, no licence was required if the site was to be occupied by only one caravan for not more than two nights or if the site was to be used for the accommodation of agricultural or forestry workers for a season. The Act gave the Local Authorities somewhat wider powers of attaching conditions to the licence than had been the case under the Public Health Act 1936, but a licence could not be refused if the applicant had been granted planning permission under the Town and Country Planning Act 1947. (This was later consolidated with amendments in the Town and Country Planning Act 1962.) The 1960 Act also extended the powers of Local Authorities in two important respects: Section 23 gave Rural District Councils the power to prohibit caravans on commons, and Section 24 gave Local Authorities the right to provide caravan sites themselves and to acquire land compulsorily for that purpose. The latter was a very considerable extension of power, but it must be evaluated in the light of a comment by Sir Arnot Wilson in his report *Caravans as Homes*: " Local authorities in general disapprove of caravan-living in principle. It seems to them a backward step in the general march towards better housing and environmental welfare, and a threat to the success of their plans for the balanced development and use of the land avalable to the communities they serve." And in fact, over the country as a whole, Local Authorities made remarkably little use of the powers available to them under Section 24 of the Act.

The Caravan Sites Act 1968 made little or no difference to Gypsies. But when, largely owing to the insistence of Mr. Eric Lubbock (then the Liberal Member for Orpington and now Lord Avebury), Part 2 of the Act was at last brought into force in April 1970, the door to further progress was opened or, at least, left ajar. The main effect was to make it " the duty of every local authority being the council of a county, county borough or London borough to exercise their powers under section 24 of the Caravan Sites and Control of Development Act 1960 (provision of caravan sites) so far as may be necessary to provide

adequate accommodation for gipsies residing in or resorting to their area." Note the use of the word "duty."
This amounts to a directive. But Part 2 of the Act also
conferred new powers of prohibiting unauthorised camping and removing unlawful encampments. However, a
Local Authority is unable to use these new powers until
it has satisfied the Minister that all reasonable steps to
provide authorised sites have been taken. Since Section
24 confers the right of compulsory purchase for the express
purpose of providing sites, it did seem that there was no
loophole. A very little space of time was to prove that
assessment was over optimistic.

There are two more Acts which can affect gypsies: the
Scrap Metal Dealers Act 1964 and the Civic Amenities
Act 1967. The first of these is important, for it requires
that anyone wishing to deal in scrap metal must register
with the Local Authority in whose area he resides. It is
obvious that this presents the nomadic Gypsy scrap dealer
with considerable problems. So far as the civic Amenities
Act is concerned it is Section 19 which is important and
this, again, affects the Gypsy scrap dealer.

I think that we are now up to date with the law, with all
the various Acts which in one way or another affect the
lives and the future of the Gypsies of Britain. Repressive
legislation against them is nothing new; as we have seen,
it has a history, in this country, going back to the sixteenth
century. The important point about the legislation we
have just been considering is that it is not directed specific-
ally against Gypsies (though many of them certainly believe that it is), but was enacted for the benefit of the nation
as a whole. Nevertheless, it cannot be denied that four
Acts, the Public Health Act 1936, the Town and Country
Planning Act 1947 and 1962, the Highways Act 1959, and
the Caravan Sites and Control of Development Act 1960,
have all been used on occasions in recent years in a repressive manner to prevent Gypsies from following their
traditional way of life.

In these circumstances what is of overriding importance

is the manner in which these Acts are interpreted and the degree of rigidity with which they are enforced by the Local Authorities concerned. And this has varied enormously from Authority to Authority and from time to time, from year to year, as the political climate has changed. Even so, the really rural Authority has always been more sympathetic, and less rigid in its enforcement of the law, than the semi-rural and urban ones. This is to be expected of course for, as already pointed out, there is often a world of difference between the attitude of the countryman and that of the townsman towards Gypsies; and public opinion still carries some force locally. The sentimental attitude (which is usually slightly condescending) is wholly urban. No countryman is sentimental about Gypsies and I have yet to meet one who regards them, let alone treats them, with condescension. The most common attitude among countrymen is tolerant indifference, faintly tinged with disapproval. The most common urban attitude is disapproval, ranging from the inactive to the openly hostile.

This open hostility can sometimes take extreme forms. For example, on April 17th, 1964 there was broadcast on the BBC Home Service a programme entitled " Born at the Crossroads ". It lasted for an hour and it was absolutely first-rate. But the most significant part of the programme was, undoubtedly, an interview with an Alderman of an important Midland Town. This man called Gypsies " the maggots of society." Later he said " one has to exterminate the impossibles." A shocked interviewer asked him if he really meant " exterminate ". He replied " why not?" It is as well to remember that Aldermen are important people, influential in the Corporation of the town they serve.

Fortunately, not everyone in a position of authority or influence held such extreme views. Dorothy Strange's *Born on the Straw* is the true story of a Gypsy family travelling the Midlands at just about this time. This couple took care to keep to the rural areas as much as possible. By so doing they avoided the worst kinds of harassment.

Indeed, they had good friends among country folk and were welcomed on their seasonal appearances. It is quite obvious, making full allowance for the possibility that the author may have viewed their world through slightly rose-tinted spectacles, that they led a very happy, if hard, life. Dorothy Strange's book provides a valuable antidote to intolerance.

Nevertheless, the Alderman quoted did represent, in its worst and most extreme form, the definite hardening of attitude towards the Gypsies that became apparent, especially in the Home Counties and the industrial Midlands, at this time. And it has to be admitted that the Gypsies themselves were in no small measure to blame for this. But that said, it must also be said that this was not really the fault of the Gypsies themselves. It was the fault of the life that modern conditions forced them to lead.

The old ways of life were dead or dying. As Ralph Wightman has pointed out, no housewife now wants handmade wooden clothes-pegs. That ancient Gypsy craft is as dead as a doornail. And this is true of all their traditional skills: flower carving, chair mending, basket weaving and the like, as a means of earning a living, are all dead. Moreover, ten years ago Ralph Wightman drew attention to the decline in seasonal piece-work on the farms, which once kept the whole Gypsy family employed from March until Christmas. That decline has continued and, in recent years, at a rapidly accelerating pace. There is now comparatively little seasonal piece-work on the farms and in the orchards, and every year there is less and less. I should now be very surprised to find a Gypsy family which is wholly employed in agricultural piece-work for nine months of the year.

But the most important factor has been the disappearance of the horse. I do not know how many Gypsy families in Britain now use a horse-drawn *vardo* as their home. The Government survey of 1965-6 gave the figure as not more than 6 per cent of the total Gypsy population.

It is certainly very much less than that today. For, now, there is no place on the roads of Britain for horse-drawn traffic. Only in the more remote rural areas, away from large centres of population, are you at all likely to see a horse-drawn *vardo* on the move. And it is difficult for a Gypsy family to make a living in remote rural areas nowadays. Each year fewer attempt it. A few of the older generation cling desperately to the ways of their fathers; the young gravitate to the towns. So the horse has been replaced by the lorry; the *vardo* by the trailer caravan.

This may be regarded as progress and praiseworthy—the Gypsy entering the mechanical age, keeping pace with the times. And, in a sense, that is true. Certainly, that it should happen, is inevitable. But with the disappearance of the horse, a way of life and, more than that, a culture, disappeared.

The Gypsy and the horse have been inseparable for years, for hundreds of years. The horse, in fact, *was* the Gypsy way of life, for it dictated the speed of living. Indeed, it would not be too much to say that the life of the family revolved around the horses—there would usually be two or three—for they had to be fed and watered and generally cared for. Ultimately it was upon them that the family's welfare (using that word in its broadest sense) depended. The horse is a living thing and a bond develops between a man and his horse, just as it does between a man and his dog. The Gypsy took great pride in his animals and their ability, and equally in the external appearance of his *vardo* with its decorative carving and the paintwork; just as his wife took the greatest pride in the spotless cleanliness of the interior. It was the pride of the Gypsy to make his *vardo* look just that little bit different and to have good strong horses and well trained dogs. Life was hard, no doubt about that. But it was not all that expensive, once you knew your way around; and you learnt the ways around at a very early age. There was always grazing for the horses on the laneside verges, and maybe sometimes there would be a convenient field at night. And

those long dogs running by the *vardo*; well, they knew a
thing or two and could be trusted to keep quiet when
silence was essential.

The pride has gone with the horse. The Gypsy wife
keeps the interior of her trailer caravan spotlessly clean; but
the fact is that one trailer caravan looks very much like
another and just the same as all the gorgio ones. It is
easy enough to replace a trailer caravan, by buying another
one. It was never easy to replace a *vardo*; you could not
buy another one, just like that. So there is not quite the
same sense of permanence attached to the trailer caravan;
not quite the same sense of pride of home, that was the
special quality of the *vardo*. And the lorry cannot be
compared with the horse. I have yet to meet a Gypsy with
a fondness for his lorry. For that matter, I have yet to
meet one with pride in his lorry, which will certainly be
second-hand and will probably have known several owners.
Above all things the Gypsy is a realist. Why bother to
paint, why bother to clean up, an old lorry? It will be
going for scrap one day. And scrap is what the modern
Gypsy knows about; scrap metal is what the majority of
them deal in nowadays.

None of this is intended in any way to denigrate the
Gypsy. I have the greatest admiration for the way in
which he has adjusted to modern conditions. But it has
to be admitted that this adjustment has often been achieved
only at the cost of increased hostility on the part of the
gorgio population. Particularly has this been the case
where dealing in scrap metals has been concerned.

You will remember that one of the main causes of complaint of the Government survey 1965-6 was that " unsightly scrap metal was littered wherever the travellers
camped." And you will remember, too, that Ralph
Wightman made no mention of scrap metal littering the
fenced lanes of Dorset. But Wightman, writing only ten
years ago, was writing of the survivors of the old tradition.
His Gypsies travelled rural areas with horse-drawn *vardos*
and they did not deal in scrap metals. Before the war,

such dealing was not a Gypsy trade.   Even today there is
very little dealing in scrap metals by rural-based Gypsies.
To deal successfully (and some have been very successful
indeed) they must be near, preferably on the outskirts of,
a town.   The Gypsy can collect scrap from the villages by
lorry, but he can sell only to a scrap-metal merchant and
these are in the towns.   He must have somewhere to
store and sort his scrap before taking it to the merchant's
yard and so he uses a bit of waste land or a roadside verge.
And it has to be admitted that what he leaves behind—
the plastic, the shells of old cars, and so on—is very unsightly.   No one can blame the people who complain and
no one can blame the Local Authority, suffering those
complaints, for taking action.   Too often, however, this
action was taken not to remedy an offence that had already
occurred, but to prevent the possibility of an offence
occurring.

Many Authorities took action to prevent unauthorised
camping, using one or other of the Acts already mentioned.
In one case a Gypsy was fined a total of £313 plus costs for
parking his own two caravans on his own land (he owned
the freehold) for which planning permission had been
refused.   Gypsies simply do not understand this sort of
thing and are naturally bitter when it occurs.   By such
means the number of camping places available to Gypsies
were severely curtailed.   Again, in some areas, considerable use was made of the Scrap Metal Dealers Act 1964.
My friend, the late Professor Charles Duff, used to maintain that in Britain there was no persecution of gypsies,
only prejudice against them.   Prejudice is often the father
of persecution and in Britain, as the mechanical age over-
took the Gypsies, prejudice steadily increased.   Indeed,
in the decade from the mid-fifties to the mid-sixties, life
over large areas of the country was made more and more
difficult for them.

With the return of the Labour Government in 1964
came recognition that a national problem existed: something which successive Conservative Governments had

consistently refused to recognise. Shortly after taking office, the Minister of Housing and Local Government (Mr. Anthony Greenwood) and the Secretary of State for Wales (Mr. Cledwyn Hughes) inspired a survey of Gypsies. (So much for Mr. Geoffrey Rippon's " difficulty of identification "!) This was carried out during 1965 and 1966 by a Sociological Research Section of the Ministry of Housing and Local Government, and the Report published in 1967 under the title *Gypsies and Other Travellers*. The report broke new ground. It was the first attempt ever made, by a Government in this country, at a comprehensive study of Gypsy lives and problems. Of course, it had some shortcomings, only to be expected of a first attempt; and *Scotland's Travelling People*, published in 1971, derived some benefit from them. But it is a most important document. Even today, when some of its figures have naturally become out-of-date, it should be read and digested by everyone in any way concerned with Gypsies. And all should take particular note of the first paragraph of the foreword, which is signed by Anthony Greenwood and Cledwyn Hughes. I quote from it:

" The world around them has altered so rapidly that their roving life can no longer be carried on without hardship—indeed the report reminds us of the remarkable fact that for most of the traveller families there is nowhere they can legally put their home: they are within the law only when moving along the road."

That, to our shame, is still true.

However, the position is better in one respect: namely that the survey was made and the report published. At least, now, people in responsible positions cannot talk arrant nonsense without fear of contradiction. No one, of course, can prevent them from airing their prejudices.

Part 2 of the Caravan Sites Act 1968 imposed a duty on Local Authorities to provide adequate accommodation for gypsies residing in or resorting to their area. At the same time, you will recall, it gave Local Authorities new powers of prohibiting unauthorised camping and of removing caravans from unauthorised sites. These new powers have, naturally, been used. But, on the whole, they have been used with quite remarkable restraint; a restraint which, I fancy, might have been less evident but for the publication of *Gypsies and Other Travellers*. The duty has, naturally, been observed or, more correctly, is being observed; for these things, in this country, take time. In some districts there has been quite remarkable progress in providing authorised camping sites. But elsewhere everything has not gone quite as smoothly as the legislators had hoped and had every right to expect. For example in 1972, Surrey County Council, in the course of duty, but anxious at the same time not to offend local residents (the residents of the wealthier parts of Surrey being known to be touchy on such matters), chose an isolated place near Caterham for an authorised Gypsy site. Caterham and Warlingham Urban District Council thereupon took the County Council to court and succeeded in getting it fined £20 for breaking the law, namely, for opening a caravan site without a licence. Surrey County Council has the duty and the power, under the 1968 Act, to open a caravan site for Gypsies; but such a site still requires a licence which only the Urban District Council can issue. It would seem that an Urban District Council can prevent a County Council from doing its duty as laid down by Act of Parliament. This is a ridiculous situation from an administrative point of view. It is also a tragic one from the Gypsy point of view.

On the other hand, there has been a case of some Gypsy families leaving an authorised site (opened for them at a cost of £20,000) because they considered the facilities not good enough and the rent (£3.50 a week) too high. According to these Gypsies the surface of the site was not hard enough and electricity was not available for every caravan. (The site had only been opened a fortnight and the installation of electricity had not been completed.) So they left, apparently preferring to seek refuge on an unauthorised site on waste ground with no hard standings and no electricity at all and, moreover, to face almost certain eviction. Complaining about the rent is understandable, almost every tenant in Britain complains about his rent. But the rest is foolish, and potentially tragic. Above all else nowadays, the Gypsies need the sympathetic understanding of the gorgios among whom they live. This is certainly no way to gain it.

But episodes like these, an Urban District Council cocking a snook at its County Council, Gypsies leaving an authorised site provided at considerable public expense for some unconvincing reason, are no more than stumbles on the steady march forward. Forward to what? Well, if you consider the nature of the legislation I have outlined above, the Town and Country Planning Act, the Highways Act, the Caravan Sites Act, Part 2 (especially the prohibitive parts, which will surely be enforced once an adequate number of authorised sites have been established by the various Local Authorities), the Scrap Metal Dealers Act and so on, there can surely be no doubt. We are witnessing the march to the virtual elimination of nomadism in England and Wales. It will take some time yet; but the end is, I think, inevitable and in sight.

Let us consider the Scrap Metal Dealers Act 1964 in more detail. This requires that anyone dealing in scrap metal must register with the Local Authority in whose area he resides. As soon as a registered dealer moves his dwelling into the area of another Local Authority he ceases to be registered. Obviously, a man who has built up a connection, which is the key to success in all businesses of this sort, is not going to risk becoming unregistered. Obviously, the man of " no fixed abode," which is the official description applied to the nomad, Gypsy or vagrant, has not much of a chance. The competition in this business is severe, but the rewards can be great. At least three Gypsies, to my knowledge, have made fortunes out of scrap metal, so the incentive to stay put is all the greater.

This, the incentive to stay put, is true not only of dealing in scrap metal; it is true of life in general in an industrial

society. The material benefits to be derived from having
a fixed abode are enormous. For example, on an authorised site there will be sanitation, main water, a hard standing, and electricity. And electricity means the television.
And that is the trap from which no one escapes.

Some Local Authorities, out of the kindness of their
hearts, provide on their authorised sites one or two standings for nomadic Gypsies. Those who use these standings
tend to be looked down upon by the Gypsies settled on the
site, so quickly does social snobbery develop. Indeed,
since the departure of the horse and the horse-drawn vardo,
the social hierarchy in the gypsy world has altered completely. Time was, and I remember it well, when it was
" blood " that counted. The Woods, the genuine Lees,
the Stanleys, the Boswells, the Coopers, the Wells, were
the acknowledged aristocracy. Now it is the money that
counts. It is the " flash traveller " with a car as well as
a lorry, with the big trailer caravan, with the television
set (especially the colour television set), and settled on a
site, who ranks highest. It is no wonder that the Gypsy on
the standing reserved for nomads is loathe to leave, and
soon tries to settle.

And, indeed, the widespread use of the word " traveller "
is symptomatic of what is happening. I cannot imagine
Manfri Wood or Daisy Lee (a man: Daisy was a nick-
name) or Jem Stanley or Charlie Draper or Joseph Cooper
or Amos Churen, the aristocracy of the Gypsies I knew as
a boy and between the wars, would ever have denied that
they were Romanies or Gypsies. I cannot imagine that
any one of them would ever have described himself as a
" traveller ". They were proud of their blood. And of
gypsies living to-day: I cannot imagine Silvester Boswell
or Clifford Lee or Wisdom Price or Britannia Lee or
Benny Smith ever describing themselves as " travellers ".
They would be far too proud, and rightly so. For it must
be remembered that those who describe themselves as
" travellers " do so because they are in some measure
ashamed, because they believe that the word " gypsy "

has acquired a derogatory meaning among gorgios and want no part of it. As I have indicated, they might have done better to describe themselves as " true Romani "!

And what happens to the Gypsies who are settled on authorised sites? Sooner or later they are absorbed into the gorgio community. For example, all those settled on the caravan site at Great Chart by the West Ashford Rural District Council have long since been housed. They have lost their separate identity. Hampshire has housed all the gypsies that once were so great a problem, and this has been done without social trouble. Gypsies and gorgios, after some initial caution on both sides, settle down perfectly well both on mixed caravan sites and on housing estates.

There are those who think that it is the most terrible thing to house a gypsy. Indeed, I have seen such an act described as " genocide ". But Gypsies have been settling in houses of their own free will for a great many years. Manfri Wood, already becoming something of a legendary figure as the last speaker of deep Romanes in Britain, married a Welsh girl and lived in a cottage at Bala. (But how deep is deep? There are still Romanes speakers in North Wales and Clifford Lee, among English Gypsies, is surely as deep as they. Nevertheless, the language is dying in Britain; even the *poggado jib*, the broken tongue, is fast disappearing, for the simple reason that the separate identity is disappearing under the stress of modern life.) Silvester Boswell, Wisdom Price, Britannia Lee, Benny Smith, are all house-dwellers, all highly respected citizens in the communities in which they live. Clifford Lee, of the highest Romani aristocracy, married an Irish girl and, without departing from Gypsy occupations (knife-grinder among them) raised three children to high status in the gorgio community. His son is an M.A. of Liverpool University and is now lecturing at an Australian University, and his two daughters are schoolteachers. This is a remarkable achievement. But this sort of thing is happening all the time, though not, of course, at so high an intellectual level. The Gypsy is being absorbed or, rather, he is entering the community of his own wish. It is a far cry from my youth when Lavendi Scamp, seeing that I was attracted by her daughter Helen (though I was but six-teen and far too shy to be anything but the most distant admirer), told me with colourful emphasis that I belonged on one side of the fence and they on the other.

Of course, being housed by a Local Authority was sometimes a traumatic experience for the elderly, those brought up with the horse and " the wind on the heath." Most of the middle-aged now want the authorised site and the degree of permanence it offers. The young really have no desire for the nomadic life and most, I am sure, would like more than the authorised site. I am sure that without exception, male and female, they do not wish to be different from the young they see all around them. A young Gypsy, whose family I have known for many years and who now live on a caravan site, is unmarried and has a good job in a garage—many Gypsies are excellent natural mechanics. He said to me not long ago: " When I gets married, I want a house with a number on the door, same as everyone else." The young everywhere want the same things from life. The radio, the television, the mass communication, have removed the barriers, and given them the same heroes, football and otherwise. Education, econ-omic pressures and, in due course, miscegenation will do the rest.

The long, long history of the Gypsies of Britain is coming to an end.

BIBLIOGRAPHY

THIS list is merely a selection, and a purely personal selection, confined to books in English, from the large number of books about Gypsies in my own library. The dates given are the dates of the copies in my possession. In a number of cases, as for example the works of George Borrow, there have been many editions.

The Journal of the Gypsy Lore Society. Old Series, 3 vols, 1888–92; New Series, 9 vols., 1907–16; Third Series, 22 vols., 1922 to date.
The Dialect of the Gypsies of Wales, by John Sampson. Oxford 1926.
(These two publications are indispensible to all students of Gypsy Lore.)
AINSWORTH, WILLIAM HARRISON. *Rookwood*, London, 1851.
ANON. *Gypsies and Other travellers*, HMSO, London, 1967.
ANON. *Report of the Commission on Itinerancy*, GISO, Dublin, 1963.
BERLIN, SVEN. *Dromengro*, London, 1971.
BLOCK, MARTIN. *Gypsies*, London, 1938. (The English translation of Zigeuner.)
BORROW, GEORGE. *The Bible in Spain*, London, 1896.
—— *Lavengro*, London, 1900.
—— *The Romany Rye*, London, 1900.
—— *The Zincali*, London, 1901.
—— *Isobel Berners*, London, 1901. (A reprint from *Lavengro* and *The Romany Rye*, with an excellent introduction by Thomas Seccombe.)
—— *Romano Lavo-Lil*, London, 1905.
BOSWELL, SILVESTER GORDON. *The Book of Boswell*, London, 1970.
BROWN, IRVING. *Nights and Days on the Gypsy Trail*, New York, 1922.
—— *Gypsy Fires in America*, New York, 1924.
—— *Deep Song*, New York, 1929.
CAREW, F. W. (pseudonym of A. E. C. Way). *No. 747, Bristol*, 1890.
CLEBERT, JEAN-PAUL. *The Gypsies*, London, 1963.
CRABB, JAMES. *The Gipsies' Advocate*, London, 1831.
CROFT-COOKE, RUPERT. *The Moon in My Pocket*, London 1948.
CUTRISS, FRANK. *Romany Life*, London, 1915.
DODDS, NORMAN. *Gypsies, Didikois and other Travellers*, London, 1966.
DUFF, CHARLES. *A Mysterious People*, London, 1965.
FRASER, Angus M. *Journal of the Gypsy Lore Society* (3), XXXII, 82-100; XLIII, 80-112.
GENTLEMAN, HUGH and SWIFT, SUSAN. *Scotland's Travelling People*, HMSO, Edinburgh, 1971.
GRELLMAN, Heinrich. *Dissertation on the Gypsies*, London, 1787. (Translation of the work published in German in 1783.)
GROOME, FRANCIS HINDES. *In Gipsy Tents*, Edinburgh, 1880. (An invaluable work.)
—— *Gypsy Folk-tales*, London, 1889.
—— *Kriespiel*, London, 1896.

HALL, REV. GEORGE. *The Gypsy's Parson,* London, 1915.
HOWARD, R. *Report on Gypsies and Other Travellers,* Hampshire Association of Parish Councils, 1961.
HOYLAND, JOHN. *A Historical Survey of the Customs, Habits and Present State of the Gypsies,* York, 1816.

JENKINS, HERBERT. *The Life of George Borrow,* London, 1912.
KESTER, PAUL. *Tales of the Real Gypsy,* New York, 1897.
KNAPP, W. I. *The Life, Writings and Correspondence of George Borrow,* London, 1899.
LELAND, CHARLES G. *The English Gypsies and their Language,* London, 1874.
—— *The Gypsies,* Boston, 1882.
—— *Gypsy Sorcery and Fortune Telling,* London, 1891.
LELAND, CHARLES G., PALMER, E. H., and TUCKEY, JANET. *English-Gipsy Songs,* London, 1875.
LEVY, JULIETTE DE BARACLAI. *Wanderers in the New Forest,* London, 1958.
LYSTER, M. EILEEN. *The Gypsy Life of Betsy Wood,* London, 1926 (a gem of a book).
MACALISTER, R. A. S. *The Secret Languages of Ireland,* Cambridge, 1937 (contains nothing about Gypsies, but gives the only full account of Shelta and Bearlagair-na-Saer).
M'CORMICK, ANDREW. *The Tinkler-Gypsies,* Dumfries, 1907.
McDOWELL, BART. *Gypsies: Wanderers of the World,* Washington DC, 1970.
McEVOY, PATRICK. *The Gorse and the Briar,* London, 1938.
MACRITCHIE, DAVID. *Scottish Gypsies under the Stewarts,* Edinburgh, 1894.
MALLESON, HERBERT H. *Napoleon Boswell,* London, 1913.
MORWOOD, Vernon S. *Our Gipsies in City, Tent and Van,* London, 1885.
PENNELL, ELIZABETH ROBINS. *To Gipsyland,* New York, 1893.
—— *Charles Godfrey Leland, a biography,* London 1906.
REEVE, DOMINIC. *Smoke in the Lanes,* London, 1958.
—— *No Place Like Home,* London, 1960.
ROBERTS, SAMUEL. *Parallel Miracles,* London, 1830.
—— *The Gypsies,* London, 1836. (Really another edition of *Parallel Miracles.*)
SAMPSON, JOHN. *The Wind on the Heath,* London, 1930.
—— *Romane Gilia,* London, 1931.
SIMSON, WALTER. *A History of the Gipsies,* London, 1865.
SMART, B. C., and CROFTON, H. T. *The Dialect of the English Gypsies,* London, 1875.
SMITH, GEORGE. *I've been a Gipsying,* London, 1885.
SMITH, HUBERT. *Tent Life with English Gipsies in Norway,* Lonon, 1873.
SMITH, RODNEY. *Gypsy Smith, His Life and Work,* London, 1902.
STRANGE, DOROTHY. *Born on the Straw,* London, 1968.
WARD-JACKSON, C. H. and HARVEY, DENIS E. *The English Gipsy Caravan,* Newton Abbot, 1972.
WATTS-DUNTON, THEODORE. *Aylwin,* London, 1900.
—— *The Coming of Love,* London, 1899.
WEBB, G. C. E. *Gypsies: The Secret People,* London, 1960.
WELLING, R. A. J. *George Borrow,* London, 1908.
WIGHTMAN, RALPH. *Abiding Things,* London, 1962.
WOODCOCK, HENRY. *The Gipsies,* London, 1865.
YATES, DORA E. *My Gypsy Days,* London, 1953.

ACKNOWLEDGMENTS

I HAVE described this book as an introduction to the history of the British Gypsies. The dictionary defines history as : " A written statement of what is known : an account of that which exists or has existed : a record : a description." This then is an introduction to what is known about the British Gypsies, not merely to what I know about them. No gorgio man or woman has ever known the Gypsies, has ever known even one Gypsy, through and through. But a considerable number of gorgio men and women have, from time to time, acquired a deep insight into various aspects of Gypsy life and thought. The *Journal* of the Gypsy Lore Society is the treasure house in which all trustworthy knowledge of the Gypsies—not only of those to be found in Britain but of those to be found anywhere in the world—is stored. The *Journal* is, in fact, the source-book of all Gypsy history. No one who would write a book about Gypsies with any claim to being authoritative can afford to ignore it. I desire to stress here, as I have stressed many times in the pages that follow, the extensive use I have made of the *Journal*. That will be obvious to all the members of the Society. It may not be sufficiently obvious to the majority of my readers, some of whom may not know of the *Journal*, and I do not want there to be any misapprehension. At the same time I must also stress that the opinions expressed are my own, unless explicitly stated to be those of somebody else.

I cannot possibly make any adequate return for the many kindnesses I have received during the preparation of this book, nor can I possibly in these days of paper shortage publish the names of all those who in one way or another have helped me during the months I have been working on it. I hope that all those whose names are not mentioned will understand that they have been omitted for no other reason and that my gratitude to them is none the less. Particularly am I indebted to Miss Dora Yates, Secretary to the Gypsy Lore Society, who has helped in innumerable ways, often I fear at considerable personal inconvenience, and who has read the book in manuscript and made many valuable suggestions and criticisms ; and to Mr. T. W. Thompson and Mr. Eric Winstedt, fellow members of the Gypsy Lore Society, the former for his great generosity in allowing me to draw so fully upon his vast knowledge gathered over many years, and the latter for his kindness in answering letters that must often have bored him immeasurably. In addition my thanks are due to Dr. N. L. Jackson, Fred Norrish, R. H. Ferry, D. St. Leger Gordon, Alice Court, Rev. I. R. Sholto Douglas, C. L. G. Smith, F. R. Hanson, Henry Clapp Smith (New York), A. P. Barranikov (Moscow), Mrs. Douglas M. Baily (Toledo, U.S.A.), R. J. Macnamara, Rev. H. Purefoy FitzGerald, Sheila Maginnis, Rev. A. A. McKenna, S.J., B. K. Ritchie, Ann Scott, B. F. D. Ashton, John Lee, Kathleen Hodgson, John Venables, Peter King, M. Lloyd-Davies, Mary Mitchell, Brigid Regan, Patrick O'Flaherty, Rev. D. M. M. Bartlett, H. T. Bent, Thomas Hannay, H. J. Massingham, Mary O'Leary, Arthur O'Leary, Frank Parsons, John Myers, Edward Blackstone, A. McC. Paul, C. E. A. de Salis, Ll. D. Boyles, Catherine Smallman, C. Henry Warren, Elsie Waddon, Emrys Evans, John Stratton, Mrs. Archie Bell, Cynthia Craddock, Henry D. Baumer (Chicago), Duncan Scott, Mark Beaumont, L. H. D. Pennyfeather, Ferdinand Huth, and Roberta Wren. I am also indebted, of course, to a large number of Gypsies, who would, I am sure, prefer to be nameless. My friend, F. H. Dickson, has once again undertaken the laborious task of reading the proofs. Finally, my thanks, my very sincere thanks, are due to one or two landowners of whose property I have occasionally made rather free use in the interests of learning, and especially to the one who caught me, but after some discussion let me go—in return for a tip or two.